Emergency Psychotherapy and
Brief Psychotherapy

Second Edition

Leopold Bellak, M.D.
Clinical Professor of Psychiatry,
Albert Einstein College of Medicine;
and Clinical Professor of Psychology,
Postdoctoral Program in Psychotherapy,
New York University, New York, N.Y.

Leonard Small, Ph.D.
Chief Consulting Psychologist,
Altro Health and Rehabilitation Services,
New York, N.Y.

GRUNE & STRATTON, INC.
A Subsidiary of Harcourt Brace Jovanovich, Publishers
New York   San Francisco   London

Library of Congress Cataloging in Publication Data

Bellak, Leopold, 1916–

   Emergency psychotherapy and brief psychotherapy.

  Bibliography: p.
  Includes index.
  1. Psychotherapy. I. Small, Leonard, 1913–
joint author.   II. Title. [DNLM: 1. Psychotherapy.
Brief, WM420 B435e]
RC480.5.B4 1978   616.8'91   77-17324
ISBN 0-8089-1057-4

Second Edition
© 1978 by C.P.S., Inc.
Box 83
Larchmont, New York 10538

© 1978 by Grune & Stratton, Inc.

First Edition
© 1965 by Grune & Stratton, Inc.

Grune & Stratton, Inc.
111 Fifth Avenue
New York, New York 10003

Distributed in the United Kingdom by
Academic Press, Inc. (London) Ltd.
24/28 Oval Road, London NW 1

Library of Congress Catalog Number 77-17324
International Standard Book Number 0-8089-1057-4

Printed in the United States of America

Contents

Foreword to the Revised Edition

In the ten years since we first published this volume an amazing degree of social change has taken place. Crimes of violence such as mugging and rape are common experiences, and nearly everyone knows personally people who have been burglarized.

The sexual revolution has led to an increased concern with sexual functioning, and divorce has increased manifold. Abortion has been legalized and homosexuality has come out of the closet.

The medical revolution has involved the advent of open heart surgery as a widely used technique, organ transplants, and dialysis for kidney disease. The aged have been discovered by the media and the problems of nearly 21 million people over 65 in the United States demand attention.

The world-wide depression has led to widespread unemployment and it is even more difficult to find stability in the constant flux of our society than it was ten years ago.

Whether changes constitute progress or decline, they bring problems in their wake. The problems are often acute, and are sometimes full-blown crises. Thus we felt that a revision of the book was indicated, taking cognizance of these changes and their attendant difficulties.

Brief psychotherapy and emergency psychotherapy has also changed since we first published this volume, from a little known field practiced by a few to one of the four basic services of every community health center.

We discuss the general history of brief psychotherapy in the text. However, there is a personal history of some decades behind it for both of the authors. In 1946 L. B. inadvertently and out of necessity participated in the Veterans Administration Clinical Program for patients treated by psychiatrists with private practices. In the beginning, the contract was for three sessions. Later it was extended to six, then to multiples of six sessions. But in the first year it was necessary to learn to do the best one could therapeutically in a few hours with a great variety of disorders presented by veterans. Simply making a diagnosis and sending them away with a few verbal pats on the shoulder was insufficient.

The next natural step came when L. B. functioned as the only psychiatrist for an active rehabilitation agency, Altro Health and Rehabilitation Services, dealing first with tubercular and then cardiac patients, followed later by patients with a primary psychiatric complaint. Again, necessity was the originator of brief psychotherapy and L. B. cannot claim he was wholly aware of what he was into. Celia Benney, then Director of Social Work and later Associate Director of Altro, pointed out his unusual approach and its success. The success was confirmed when the staff of social workers who were at first highly critical, also began using the technique with patients, with encouraging results.

The other author (L. S.) was first exposed to the notion of abbreviated psychotherapeutic procedures during World War II as a clinical psychologist in Army psychiatric hospitals. The sheer demand for therapeutic services for the swelling number of psychiatric casualties prompted inventive variations and concentrated programs of psychotherapy. Most important, these experiences demonstrated that effective change was possible, even probable, in a wide variety of disturbances. Later, as consulting psychologist at Altro, L. S. participated in the individual therapeutic planning for several thousand patients presenting psychiatric, social, and physical disabilities.

After Altro, the authors worked together at the pioneering *Trouble Shooting Clinic* at Elmhurst General Hospital, sharing a variety of professional experiences in the course of several years of brief psychotherapy of more than fourteen-hundred walk-in patients.

Since the first edition appeared we have added to our experiences with brief and emergency psychotherapies in private practice, community mental health outlets, the emergency service of a social agency network, and in demonstrating and teaching the procedure in a large variety of other settings. Watching the progress in the field across the country and the changes in our society, and bulwarked by our own expanding experiences, a revision of our book appeared appropriate. Brief and emergency psychotherapies are increasingly proving their significance in overall mental health care. We hope that our effort will be useful in demonstrating that what was once possible has become practical and feasible.

Acknowledgment

For valuable editorial assistance
in the revision of this volume,
the authors would like to thank
Mary Ellen Beveridge.

PART I

Basic Principles and Methods

1

The Roles of Brief and Emergency Psychotherapies

Brief psychotherapy is best defined by its qualifier: it is limited to a few treatment sessions utilizing specific techniques for the attainment of a specific therapeutic goal. A high degree of conceptualization is required throughout the therapeutic relationship and a careful choice of interventions or noninterventions. Brief therapy also involves—for both the therapist and the patient—activity that is more carefully goal-directed, as compared to some of the longer-range therapies.

We shall enlarge later upon this brief definition. It is important to point out now, however, that brief psychotherapy in principle can be applied to any kind of emotional problem. If it is utilized in an emergency situation we speak of it as emergency psychotherapy. The only difference between emergency psychotherapy and brief psychotherapy is that emergency psychotherapy provides help for the psychological emergency as its specific goal within the brief therapy. Otherwise the same basic principles apply. Some specific principles pertaining to the nature of the emergency may dictate the specific conceptualization and activity of the therapist.

Crisis intervention has been conceptually separated by some authors. We do not believe there are basic conceptual and theoretical differences between crisis intervention and emergency psychotherapy, as we will point out later.

THE COMPELLING NECESSITY

A public increasingly aware of the importance of mental health is making growing demands for mental health services of all kinds. At the same time such measures as the Community Mental Health Act provide means for offering more of the services than ever before.

Emergency psychotherapy, other forms of brief psychotherapy, and associated measures play at least a twofold role in the situation. One role emerges in response to the shortage of competent personnel: to meet the demand for psychotherapy, provide brief psychotherapy to help those with the most urgent problems, or offer just enough help to effect, at least, the difference between the person being crippled by an emotional disorder and being able to carry on—even though far from optimally—until in some cases extensive help is possible.

Brief therapy may also serve in a preventive role: in many situations immediate treatment, albeit brief, forestalls the progression toward ever more serious maladaptations until the person is seriously and chronically disordered.

Thus, while the suggestion to truncate psychotherapy is a serious matter, the reasons for advancing the suggestion arise from causes equally serious.

The Needs of Individuals

Many people present themselves for psychotherapy only in crisis; once the crisis has passed, motivation for continuing in-depth exploration diminishes or disappears. Every psychotherapist must ask himself whether he has a responsibility to people in such situations. Our belief is that the psychotherapist is responsible for helping people as best he can within the limits of their motivations and their availability for psychotherapeutic intervention.

In almost everyone's life there are situations that may lead to major psychological problems. Birth, marriage, death and injury, the family crises of financial problems, children in trouble and parents in disagreement pervade the existence of all human beings. The psychotherapist can no more refuse to treat these problems with brief psychotherapy than the physician can refuse to stop arterial hemorrhage because the patient needs a prolonged course of kidney treatment.

Brief psychotherapy used in situations other than crises has some advantages in its own right over traditional psychotherapy. It avoids the secondary gain from the dependence in long-term therapy. Treatment provided promptly, with some relief of an acute disturbance, can prevent chronicity. It can also prevent life circumstances from becoming irreversibly harmful, as they might in long, drawn out therapy. Above all, if brief therapy is available for an acute disturbance, it is likely to be greatly more efficient than any kind of treatment begun after chronicity has taken its effect.

There is also the financial advantage of the lesser direct cost to the individual. Where symptomatology interferes with performance of one's occupational and social tasks, brief psychotherapy provides a means to minimize disruption of the individual's life and that of his family or economic unit.

CRISIS INTERVENTION AND BRIEF/EMERGENCY PSYCHOTHERAPY

Crisis intervention found its specific origins in Lindemann's work with the bereaved in the Boston Coconut Grove fire.[112] Caplan, working with Lindemann, later defined crisis intervention as "a state provoked when a person faces an obstacle to important life goals that is, for a time, insurmountable through the utilization of customary methods of problem solving. A period of disorganization ensues, a period of upset, during which many different abortive attempts at solution are made. Eventually some kind of adaptation is achieved which may or may not be in the best interest of that person and his fellows."[56] A theory of crisis intervention subsequently developed which some authors[135] see as a distinctive to brief or emergency psychotherapy. The basis of crisis theory for these writers lies in the idea that a relatively stable personality reacts to a crisis by being almost overwhelmed, and then adapts or maladapts in due course. Crisis intervention presumably attempts only to return the "organism" to the level of previous functioning.

While crisis intervention may begin with the purpose of returning the patient only to the premorbid level, it would be difficult to limit or interfere with the possibility that the patient might spontaneously reach higher levels of adaptation. The nature of learning makes this almost automatic for many people.

The dynamics of crisis reaction do not seem to be in any way different from ordinary symptom formation, psychiatric or somatic. In acute physical illness the body meets a bacterial or viral invasion with immune bodies or other defenses, and although incapacitated, begins to adapt to the invasion.

In a few instances the body is left more vulnerable, as in cases of pneumonia.* In other diseases (especially the viral ones), immune bodies produced reactively give temporary or even lifelong protection against further infection, permanently establishing a better way for the body to cope with illness.

Neurotic and even psychotic symptomatology, in response to traumatic situations, follows a very similar pattern. Many symptoms clearly are attempts at adaptation and problem solving which succeed in varying degrees and may leave one stronger than before the traumatic situation. There seems to be no basic difference between the dynamics involved in such instances and those described in crisis theory. We therefore believe that the terms "crisis intervention" and "emergency psychotherapy" are interchangeable. We maintain, furthermore, that helping a person deal with an immediate crisis or emergency simultaneously may be an attempt to reach a better level of general adjustment than existed before. Emergency psychotherapy or

---

*Pneumonia lends itself particularly well to a discussion of crisis theory. Internal medicine used to speak of "crisis" as being that stage of pneumonia characterized by the highest temperature, just before the turning point leading to debility and possibly death, or recovery.

crisis intervention follows basically the same principles as brief therapy in noncritical and nonemergency situations. A further discussion of crisis appears in Chapter 3.

FIVE-SESSION THERAPY AS OUR BASIC MODEL

Though the concept of five-session therapy in our basic model is by no means a rigid one, there is a sound basis for making five sessions the basic form: Statistics show that most patients coming to out-patient clinics break off after five visits. If this is what the average consumer of psychotherapy wants, especially in out-patient clinics, it is more rational to tailor therapy to his actual likelihood of attendance than to plan long-range therapy and accomplish very little because the patient fails to return after the fifth session.

The Needs of Society in Community Mental Health Programs

The Report of the Joint Commission on Mental Illness and Health in 1963 told us that about 17 million people in the United States have emotional problems which require treatment. This number has since increased, of course, with the growth of the population.

Increasing the recruitment and training of psychotherapists or effecting reduction of the growth of the population would contribute partially to a solution of the nation's mental health problem. Extending the availability of extant psychotherapists as much as possible is another approach, one more immediate than the preceding two approaches. Our thesis is that the development and utilization of brief psychotherapeutic procedures immediately contributes something substantial to the alleviation of the enormous mental health problems of the United States.

With the passage of President Kennedy's Community Mental Health Act and the creation of community mental health centers across the nation, brief and emergency psychotherapy has become one of the four cardinal requirements of every community mental health center. Since the first edition of this volume there has been a tremendous increase in community mental health centers, specifically psychiatric first aid clinics and hot lines. At the same time, in the roughly ten-year existence of community mental health programs organized under the auspices of the National Institute of Mental Health, community psychiatry, community mental health, and the mental health centers have undergone a number of great changes.[26] The initial enthusiasm of the "movement" led to some excessive expectations: Mental health professionals became entangled in a variety of socio-political problems that they were not especially well equipped to handle, and problems of quality control arose of the services made available. As will happen so often with new therapeutic modalities, the expectations were not only excessive but led to peculiar phenomena of their own. The antipsychiatry movement took many of its roots from a combination of community mental health philosophy and anti-establishment feelings, leading to the proposition that psychiatric hospitals were instruments of the establishment. Even the American Civil Liberties Union took a stand against commitment and serious attempts were made to do away particularly with state hospitals: all treatment was to be offered in the community, on an ambulatory basis. Since then, studies such as Pasamanick et al.,[26] at first strongly supportive of care in the community, have reversed themselves after they demonstrated that patients did not do better when cared for in their own homes rather than in a hospital. In New York especially, new mental health regulations had led to the near-emptying of state hospitals by patients poorly equipped to handle life in the community, much to the disservice of both the communities and the patients. California had led this movement, which to a considerable extent was economically inspired by the hope of doing away with hospitalization costs.

A sobering came with these developments. It is now quite clear that hospitals have a role to play. Some psychiatric die-hards, on the other hand, would now just as soon swing the pendulum to the other extreme and write off community psychiatry and community mental health as a pipe dream.

The fact is that the community mental health *viewpoint* is constructive and as likely to stay as Social Security. It is only reasonable that state facilities, usually far removed from the homes of the patients and thus almost enforcing their neglect, play a lesser role and that care in these facilities be modernized. In New York State the current effort involves out-reach programs, staffed by personnel no longer needed in state hospitals because of the reduced number of patients there. These clinics serve patients placed in various communities in some proximity to the state hospital or in the catchment area. In most of these clinics brief and emergency psychotherapy plays an important role.

Community mental health must actually be considered an aspect of public health and preventive medicine. In this sense brief therapy has a role to play in all three of the phases of public health—that is, primary prevention, secondary prevention, and tertiary prevention.

Primary prevention is concerned with the treatment of presenting problems or situations that may lead to illness by fostering the enabling conditions for illness. Treatment in the form of brief therapy can deal with some but not all of these problems. In malaria prevention, engineers, not physicians, dried swamps and covered them with oil to interfere with the breeding of anopheles. Likewise, in mental health not all primary prevention falls within the task of the mental health professional. Slum dwellings, poverty, unemployment, and discrimination are all factors which lead to mental health problems and which are best dealt with by social, economic, and political changes.

Primary prevention does play a role for the mental health specialist in instances where he recognizes a situation that is likely to lead to psychopathology and so alters the situation to make psychopathology less likely. Often a mother presents herself for treatment and one becomes aware that her child is likely to suffer considerably and to develop pathologically within the given family setting. Primary care must then be directed toward altering the situation in a way that offers preventive measures for the healthy development of the child. Bellak[31] has suggested that all children, at least at the time they enter elementary school, be screened by a mental health professional for incipient pathology either in the child or in the family constellation. Controversy can be avoided if one simply includes the grossest problems for a beginning. Having an alcoholic father and a mother addicted to heroin is likely to lead to pathology in the offspring and whatever can be done to alter the family situation for the child probably will be constructive. Although such intervention can be compared to the school authorities' decade-long insistence on the vaccination of children before they could enter school, this suggestion has aroused a great deal of antagonism and concern over civil rights.

Consider the following as an example of one way in which brief psychotherapy might serve as a preventive role in a community psychiatry program. Hilgard and Newman,[86] studying the onset of symptoms in a large state hospital population, found, particularly among the female population, a high incidence of what they termed "anniversary psychosis." A significant percentage of these women patients suffered a break when their oldest child reached an age at which the patients themselves had lost their mothers. Thus, Mrs. Jones had lost her mother when she was six; she suffered an acute psychotic break when her oldest child reached the age of six. Presumably this coincidence produced a variety of conflicts in Mrs. Jones. We could hypothesize that she identified with her own daughter and experienced a great deal of anger, jealousy, and fear. Another hypothesis could be that she identified the daughter with her own mother and reversed the psychological positions, suffering a considerable stress from that reversal.

It is conceivable that community programs could develop to the point where computing machines would bring to our attention the approach of such anniversaries. The harmful effects could then be forestalled by preventive brief psychotherapeutic procedures. Surely there are many clearly circumscribed situations which predictably will lead to catastrophic emotional reactions; these in turn could be predictably prevented if identified and treated before rather than after the fact.

Caplan[56] has spoken of the emotional "typhoid Mary," the carrier of emotional disorder, the person who contributes largely to psychological tension in a family, in a small community, in a factory, or in some other circumscribed setting. There are classes in schools or whole neighborhoods where a great deal of tension stems from one disturbed adolescent. The intervention of competently trained psychotherapeutic teams could go a long way toward forestalling the contagious influences of such people. A major need in prevention is the technique of identification and prediction. Another major need is the brief psychotherapeutic procedure.

Let us choose a simple individual example. A young woman came to the Trouble Shooting Clinic for various problems in her family life. Among them was that her younger sister had recently settled with the woman's family and created some imbalance in the family pattern. Her young son, who previously had slept in a small room now occupied by his aunt, had now joined his parents in their bedroom, and in fact shared their bed. This set-up was particularly awkward because he had developed nightmares and occasional bedwetting.

Under the circumstances, it was unnecessary to explain the Oedipus complex to her, or the importance of the primal scene. All that was suggested was that the young boy would be better off in a sleeping bag on the kitchen floor than sharing the conjugal bed. It was gratifying to hear that the change was made and that both the nightmares and the bedwetting stopped.

Actually, this case falls between primary and secondary prevention, but it makes the point. The symptoms had not yet hardened into a structure and were therefore easily reversible. Therapists have seen adults who were raised under similar circumstances and who developed a character structure primarily concerned with excessive defenses against passivity, or adapted with homosexual tendencies or fear of homosexual tendencies.

For instance, one middle-aged man who was seen in a cardiac clinic had had a similar childhood and apparently had spent all of his adult life as a super-macho truck driver and bus driver. This fact may or may not have had something to do with his early coronary infarct, if stress indeed contributes to coronary infarcts. However, his restlessness and his need for activity were so great that he moved a piano soon after his first coronary only to have another infarct ensue. An earlier part of his psychological problems had also been enuresis, and later in life, premature ejaculation.

It is in the area of *secondary prevention* where brief and emergency psychotherapy plays its most conventional role in the treatment of acute problems and crises in order to prevent them from becoming chronic problems. For instance, a young woman presented herself to the Clinic with a subway phobia, which in turn kept her from going to her job. Without means to earn an income, she would have been forced into dependence on public assistance, and secondary gains would have resulted from the enforced passivity. If the subway phobia had been permitted to persist for any length of time, it probably would have increased, in the nature of phobias, to include other phobic mechanisms. Along with the loss of income, depression and loss of self esteem would have appeared; she probably would have become a chronic psychiatric patient. Brief intervention made it possible to treat the phobia successfully enough to enable her to take a job again, and if necessary, to continue treatment under private care.

Tertiary prevention: The revolving door phenomenon has been one of the regrettable results of the improved care of psychotics by pharmacotherapy and community mental health provisions. Too many patients discharged into the community have promptly returned to the hospital within a year. It is estimated that only 20 to 40 percent of those returned to the community manage to integrate well enough to become active or self-supporting without troublesome pathology.

Brief therapy can serve an important function in the prompt treatment of acute exacerbations of chronic psychosis. One woman had adjusted quite well after two previous hospitalizations, but she became actively psychotic again when her son left the household. She developed delusions of people spying on her, she ripped the phone out because she thought people were listening in, she failed to appear at her job, and she became a recluse because of her fear of this spying. Prompt and brief therapy made it quite clear that her delusional and hallucinatory phenomena were compensatory for the loss of her son; indeed, she wanted someone to take an interest in her in his absence. After working this through in a few sessions she lost the acute symptomatology and was able to resume a reasonably normal life in the community.

In this particular way brief therapy plays a major role in maintaining psychotics reasonably well-adapted in the community, rather than making it necessary for them to be repeatedly hospitalized.

IN THE GENERAL HOSPITAL

It is accepted practice to prepare patients for surgery with fluids, antibiotics, and whatever else is needed; afterward, in the recovery room, immediate sequelae and complications are cared for. Preoperative and postoperative psychotherapy should also be provided whenever someone has an amputation or other emotionally traumatic surgery. During the preoperative preparation, brief psychotherapy could be addressed to the meaning of the particular trauma or loss. It would, for example, go into the meaning of what losing an arm might mean occupationally, what it might mean to the patient's self-esteem, what its influence might be in arousing his need for passivity. Hysterectomies, prostate operations, and many others arouse specific problems.

The presence of a psychotherapy team in the medical-surgical emergency room 24 hours each day has also established that among those patients coming in with symptoms of appendicitis or of a heart attack, there are actually many anxiety and panic reactions or a variety of other emotional problems which are treated on a brief psychotherapeutic basis. This appears to be particularly true at night when the incidence of emotional and psychosomatic problems is very high.[28]

INDUSTRY AND BUSINESS

Brief therapy has also played an increasing mental health care role by way of the private sector, in industry and business. Many large companies have availed themselves of brief therapy either within the organizational setting or through special contracts with private practitioners, Mental Health Association clinics, or other facilities. Care outside the corporate framework probably has advantages in that patients feel more assured that data will not be used against them under these circumstances.

THE HOT-LINE SERVICE

Hot lines, especially suicide emergency lines, have come to play an increasing role nationally and internationally. Such services often are permanently listed on the cover or inside cover of the telephone directory. They are available around the clock, with emergency psychotherapy the method of choice in dealing with potential suicides. As one example, the Westchester Mental Health Association has found particularly useful an arrangement in which the Mental Health Association staff receives the calls from 9:00 A.M. to 5:00 P.M., and two local hospitals respond in the intervening hours and on weekends to the same hot-line number.

OUT-REACH PROGRAMS: THE TRAVELLING CLINIC

Out-reach programs are funded in different forms, most recently as part of the decreased emphasis on state hospitals. Some state hospitals have created their own mobile teams that visit patients and offer active intervention. Psychotics, who are often unwilling or unable to seek help, can be reached under these circumstances with brief therapy or a combination of psychotherapy and drug therapy. At other times the mobile team can arrange hospitalization if necessary.

OVERVIEW OF BRIEF PSYCHOTHERAPY AS THE TREATMENT OF CHOICE

Throughout this volume we will call attention to the efficacy of a brief psychotherapeutic approach to a wide variety of emotional and personal problems—depressions, anxiety states, depersonalization, somatic disorders, sexual dysfunctions, crises and emergencies of many kinds, and age-specific problems such as aging, grief, and mourning, among others. We will cite research demonstrating a degree of effectiveness that indicates the significant role of brief psychotherapy among the mental health services. *The effectiveness of brief psychotherapy derives from the clarity of conceptualization necessary for its practice.*

Many personal and social conditions will be cited where a brief approach is desirable. Primary among these conditions is the pressure of a large population needing and increasingly demanding mental health services. As we have already pointed out, an effective brief approach is a major device for meeting this demand. The premiums for mental health services under prepaid insurance plans can be held to reasonable levels by the effectiveness of brief psychotherapy. The emerging concept of health maintenance organizations emphasizes the role of preventive measures in holding costs in check; brief psychotherapy is effective in preventing acute conditions from becoming chronic. A large segment of the population views the effectiveness of any therapeutic service—medical or psychotherapeutic—largely in terms of the brevity of treatment and the immediacy of its results. These persons shun long-term approaches. There is the urgency of other human circumstances, such as emergencies and incapacitating traumas, where the threat to life or the integrity of the personality demands an effectively prompt intervention. There are persons whom we perceive diagnostically as having tendencies that long-term treatment threatens to intensify, such as susceptibility to dependence or excessive dissociation in the self-observing process. There are chronically psychotic individuals whose psychosis cannot be significantly altered by thousands of hours of psychotherapy, but who can be sustained at a reasonably productive level of functioning by occasional brief intervention when episodic stress threatens to induce decompensation or regression. There are persons who can be described as reasonably normal and healthy, for whom long-term therapy is not indicated but who can be helped quickly with brief therapy to resolve critical situations that provoke anxiety, depression, and confusion.

Experience with brief methods over the last decade supports the conclusion that brief psychotherapy is not a second-best intervention, a band-aid form of treatment born merely of a huge supply/demand problem to stem the tide of emergent events in human life, or a "little is better than nothing" rationalization to be thrown into the breach. In all of these circumstances, brief psychotherapy can be effective; and as such it is not only desirable, but often the treatment of choice.

ADMINISTRATIVE IMPLICATIONS OF BRIEF THERAPY PROGRAMS

To utilize brief psychotherapy as the method of choice in any organizational setting, administrative provisions are essential. Ideally there should be no waiting list. In the original Elmhurst Trouble Shooting Clinic it was often possible to see people within an hour of their initial appearance at the Clinic. Since some were mothers with small children, a playroom managed by volunteers was made available while the mothers were interviewed.

There are two kinds of intake methods for our purposes. With the first, the director of the clinic conducts all intake interviews. He then assigns a therapist, discussing with him all basic aspects of the intake interview, and establishing a direct personal contact between patient and therapist while present. If the director is a physician, this method fulfills any legal requirements that the patient must see a physician. If the primary therapist is not available due to illness, vacation, or departure, the director, as the first person to have seen the patient in an administrative capacity, can also serve as interim, full-time, or auxiliary therapist. If the director has medical qualifications, he is available to oversee drug treatment and other medical aspects. By taping the initial interview, the director can make the basic facts and first impressions available to the therapist assigned to the patient.

With the second method any therapist with a free hour takes the next patient for an intake interview and continues with subsequent therapy. Many appointments are broken and someone is usually available, even if scheduling is tight. This method involves no interference or disruption of contact. However, no supervision or knowledge of the patient by another therapist is provided if the primary therapist should need substitution or supplementation: substitution in the case of illness, vacation or job change; supplementation if excessive transference or countertransference problems make it desirable to have an auxiliary as well as a primary therapist.

Professional and Related Aspects

PROFESSIONAL RESISTANCE

Professional resistance to brief therapy stems from two important factors. First, many excellent therapists, trained in the theory and practice of psychoanalysis, feel like charlatans doing anything less. The second factor has as much to do with training as with character structure. The idea of passively listening and engaging primarily in interpretation is based as much on psychoanalytic theory as on the personality of many of us in this field. Psychotherapists are clearly different from salespeople or even attorneys in terms of aggressiveness and the wish to manipulate. We are often patient, waiting, supportive, and relatively passive people who serve well as mothering figures. Very often psychotherapists are also relatively shy and use the professional situation, sometimes excessively and inappropriately, for the accomodation of their need to be passive, as well as of other difficulties in object relations. Therefore the idea of actively listening and questioning, then immediately collating this information, making decisive plans for interaction, and, if necessary, taking a variety of active steps other than interpretation, is difficult for many. Also, active interventions are sometimes seen as a form of playing God.

The reply to these objections is that we have slowly learned that it is impossible not to have some value systems of the therapist enter into the therapeutic process, even when the therapist is not active. Once patients come to us our responsibility is not different from that of surgeons: We share all available facts with the patient, then give some options and make some contract. Once the patient enters into that contract it would make no more sense for the therapist to hesitate to do what he feels is necessary and correct in his best professional judgment than for the surgeon to wake the patient during surgery to ask if he has a preference as to procedures. People come to us because of our expertise; as long as we exercise it to the best of our knowledge and ability, we stand on ethical grounds.

On the other side, there is no question that therapy, especially brief therapy, can be used for acting out one's own impulses. This pitfall must be guarded against as much as excessive passivity. In addition to knowledge and skill and having been analyzed, the ideal therapist has a well-sublimated rescue fantasy. Some sublimated form of wishing to be Dr. Kildare without believing in magic or in one's omnipotence can be a useful quality in our helping and healing profession.

BRIEF THERAPY AND PRIVATE PRACTICE

A number of patients in private practice come either with crisis situations or relatively circumscribed problems for which brief therapy suffices, and may in fact be the procedure of choice even though the patient can financially afford longer treatment. There are relatively acute situations, either precipitated by life circumstances such as the loss of a loved person, or developmental crises in adolescence, middle age, and old age for which brief therapy is often the ideal procedure quite independent of considerations of available time, manpower, and money.

It is also to the therapist's benefit to practice a variety of therapeutic modalities. Psychotherapy puts heavy stresses and strains on the therapist.[38] Complementing relatively passive long-term psychotherapeutic or psychoanalytic practice with relatively active brief therapy provides a change in pace, often with a refreshing and energizing effect.

POTENTIALITIES FOR TRAINING IN PSYCHOTHERAPY

The very length of psychoanalysis and intensive psychotherapy imposes limits upon the methods of training for them. It is not feasible to record their processes photographically and aurally for educational and training purposes. It is not feasible for the student to spend years behind a one-way screen observing the experienced therapist at work. Consequently, we have developed the methods of undergoing personal therapy and undertaking therapy with supervision for the training of the young psychotherapist. Learning based upon direct observation of the teacher, and supervision based on direct observation of the student could improve the overall quality of training. Many more clinical experiences with varieties of personality and varieties of aberration could be incorporated in training if condensed exposure to patient problems were added to the training regimen of advanced students by means of live or taped observation of brief psychotherapy as practiced by the teacher.

Now the young therapist is seldom observed critically *in situ* as he works. Traditionally, he reports *after* the fact to his supervisor, with the report suffering the attenuation of time and repression. Moreover, the young therapist seldom is required to conduct more than three cases under supervision. Under careful and current control by the teacher, advanced students might even undertake brief psychotherapy with a much larger number of selected patients. Brief psychotherapy might thus provide opportunity for wider clinical experience as well as more direct supervision of trainees.

POTENTIALITIES FOR RESEARCH IN
PSYCHOTHERAPY

The length of time that ordinary psychotherapy takes becomes one of the problems of its evaluation. Brief psychotherapy not only has the advantage of producing results sooner than more conventional psychotherapy, and therfore of providing a chance to follow-up its potential for therapeutic success, it is also—at least in our practice—a highly structured process with clear conceptualization and methodology. It is therefore especially easy to test hypotheses. The preferred procedure of repeated prediction and judgment is similar to the one described by Bellak and Smith,[19] and in the study of brief therapy at Elmhurst General Hospital reported in Appendix A. Because a great deal of activity takes place in brief therapy, it is especially easy to have some clinicians formulate a treatment plan for a given patient, while others judge the process and conduct of a given session. This method is useful for establishing whether judgments can verify conceptualized predictions, based on session-to-session observations made by independent teams of clinicians. If, for example, the statistical method of intensive design employed by Bellak and Chassan[29] and Bellak et al.[35] is used, control samples are not needed. Time sampling and using the patient as his own control can be used for a study of process, rather than relying on an attempt to match samples. Aside from being used to evaluate the effects of psychotherapy, brief psychotherapy lends itself especially well to the research and investigation of different hypotheses regarding various psychopathological conditions.

2
Definitions, Theories, and Principles of Brief Psychotherapy

The approach to emergency psychotherapy and brief psychotherapy presented in this book is derived in large measure from the orientation, training, and specific experiences of the authors in the theory and practice of psychoanalysis. In this chapter we set forth these concepts we have found that explain and make feasible short, time-limited interventions with some people in emotional distress. These concepts derive largely from psychoanalytic theory. They emphasize the importance of causality in producing emotional stress, the identification of specific causes through diagnosis, and ego function assessment in the reversal of disorders.

We have also derived therapeutic interventions from theoretical and practical experiences associated with psychoanalytic emphases other than our own, and from orientations other than psychoanalytic. These sources are presented in Chapter 3. From an amalgam of psychoanalytic and other theoretical concepts we have evolved a body of basic procedures for brief and/or emergency psychotherapy. This chapter and the next introduce these procedures.

WHAT IS PSYCHOTHERAPY?[40]

Psychotherapy is basically a very simple process involving unlearning, learning, and relearning. We are the product of our own cognitive past. We bring our unique biological Anlage into our experiental world which has a structuring effect on the way we register, store, and retrieve our experiences.

Psychotherapy—that is, dynamic psychotherapy—concerns itself with understanding the effect of specific life experiences on the human organism. It attempts to understand the accumulated apperceptive mass which affects contemporary cognition. It further attempts to help untangle or otherwise modify those past apperceptions which maladaptively tend to affect contemporary feeling and behavior, and the responses derived from them. Past distortions are restructured by the therapeutic alliance between the intact part of the patient's self and the technical and human role of the therapist. As Freud noted, after we help the patient lose his neurotic troubles, he still has to deal with civilization and the discontent it entails.

The acquisition of the individual's apperceptive mass is a complex process. Personality structure, and the lack of it, is a subtle matter and it takes time and skilled technique to bring about more adaptive modes than the patient previously acquired.

Categorically, methods of psychotherapy are more effective when:

1. The sounder the basic hypotheses are, concerning psychology of personality;
2. The more rigorously the method's conceptions of psychopathology are interrelated with this theory of personality; and
3. The sounder the propositions are for reversing problems perceived in terms of a clearly formulated theory of restructuring by unlearning, learning, and relearning.

To question whether psychotherapy is effective is inappropriate; one might as well ask whether learning is effective. The only legitimate question is *how* effective a certain form of psychotherapy is with a certain person under certain conditions. Quite clearly the effectiveness will be limited by personal and technical factors and by limitations, in principle, to learning, unlearning, and relearning of early, consistently repeated, and traumatically forceful experiences. Like any potent therapeutic modality, a particular method may at times be negatively effective.

Classic psychoanalytic theory embraces the most detailed and complex hypotheses concerning the acquisition of experience in interaction with maturational phases, as described for instance in the propositions concerning libidinal development. It is a particularly good learning theory in this sense of the phase-specific interaction of biological development and experience. Since Freud, much has been added by others, and much still needs to be added concerning the strictly cognitive aspects of the organization of experience. Implicit in psychoanalytic theory are such academic psychological concepts as the *law of primacy* and the *law of frequency and intensity*. Although Freud's theories of dream formation and dream interpretation are splendid examples of Gestalt formation, psychoanalytic hypotheses have not been stated systematically, in the experimentally verifiable propositions of Gestalt psychology.

In psychoanalytic psychology, psychopathology is closely and logically

related to the hypotheses of psychological development. In turn, psychoanalytic psychotherapy is closely interrelated with the hypotheses of personality
development and psychopathology.

Psychoanalytic psychotherapy does not treat the therapeutic process
sytematically enough as a learning, unlearning, and relearning technique.
Freud was primarily preoccupied with learning by *insight,* at least explicitly.
Implicitly, the concept of working through also involves learning, unlearning, and relearning by *conditioning.* Learning by *identification* with the
therapist is a third process of the therapeutic change, although the implicit
concept of transference has not been systematically stated in terms of learning theory.

Percept becomes structure, as psychoanalytic theory postulates. The
acquisition of structures follows certain dynamic processes. Not everyone is
happy with the structures Freud formulated. The tripartite model of id, ego,
superego has a number of limitations. However, with some necessary
changes and modifications, it is basically quite compatible with object-
relations theory as described by Edith Jacobson[93] and Otto Kernberg.[103]
This theory primarily involves a different and possibly supplementary way
of describing the acquisition of certain structures or "introjects." Experimental demonstration will have to establish that one kind of theory is more
useful than another for techniques of changing maladaptively acquired structures by different forms of therapeutic relearning.

The important fact is not to reify any kind of structure. Rapaport[139] used
the felicitous phrase that "structures are processes of slow rate of change,"
which is the only way experiental structures make sense. Psychotherapy is
then concerned with the regrettably slow change of those structures which
need changing to permit one to live with less maladaptation and less subjective pain and dangers for others.

Psychotherapeutic technique concerns the propositions necessary to
bring about optimally the changes in structure and dynamics for better adaptation. Insufficient systematic attention has been paid to the means for optimal and quick learning by verifiable techniques predicated upon
psychoanalytic theory.

Nevertheless, compared to others, the psychoanalytic psychotherapies
are markedly superior learning processes. Behavior therapy, once again in
the limelight, is most of the time an overly simplistic personality theory
excessively limited to learning by conditioning. Predicated upon this, learning theory is a similarly limited theory of therapy. Its usefulness is therefore
limited, primarily as an adjunct to other therapies.

Existential psychotherapies are unduly limited to propositions concerning the experience of the self, and their orientation is so anti-intellectual as to
be of little scientific value. They do not have a hierarchy of propositions that
lend themselves to an orderly statement of a personality theory or a theory
of therapy. Mysticism and its derivations in the form of various "guru"

notions are predicated on denial that is understandable in view of the terrible history of Eastern peoples, but hardly adaptive for them or anyone else.

The most popular fads in psychotherapy are usually predicated upon the short-term benefits of catharsis. Dianetics, EST, or primal scream make little difference; they involve a short-lived change in response which, if it includes no miracles in relearning, cannot affect the long-acquired structures. At times they work by modifying the superego temporarily in the proposition of living now, for oneself. This form of "giving permission" may have its limited validity when the supergo is too severe, but it hardly holds any promise of lasting effects.

Carl Rogers, in his earlier client-oriented therapy and later in joining with other encounter therapies, has most widely overestimated the value of simple confrontation with one's maladaptive patterns and the spontaneous learning gained by such insights. Seeing personality development and its maldevelopment as a long learning process over time, makes it conceptually impossible to accept short cuts in learning, without operations carefully predicated on complex theories and subtle techniques.

The only exception to this rule is that carefully planned brief or emergency psychotherapy, based on clearly formulated propositions derived from psychoanalytic theory, indeed may lead to relatively extensive and quickly attained changes—or at least beginnings of changes—which under fortunate circumstances may continue autonomously once set in motion.

Anatomical and physiological processes, also of slow change, can be considered as part of the structure influencing cognition. It is very likely, for instance, that some biological substrata will be found at least for some of the psychoses. However, it is also entirely possible for a condition caused at least in part by a clearly defined biological process or defect to lend itself to purely psychological treatment. For example, a percentage of schizophrenics may suffer from this symptomatology because their cognitive processes are affected by a biochemical abnormality interfering with registration, storage, and/or retrieval of data. Biochemical treatment might help such patients perceive reality in an undistorted way from the time the chemotherapy took effect. It appears unlikely at this time, however, that any amount of biochemical agents would "unscramble" the stored faulty data affected by biochemical forces in the past. Psychotherapeutic reconstruction would be necessary to undo the effect of previous cognitive distortions.

If this sounds too fanciful, one must keep in mind that many people have been "talked down" from a chemical psychosis induced by LSD or some other agent by a more or less skilled verbal intervention. Psychological forces have been used to treat various degrees of cognitive distortion caused by dyslexia or minimal brain dysfunction, and to undo the cortical disturbance of cognition of space, the self, and the spoken word.

These observations are made advisedly for the benefit of those who bury psychotherapy and especially psychoanalysis at regular intervals, while hoping for some biological psychiatric equivalent of Paul Ehrlich's magic bullet. So far, psychotropic drugs treat symptoms relatively well. If the dopamine hypothesis or catecholamine hypothesis or some relative thereof should become successful, we can only hope that it will halt the psychotic process, and eventually even prevent it in some individuals. At present the process cannot be imagined by which biochemical agents would undo a life history of effects of biochemical forces, leaving the organism prey to a low stimulus barrier, a poor self-boundary, a symbiotic relationship, and the consequent disturbance of symbolic processes and object relations.

Aside from naively questioning the value of psychotherapy in principle, being confused by reductionistic fads, and confounded by the role of biological factors, there are other unnecessary sources of misconception. Some suggest that it is the nonspecific effect of a suitable psychotherapeutic personality with a benign interest that is therapeutic, and that specific hypotheses of different schools are unimportant.

One can compare this notion to the well-established fact that placebos may lead to a 50 to 60 percent improvement: Most acceptable drugs must be established as doing significantly more. There is indeed some general psychotherapeutic "placebo effect." A well-meaning therapist could also be compared to the provision of bed rest, fluids, and reliance on *vis medicatrix naturae*—the spontaneous healing forces of nature of homeopathic medicine.

However, one would not want to use a placebo instead of digitalis. Penicillin is still the preferred treatment for a serious streptococcal infection, rather than simply bed rest and fluids. Having a human therapist with a therapeutic personality is not unimportant in both general medicine and psychotherapy, but in addition, a well-trained therapist provides specific interventions that are predicated on specific hypotheses about personality and psychopathology, and work with interlocking propositions concerning optimal technique.

Technique consists of a carefully formulated series of interventions which promote the therapeutic process in an orderly and predictable way. Technique, predicated on the psychoanalytic theory of personality and psychopathology, creates the optimum conditions in which the patient can become aware of apperceptive distortions, conflicts, and wishes. It provides an orderly sequence for learning, unlearning, and relearning by creating and maintaining an optimal motivation, and avoiding both excesses of anxiety and premature absence of anxiety so that learning by insight, conditioning, and identification leads to a restructuring of the personality.

Technique then is crucial, as long as the therapist does not maintain that one invariable technique must fit all patients. The invariant principle is that theory be adapted to the specific patient to allow for greater or lesser parameters from a hypothetical standard.

Guided by technique, the therapeutic process consists of several steps.

The patient *communicates*. We listen for common denominators in his cognitive distortions. When we understand them, we decide on any one of a dozen or more possible interventions, depending on what seems most useful at that point. This intervention is called *interpretation*. If all goes well, the patient gains some insight by seeing the common denominator in his apperceptive distortion of the historical, contemporary, and therapeutic relationships. Oversimplified, this means that he perceives a new Gestalt, one less affected by forces of the past and more affected by the reality of the social consensus. After he leaves the office, he applies learning by insight to a wide range of reality situations: Even the cop on the beat is perceived in a somewhat changed Gestalt derived from the restructuring of the therapeutic situation. Often, this process of restructuring takes place in the transference as well as in reality. It constitutes a slow learning by *working through,* which largely involves a form of learning by conditioning. Learning by *identification* with and introjection of the therapist also plays an important role. Strictly technical considerations involve the choice of areas for intervention, methods of intervention, and sequence of the areas and methods chosen, as we will discuss for brief therapy specifically.

We and our colleagues previously demonstrated both for classical psychoanalysis and brief psychotherapy that this technique can be carried out in a scientifically lawful way.[19,30] We were able to agree with satisfactory statistical validity and reliability on what forces were at play, and predict what intervening forces would produce a given effect in the patient's productions. This statistical validity does not mean we can rest on our laurels. A great deal of systematic and experimental verification, modification, and rejection is necessary in the interacting basic propositions of the psychology of personality, psychopathology, and psychotherapy.

We urgently need variations of more effective therapeutic learning techniques. The sooner we have a national research center and clearinghouse for systematically dealing with this problem, the sooner we will have satisfactory solutions.

BRIEF AND EMERGENCY PSYCHOTHERAPY FURTHER DEFINED

Psychotherapy can be a reasonably good science. Inherent in its practice are a variety of hypotheses that both require and permit explication. Stating hypotheses permits us to test them in clinical practice. Moreover, their very statement in large measure protects the therapist from being swayed by personal motivations, hunches, intuition, kindness, and a host of other inappropriate determinants. The practice of brief psychotherapy particularly requires that the therapist operate from a set of firmly rooted facts and substantial hypotheses. The brevity of the treatment itself demands the highest possible order of precision in thought and the utmost economy of intervention. Brief psychotherapy, as defined here, is to be accomplished in the short range of one to six therapeutic sessions of customary duration (45–50 minutes). Most especially, brief psychotherapy is not easy therapy. The therapist must be acutely alert to every meaningful communication, while rapidly formulating the common denominators, filling in the omitted parts from his vantage point of uncommon sense, and almost simultaneously deciding upon the most fruitful intervention, which he balances against his assessment of the patient's ego strengths and real-life circumstances and conditions. In brief psychotherapy, the therapist does not have the time to wait for insight to develop; he must foster insight. He does not have the time to wait for working through; he must stimulate working through. And where these basic aspects of the therapeutic process are not forthcoming, he must invent alternatives. Brief and emergency psychotherapy is thus properly a specialty for the experienced practitioner, and one that requires full use of his capacities. The brief therapeutic process must be thus understood if it is not to be gravely misused.

Brief psychotherapy is a much foreshortened application of traditional psychotherapy, called into being either by the life situation of the patient or by the setting in which treatment is offered. Emergency psychotherapy is brief psychotherapy applied in special situations of crisis and exigency.

Basic Theoretical Propositions

Brief psychotherapy as set forth in this book has its roots in orthodox psychoanalytic theory. The psychoanayltic orientation appears to offer the most systematic hypotheses available, hypotheses which lend themselves most readily to clinical verification and, in the long run, it is expected, to experimental verification, modification, or exclusion. These must be considered relative statements: some aspects of Freudian theory, major and minor, are far from proved; other contributions have much to offer to the understanding of human behavior. Nonetheless, the fundamental procedures of brief psychotherapy are derived from the understanding of human behavior, normal and abnormal, contained in orthodox psychoanalytic psychology.

Without reviewing or abbreviating psychoanalytic theory, attention must be directed here to several fundamental concepts in Freud's theoretical structure. Upon these the comprehension of symptoms and complaints and the choice of intervention in brief psychotherapy are based.

DETERMINISM

Freud first applied and demonstrated the principle of causality in the form of psychic determinism: each effect, cognitive process, or behavioral act is the result of a specific cause or set of causes and, in turn, is itself the cause of other effects. The practice and theory of free association, the assignment of meaning to symptoms, and the interpretation of dreams are all based upon the assumption of causal connections operating unconsciously.

The theoretical structure of psychotherapy and psychoanalysis stands upon a bedrock of psychic determinism. The therapist must assume that every act has a cause; the concept of determinism commits him to search for it in each instance. Thus we seek precipitating causes in recent events and underlying causes in the historical past, both within the individual and in his culture. Establishment of causality becomes a necessary step in the selection of intervention: what has been done must be undone or redone. Undoing a symptom requires intervention with awareness at the level of the causation.

Since the end of the nineteenth century, the concept of determinism, along with its more general counterpart the "law" of causality, has undergone a good many changes along with the scientific framework from which Freud formulated his ideas of determinism.

Freud's concept of overdeterminism itself incorporated some notion of an act being caused by more than one factor (*see* Overdeterminism). One development of this thought in medicine is Selye's field theory of illness in which illness is seen as caused by a whole matrix of stresses, not by a single disease agent. Another modification of determinism is dictated by the effect of Heisenberg's uncertainty principle in physics, by probability theory and statistics based on it. Causes and effects are, therefore, no longer thought of as links in a rigid chain, but rather as events which one may expect to be linked with each other in a very *high degree of probability.*

Nevertheless, for practical purposes of psychotherapy, especially brief psychotherapy, it is as reasonable to think in strictly empirical terms of causal relationships as it is, for example, necessary to do so in mechanical engineering.

OVERDETERMINISM

The progress of an individual's psychotherapy often establishes that a given effect is the result of several forces arising both genetically and currently. The experienced therapist is not surprised, therefore, when treatment of one cause does not modify the effect; he continues his search for additional causes. The "working through" aspect of psychotherapy especially requires that the therapist keep in mind the principle of overdeterminism, finding that as one causal sequence is worked through the necessity arises to search for others and, in turn, to work through these.

CONTINUITY OF PERSONALITY AND UNCONSCIOUSNESS

Perhaps the most startling and successful achievement of psychoanalytic theory has been to bridge the seeming discontinuity of manifest behavior: For example, our ability to now order into a continuum dream content, and the thoughts and concerns of the day preceding the dream and those of the day subsequent to the dream. Common parapraxes such as slips of the tongue, misnaming, misspelling, etc., are simple examples of apparent discontinuity to which meaning is usually brought by the construct of the unconscious.

Linking the concept of the continuity of personality with that of unconsciousness permits us to determine past causes for contemporary effects. Freud did not state explicitly a concept of continuity of personality. However, the concept is implicit in his contention that all of the essentials of the personality are established by the fifth year. Differences of behavior in later life are presumably explained by shifts in the intrapsychic system, a quasi-closed system, in that the person is in constant interaction with the environment. It might be better to say, therefore, that the theory of continuity of personality implies that after childhood, responses to the environment take place over a certain *limited range of variations* which are largely predicated upon earlier established structures.

The question of "sameness" of the personality, intrinsic to the matter of continuity, is of course a theoretically complex one, somewhat beyond the scope of this volume. Suffice it to mention that, of course, different configurations or *Gestalten* can result from the sum of parts, somewhat as in a kaleidoscope. In psychoanalytic terms, a large variety of combinations of drive and defense are equally possible.

Allport's theory of the "autonomous functions,"[4] White's motivational theory,[170] and other less genetically oriented theories of personality have not played much of a role in clinical work, but they are nevertheless important constructs and in no way mutually exclusive to psychoanalytic propositions.

HOMEOSTASIS

Jones[97] has described how Freud wrote of constancy of organismic and psychic phenomena, thus anticipating broadly the later concept of homeostasis advanced by Cannon, and more recent applications of this concept to psychological phenomena, e.g., by Menninger[75] and by Bertalanffy.[47] The pleasure principle of Freud's theory implies that the organism has a tendency toward the gratification of drives—that is, toward a state of equilibrium—perceptually, physiologically, and in other ways.

The reality principle, dramatically opposed to the pleasure principle, is a result of the learning of detour behavior by the ego which inhibits the immediate, direct gratification of drives consistent with cultural demands. Freud[74] and Hartmann[84] have both pointed out that in animals the instincts lead to gratification and survival, whereas in man the ego is required to mediate between drives and reality in order to achieve gratification. Freud's contention was that increasing civilization requires increasing interaction between individuals and, therefore, increasing regulation of individual behavior. This increases conflict, which in turn requires more frequent and more complex detours to achieve permissible drive gratification.

Symptom formation in this sense was seen as an unstable compromise effort between drive gratification, on the one hand, and inhibition of the drive by learned behavioral patterns, on the other.

In the newer concept of psychic homeostasis, it is necessary to keep in mind the structural aspects of the personality as well—the id, the ego, and the superego. One must identify the balances between these aspects of the personality: The strength of drives in relationship to the strength of the various functions of the ego for mediating these drives; and the strength and quality of superego counterdemands upon the ego in a total metapsychological setting—of genetic, dynamic, economic, adaptive, topographical, and structural nature.

Differentiation from Psychoanalysis

Having established the roots of brief psychotherapy in psychoanalytic theory, we must differentiate brief psychotherapy from psychoanalysis in terms of goals and other factors.

GOALS

Emergency psychotherapy is a method of treatment for *symptoms* or *maladaptations* demanding the quickest possible relief because of their crippling or endangering nature as, for example, in the case of exposure to catastrophic events. The goal of brief psychotherapy is limited to the removal or *amelioration* of specific symptoms: It does not attempt the reconstitution of personality except that any dynamic intervention may secondarily and, to a certain extent, autonomously lead to some restructuring. In its symptom-directed orientation, brief psychotherapy seeks to improve the individual psychodynamic situation sufficiently to permit the person to continue functioning, to allow "nature" to continue the healing process, and where indicated, to increase the self-supporting ability of the individual sufficiently so that he may be enabled to continue with more extensive psychotherapy. For example, a patient may display a disturbed equilibrium between the push of drive and the demands of reality, or between the push of drive and the demands of the superego. The goal would be to help such a patient with intervention to a point where spontaneous changes occur which enable him to continue to function and perhaps achieve additional desirable results on his own. Achieving homeostasis where equilibrium has been disturbed, even if the homeostasis is achieved for a brief time only, provides the individual with both the realization that improvement is possible for him and with the motivation to continue to search and work for it.

The symptom-directed efforts of brief psychotherapy are necessarily relative. Even in intensive psychotherapy one does not always reduce symptoms to the vanishing point. Particularly in brief psychotherapy, we are concerned with degrees of amelioration, with the limited goal of at least some improvement in functioning, with the goal of decreased subjective difficulty, and with the goal of increasing strength to the point where the individual avails himself of more substantial treatment as a result of improved earning power or improved motivation. But at the same time, we would stress that for many people relatively limited psychotherapy may in itself be sufficient to help them achieve a point from which they continue autonomous improvement; this phenomenon is well-known in all of medicine, whether it is conceptualized in Selye's terms or in the hopeful notion of homeopathy's *vis medicatrix naturae*.

TIME FACTORS

Obviously, in emergency psychotherapy the pain or danger to which the patient is exposed requires that intervention be immediate with some degree of relief obtained as rapidly as possible, most often within the first therapeutic session.

We may, however, designate as brief psychotherapy a span of from one to five sessions (or any reasonably limited number of sessions). Often the time period of brief psychotherapy is automatically established by the setting. Many universities offer short-term psychotherapy in their mental health facilities, defined as a certain number of visits, usually under 20. Fullest possible utilization of the clinic facilities of a large municipal hospital might require a shorter range of sessions.

METHODS

Traditionally, psychoanalysis employs the method of free association to promote the determination of causality, to establish the transference, and to promote insight based on interpretation derived from the material produced by free association. The patient traditionally lies upon a couch with the analyst seated behind him, a situation designed to facilitate free association and to help the analyst maintain some lack of structure of the immediate situation.

In brief psychotherapy free association as such is not a basic tool except as it may arise in response to specific stimuli from the therapist, as, for example, when he pursues the securing of an informative and pertinent history. Nonetheless, free association cannot be considered inoperative in brief psychotherapy. Any human exchange which permits a relatively free response even to an ordered stimulus involves free association to a degree. One might view the operation of free association as spread along a continuum in psychotherapy, with the fullest degree being achieved in the psychoanalytic method and a more restricted degree operating in the brief psychotherapeutic situation.

In brief psychotherapy the patient does not lie upon a couch, but sits vis à vis the psychotherapist. This procedure stems both from the goals and the methods employed, and from the time limits.

In psychoanalysis, interpretation is the analyst's chief device to facilitate insight. This is true as well in brief psychotherapy. However, interpretation is, as we shall see, modified considerably in practice by the demands of the immediacy of the situation. Very often interpretation is employed in situations where it would never be so used in the psychoanalytic process. Most importantly, interpretation—that is, psychodynamic intervention—in brief psychotherapy is coupled with other types of intervention (medical, environmental, etc.) never or rarely employed in traditional psychoanalysis. Moreover, the merit of a given interpretation as judged by its ability to produce insight is a relative matter in brief psychotherapy. Since its goal is the relative amelioration of symptoms, the effectiveness of the interpretation in producing insight is similarly judged in a relative way.

The analysis of the conflictual transference is considered to be the basic curative aspect of the process, in which there is produced within the analytic situation a repetition of the original parental or other relationship. The use of transference will be dealt with in detail in a later section, but here we should state that in brief psychotherapy positive transference is sought and maintained from the beginning to the end. It is not "permitted to develop," but rather is encouraged and elicited. With symptom removal or improvement as its goal, brief psychotherapy presents the therapist as a benign, interested, helpful, and intervening person. The positive transference is fostered and taken for granted. The emergence of negative transference is avoided as much as possible and referred to only on rare occasions when it can, in a helpful way, be related to other manifestations or when it stands in the way of therapeutic progress.

INDICATIONS

The indications for brief psychotherapy are several. All other things being equal a strong plea can be made for making brief psychotherapy the *intake method of choice,* especially in out-patient clinics and agencies. It is true that necessity plays a role: Available personnel and time, the willingness of patients, and the admonition, as Leighton said, that "In the care of the few we have to keep in mind the needs of the many play a role."

Brief psychotherapy is a treatment form which often has advantages over other forms. If it is routinely considered the method of choice we will be able to do away with waiting periods and probably provide more effective goal-directed service than in long-term therapy.

From a theoretical standpoint there is much to be said about the advisability of brief therapy. While it is yet to be proven by research, clinical experience is consistent in demonstrating that repeated episodes of brief therapy over time may be more beneficial than the long-term psychotherapeutic process.

The theoretical basis for this lies in learning theory. If the patient has reached some level of adaptation, "silent learning" as academic psychologists call it, may take place. Also in accordance with learning theory, dispersal of training is very effective. It is generally better for a child to try to memorize a few lines from a poem one day, try again the next day, and again the following day, rather than attempt to memorize the whole poem at one sitting. Similarly, a patient seen in brief therapy may profit from a resolution in the first session, learn a good deal before coming to the next session, and learn it more effectively on the principle of *dispersal of training*.

In view of these advantages of brief psychotherapy we suggested in Chapter 1 definite administrative arrangements with regard to using brief therapy as the method of choice from intake through follow-up.

CONTRAINDICATIONS TO BRIEF PSYCHOTHERAPY

Our clinical experience has shown that brief psychotherapy may be of at least some usefulness in nearly every kind of emotional disturbance. Even in a young girl with a very marked narcissistic character disorder, it was possible to make her behavior at least somewhat ego-alien and possibly establish conditions for further spontaneous changes. Psychotic conditions have also responded well.

The first and most obvious contraindication to brief psychotherapy is obviously in those cases where it was tried and found not to suffice. Furthermore, if circumstances permit more prolonged treatment, there are a number of situations where extensive psychotherapy or classical psychoanalysis remain the treatment of choice. Character disorders outstandingly fall into this category. These are usually subtle conditions, not necessarily causing sufficient palpable discomfort to provide very good motivation for a change.

In fact, in all conditions where extensive restructuring of character and personality is desirable and feasible, brief psychotherapy is not the treatment of choice, except for clearly limited goals. This will include psychoses, as well as subtle and pervasive psychoneuroses and sociopathies in which acting out plays a marked role.

Much of what we have said about indications and contraindications of brief psychotherapy is rather obvious. There is an interesting clinical area where a good deal of dissension might exist with regard to the therapy of choice: In those conditions and people where some might think that long therapy or psychoanalysis might be indicated, others might feel that the disadvantages of prolonged dissociative processes, stimulation of secondary narcissism, and induced psychological validism militate for brief psychotherapy. No more can be said than that the relative advantages and disadvantages of brief versus prolonged therapy should be more carefully weighed than they seem to have been heretofore, even if prolonged psychotherapy or psychoanalysis is in principle available and possible.

THEORY AND PRINCIPLES OF BRIEF PSYCHOTHERAPY

Psychotherapy succinctly defined is *a verbal or otherwise symbolic interaction of a therapist with a patient, guided by an orderly and integrated series of concepts, and directed toward beneficial change in a patient.* Emphasis is placed upon the necessity for an orderly series of concepts guiding the therapist's interventions; these must be based logically upon a personality theory and propositions concerning diagnosis, the dynamics of the illness, and the treatment of causes and/or effects. This definition, however inadequate, does serve to exclude treatment by instinct, intuition (except as a preconscious form of conceptual thinking), art, faith healing, or by general philanthropic strivings. It is intended to set the frame of reference for an orderly methodology.

Logically derived guiding concepts must be the basis for all forms of therapy, whether analysis, intensive psychotherapy, emergency psychotherapy, brief psychotherapy, drug therapy, electric shock, or insulin coma. A proposition concerning treatment based upon logically guiding concepts merits exploration, attention, and research. Any others represent only random trial-and-error efforts to help a patient, inappropriate to the present stage of development of the science.

We must further keep in mind that in most instances *general* guiding principles of psychotherapy will be insufficient except for superficial, temporary success. Beyond the universalities of human behavior, each individual is unique, with unique patterns of disturbance, a unique ego structure, and a unique personal history. General principles must not be mistaken for the whole of psychotherapy, as has so often been the case. The psychotherapy of an individual encounters problems different from those of any other person. Treatment methods not painstakingly anchored to extensive diagnosis and specifically planned prescriptions of therapy are inadequate. Any general prescription of relationship therapy, communications therapy, work therapy, family therapy, group therapy, or psychoanalysis of any persuasion is insufficient if not accompanied by specific propositions as to diagnosis, dynamics, and therapeutics tailored to one specific person.

This section will set forth the theories and principles underlying brief psychotherapy, theories, and principles whereby the therapist proceeds from a general conceptualization of human behavior to specific propositions concerning the behavioral problems of the individual patient.

Three basic processes are common to dynamic, psychoanalytically oriented psychotherapy: communication, insight, and working through. They apply in brief psychotherapy and merit comment here.

Communication: Patient to Therapist

As in all human interactions, communication is the basic first step. The patient informs the therapist of his problems, his history, and his contemporary life. The patient's communications take many forms. They may be strictly verbal, as reporting, description, or free association. Communication also occurs through facial expressions and other motor acts: The patient may bite his fingers, wrinkle his face, wriggle in his chair, shake his foot, pull at his ear. Recounting of dreams provides a level of communication in which the patient does not at the time participate with full knowledge of the content of his communication. Speech, of course, is the basic medium of communication in psychotherapy. The patient's choice of words, the pace of his speech, the style and method of delivery, the emphasis or lack of it, all may communicate important information to the therapist. Adjunctive measures for fostering communication from the patient to the psychotherapist may be used when the patient finds verbalizing difficult, as we shall later describe. We refer here to the appropriate use of psychological tests, certain drugs, and hypnosis.

The Therapist's Insight

As the patient communicates, the therapist is alert to recognize common denominators in his behavioral pattern, as well as thoughts, feelings, and experiences, particularly as these relate to his symptoms. Behavioral and experiential patterns must be quite broadly defined. Principally we speak of horizontal patterns (the contemporary patterns) and of vertical patterns (the genetic precursors of contemporary behavior). In addition to these behavioral configurations, the continuous study of behavior in relationship to the psychotherapist is important. The task of the psychotherapist is to find the common denominator in these three general, broadly grouped patterns of behavior and experience. The common denominators contain the explanation for the patient's present mode of behavior, both adaptive and maladaptive.

Interpretation: Communication from Therapist to Patient

The therapist is now equipped to communicate his insight to the patient by means of interpretation. The goal is to give to the patient the therapist's understanding of the meaning of the common denominators of his various behavioral patterns. It is well understood that because interpretation consists of pointing out the common denominators in different behavioral patterns and feelings, there may be many different levels of interpretation. Also, of course, some interpretations interlock with others, and therefore a good deal of interpreting is often necessary to restructure the past apperceptive mass. It is well understood also that the therapist uses types of intervention other than interpretation in the strict sense. Any number of preparatory verbal interventions may be necessary before interpretation itself is appropriate. Thus, before presenting a definitive interpretation of certain behavioral patterns and feelings, the psychotherapist may elect to offer a number of other partial or lesser interpretations designed to lead the patient himself toward the major insight the therapist has discovered, to prepare the setting for the communication of the insight, or to test the patient's readiness to accept it.

Attention may have to be directed to an area first in what might simply be called "focusing" remarks. At times, additional information has to be given in order to have an interpretation make sense.*

The therapist must be as aware of his own speech as he is of the patient's. His choice of words, his pace, his stresses or emphases, his imparting of warmth, quizzicalness, even reproval will be understood by the patient as clearly as will the literal content of his speech.

The Patient's Insight

If all goes well, insight on the part of the patient will follow. We define insight as the patient's perception of the pattern or configuration in his experience, feeling, behavior, and thinking. The manifestation of insight by the patient may take many forms. Borrowing from an old academic psychologist, we may say that it can be manifested as an "aha!" experience in which there is a sudden "closure" of understanding. In another instance, the insight may seem, like the dawning of day, to rise slowly and gradually enter the patient's consciousness. The insight may be manifested in the form of laughter, which psychoanalysts term "symptom" laughter, a sign that something has clicked; it may be expressed by crying, by anger; it may be preceded by manifestations of anxiety. Insight, properly speaking, therefore, is both the intellectual and emotional perception of common denominators in the experiential pattern. The ultimate degree of insight is achieved when such emotional and intellectual understanding is related to patterns as

---

*There are, of course, many other forms of communication. Strupp,[165] for instance, in his analysis of the variety of interventions by the therapist includes silence and passive acceptance, among others.

they exist in the contemporary life, the transference, the earlier life, and particularly to the relationship between conscious and unconscious motivation.

Working Through

Having understood or learned to perceive certain common denominators in his behavior, we now expect the patient to apply what he has learned; e.g., if the patient has learned that he projects onto his boss a hostility felt for his uncle, we can now expect that upon his next encounter with the boss he will continue to feel hostile but will remember the discussion of the hostility and its projection. Accordingly, he will at first modify the hostility volitionally. After a while, we would expect, as with all learning, a shift from volitional control to a more automatic, unconscious control, to the point where the patient no longer projects the hostility. Perhaps an even earlier step in working through occurs when the patient extends his insight to see that he behaves in the explicated fashion not only in situation "X" but also in situation "Y" and then proceeds to establish a common causality.

Working through, therefore, is a process whereby the patient applies the newly acquired insight to a variety of situations for which the same patterns hold true. His awareness of his manifest behavior and its causes are thus increased. This is essentially a learning process, through which the patient's behavior is changed; by metapsychological restructuring, therapeutic changes are brought about as the understanding strengthens the ego, and as the ventilation relieves the pressure of drive or brings about a modification of superego pressures.

Very often indeed, working through does not accomplish the desired result of a symptomatic change. The therapist is left then with the question of whether the insight is inaccurate, or whether other causes for the same behavior still remain unexplained. Most often the latter is the case, and both the patient and the therapist encounter overdetermination of a specific symptom. The therapeutic process is then repeated until the two or more determinants of the behavioral pattern have been elucidated and worked through.

These, then, are the general principles of dynamic psychotherapy which apply as well to brief psychotherapy. Aside from these dynamic considerations, structural evaluation in the form of ego functions also is very important for diagnosis, treatment, and prognosis. Ego functions assessment in relation to these problems is discussed in detail in Chapter 4.

3
Other Sources of Theory and Principle

The practice of psychotherapy is probably as multifarious as its practitioners. Individual practices based upon the same body of theory have many different and selective emphases.

So it is with the brief psychotherapies. The records of the early developmental years of psychoanalysis (Ferenczi, Stekel, and Freud himself) contain patients' expressions of gratification for quick reversals of neurotic conditions. (Stekel actually operated an Institute for Active Analysis in Vienna, where he practiced what we now call brief psychotherapy.) Such references occurred even during the heyday of psychoanalysis after World War II. The first of these post-war expressions in America was probably the influential *Psychoanalytic Theory* by Franz Alexander and Thomas French,[3] which proposed that there were principles within psychoanalytic theory and practice that could be utilized to make psychotherapy shorter, and hence more efficient.

Almost 20 years passed before concentrated efforts to evolve a brief therapy appeared in the United States and in England, undoubtedly in response to increasing demands for psychotherapy to serve all classes of people. These efforts produced a spate of therapies rooted in psychoanalysis which shared some fundamental concepts although they emphasized different aspects of the mother-therapy. Here we will review these other sources.

PSYCHOANALYTIC SOURCES

The essential common denominator among the psychoanalytically derived brief therapies is the concept of "focus," the concentration over a brief period of time upon the resolution of a specifically identified conflict, or the pursuit of a specifically identified goal. In all the approaches, the identification of the goal is made from a comprehensive psychoanalytically guided diagnosis of the patient's difficulties. Technically, the commitment to a focused goal, arrived at early in the therapeutic relationship, implies a modification and at times even an abandonment of the psychoanalytic commitment to the process of free association, and to the development and analysis of a transference neurosis. But it is important to stress that transference manifestations and periods of free association are incorporated into these brief therapies.

Bellak emphasized these points in a paper published in 1952.[14] In this paper he set forth the nucleus of the formulation on which he later based his approach to The Trouble Shooting Clinic, and from which his approach to brief therapy originates.

In England (1955) Michael and Enid Balint organized a study group for the development of a short-term, limited-goal psychotherapy. Five years later, when the group terminated, Balint concluded that the new techniques were supplementary to and not antagonistic to psychoanalytic theory and practice. The impact of this study group's efforts are most clearly and fully available in Malan's book, *A Study of Brief Psychotherapy*,[118] describing an analysis of the treatment of 21 patients by seven therapists employing a relatively active, focused, interpretative technique within the context of an "objective emotional interaction with the patient."

Malan's description of the use of interpretation is perhaps the most important element to single out here. He postulates "focus" as a goal to be formulated in an "essential interpretation." Ideally, if this essential interpretation were made under conditions that would insure insight in the patient, resolution of the conflict would most likely occur. The essential interpretation is seldom feasible in this manner; the focus, however, directs the therapist. The patient is guided toward the essential interpretation by partial ones. His movement toward the desired insight is encouraged by reinforcing communications from the therapist. Movements away from the interpretation by the patient are discouraged, most usually by inattention from the therapist.

Balint, in a posthumous publication,[8] reports that the independent discoveries by the patient increase in proportion to the number of the therapist's interventions as brief therapy moves toward termination. Balint emphasizes, as does Malan, a solely interpretative approach to the resolution of focal problems, and views so-called active therapies as manipulative. He utilizes structured record forms to initially identify and keep the therapeutic effort directed toward the goal, completing such forms after each diagnostic and therapeutic session.

In the United States, contributions to theory and practice of brief psychotherapy came largely from workers in New York City, Los Angeles, and Boston. Aside from Bellak,[14] Wolberg[172] offers a brief, active psychotherapy that identifies its focus in "target" symptoms, and encourages the patient's insight through interpretation, the resolution of resistance as soon as it is encountered, and the avoidance of the development of a transference neurosis.

H. J. Parad's[135] review of the variety of crises in the human life cycle (grief, parenthood, premature birth of a child, school entry, middle and later years, relocations, suicide, and deaths of others) stresses the propitious moments for change in the life cycle. Jacobson,[95] of the Benjamin Rush Institute in Los Angeles, stresses his practice of brief psychotherapy as pertinent for a population not able or willing to tolerate long-term therapy. He indicates also that a brief approach is especially useful for people accustomed to concrete thinking and to practical resolutions of their problems.

Sifneos,[152] of the Beth Israel Hospital in Boston, describes anxiety provocation as the chief impetus to the quick resolution of conflict. Essentially opposed to time limits on psychotherapy, he holds that short-term therapy can be facilitated by establishing a therapeutic alliance with the patient, identifying the problem to be solved, and using positive transference as the major therapeutic tool. Anxiety-provoking queries are used to elicit data needed to formulate or modify the psychodiagnostic elements of the conflict. Anxiety provocation is also the intent of statements that encourage or prod the patient to examine and experience a conflict more directly, and by experiencing the conflict, learn new ways of solving problems.

Although the psychoanalytic contributors to brief psychotherapy agree without exception on the importance of a selected focus, goal, or target in facilitating the resolution of conflict within a short time, they are far from agreement about the duration of a brief psychotherapy. Their procedures range from the specific minimum of five sessions preferred by the authors, to Sifneos's insistence that the patient should be given as much time as he reasonably needs within the context of the short-term situation.

One may well ask, therefore, what significance if any is assignable to the time-limiting factor when it is introduced. As will be developed later in this chapter, the authors believe that the predetermination of a time limit creates an expectancy within both the patient and the therapist that then influences the outcome in teleological fashion.

Mann[120] identifies time as the central issue in a theoretical structure derived from his conviction that long-term therapy generally leads to increasing dependency and diffusion, rather than focusing of content. He is concerned that the therapist avoid increasing the already existing dependency needs that the patient brings to therapy. He believes that in his observations of the course of long-term treatment, a point is reached where additional time no longer serves the goal of therapy but rather encourages the patient's search for gratification of infantile needs.

Time is postulated by Mann as first having a purely subjective, existential quality for the individual, embracing the first physiological experiences and encounters with the external world and its physical and human forces. These subjective meanings of time intrude upon and intertwine with a sense of concrete real time that is acquired later, as the cognitive abilities mature. In his therapy, Mann observes that limiting real time provokes the emergence of existential time–meaning and makes the earlier material available for resolution. To test his theory, Mann arbitrarily elected to offer patients at the Boston University Psychiatric Clinic a 12-session treatment in which a central therapeutic goal was identified and agreed upon at the first session.

Ample evidence can be obtained from this perusal of psychoanalytically based, brief psychotherapies to confirm the early findings and prediction of Alexander and French that within psychoanalytic theory and practice are principles that can guide efforts to make psychotherapy shorter, at least for many individuals who need emotional and psychological help.

In comparison to these methods of brief psychotherapy, the procedure of our own five to six session therapy is technically simpler. It is also closer to the basic model of psychoanalytic psychotherapy without necessitating any special provisions. Extensive reviews of methods of brief psychotherapy other than our own can be found in Small,[156] Barten,[9] and Barten and Barten.[10]

LEARNING THEORY

Modification of behavior is the goal both of learning efforts and of psychotherapy. The two endeavors have much in common. It is our thesis that psychotherapy is a learning process, that the psychotherapy of each patient consists of different problems of learning, and that therapy must be specifically fitted to the particular patient as understood diagnostically. The rational approach to psychotherapy must be tied to the explicit question, "How can this patient best unlearn, learn, relearn, or learn differently what is required in order to lose certain symptoms, master certain functions, or change the structure of his personality?" Psychoanalysis and dynamic psychotherapy are based primarily upon the learning acquired by insight, the relatively sudden perception of connections, accompanied by affective changes. This concept parallels precisely the concept of insight or closure inherent in the Gestalt theory of learning. "Transference cures" in psychotherapy may be viewed on the other hand as a special learning situation, predicated, for better or for worse, on the exceptional motivation provided by the patient's intense relationship to the therapist. If not accompanied by some insight and working through, such symptomatic changes tend to be unstable. Learning theory (concerned as it is with methods of learning, obstacles to learning, heightening the effects of learning) offers much of value for the psychotherapist, particularly in the practice of brief psychotherapy. We review first some of the fundamentals of learning theory and then relate them specifically to the process of psychotherapy.

Learning Theory Reviewed

TRIAL AND ERROR

The theory of trial-and-error learning holds that new adjustments require a drive which the habit equipment of the individual is inadequate to satisfy. Drive may be defined as a persistent, stimulating condition either within the individual or in the environment. Drive, conceived as a state of tension, requires release.

Blocks to the release of this tension are encountered, and the individual resorts to random movements because of inability to discharge the tension. These movements may lead to chance success. This experience in turn leads the individual to select among the random movements those which have led to success; the end result is a fixation upon the movement which resulted in the discharge of tension or the achievement of satisfaction.

Selection of purposive movements is a central problem in the trial-and-error theory of learning. In the examination of the problem of selection the principles of frequency and recency have come to the fore. The principle of frequency assumes that repetition tends to fix an action pattern. This principle, borrowed from general learning theory, does not suffice, and psychologists have turned more to an explanation of selection based upon the operation of motivation, conditioning, and inhibition of antagonistic responses. The inhibition of antagonistic responses would appear to be of primary concern in psychotherapy. Logically, one cannot approach and recoil at the same time. The likelihood is that one or the other action will dominate, or that some third response will result. Psychodynamically and metapsychologically, we perceive the action of antagonistic components in the personality: Ambivalence is one example, the antagonism between drive and superego is another. In psychotherapy the learning problem may require the decrease of one motivation and the increase of another, the lowering of one antagonistic response and the reinforcement of the other.

CONDITIONED RESPONSE

Conditioning involves the establishment of new integrations. Two unrelated stimuli become associated or integrated as a result of conditioning. As the two stimuli are repeatedly presented in tandem, a connection is gradually formed, so that the presentation of one stimulus alone will elicit the response appropriate to the second stimulus.

The concept of reinforcement in conditioning theory is especially pertinent. Experiments established that frequency and repetition alone are not enough to reinforce or maintain the conditioned response. If, after conditioning, the conditioned stimulus is presented without the original reinforcing stimulus, the transfer of response is gradually extinguished. Thus the general law of exercise was found to be inadequate and the addition of reinforcement was necessary. In diagnosis, we are concerned with the emotional factors which led to the establishment and particularly the maintenance or reinforcement of the symptomatic behavior. In the treatment of that behavior, we become concerned with reinforcements in the psychotherapeutic procedure which assure that the newly acquired response will persevere. Discovery, on the couch, of paths to satisfactions in life must be reinforced by real experience.

Clinical experience often shows that following the cessation of psychotherapy, its effect may become extinguished, in the sense that the old symptoms return and the patient must return for additional psychotherapy or reinforcement.

GESTALT

Gestalt psychologists have opposed both conditioning and trial-and-error learning theory as mechanistic and essentially physiological. The Gestalt psychologists maintain that learning is not merely an addition of simple parts, but rather is an interacting system or configuration which has its own properties and qualities. The whole of the personality or the individual is something entirely new and different from the simple parts which go into its composition. They hold, too, that the stimulus to which an organism responds is never a simple physical quality; it is always a stimulus with meaning, a stimulus in relationship to something else.

The Gestaltist does not deny the existence of trial-and-error or conditioned learning, but insists upon a different interpretation of the observable facts. He maintains that the experimental conditions which led to the establishment of these theories prevent the subjects from obtaining an insight into the whole and its significant relationships. The Gestaltist believes that our learning acquisitions are typically more dramatic and rapid, more purposive and directed than the other theorists would allow.

Cole[59] notes that closure or sudden learning appears to have taken place in some of the studies conducted by Thorndike, the primary advocate of trial-and-error behavior. This observation leads Cole to several conclusions worthy of note here. He believes that no single form of learning is typical for all situations or all individuals; regressions in learning, that is, primitive types of learning errors, appear with novices and children, or where the mass of stimuli confronting the learner is too complex and confusing, or where motivation is ambiguous, confusing, or lacking in intensity.

Cole further believes that closure occurs as a learning pattern among the more experienced, more mature, more highly developed or organized individual; or where the stimuli are few enough in number or so related and grouped that significant factors stand out and hence result in a directive, selective, and integrated type of response; or where the individual's motivation is definite or intense enough; and where his past experience provides the setting for an adequate response in the present.

The significance of the Gestalt view of learning for psychotherapy is that material properly ordered for an individual will eliminate blundering, that the monotonous, discouraging routine or practice can be replaced or considerably reduced by insight, and that in essence a grasp of a problem or a situation is more important than frequent repetition.

The Tension-Reduction Model Questioned

Seward[149] has furnished us with a review of recent developments in the theory of motivation. Learning theorists have been striving to establish more clearly the roots and operation of motivation, particularly as it applies to social behavior. In their efforts, the idea of instincts has given way to that of biological drives, and these in turn to the concept of conditioning of social motives which are not considered to be innate. Allport[4] proposed a *functional autonomy of motives,* thus questioning the tension-reduction model of learning. According to Allport, behavior eventually splits off from its original motivation and becomes motivation itself—what formerly were *means* become *ends.*

Parallel developments came to question the notion (basic to the theory of functional autonomy) that such motives are learned: Woodworth[173] suggested that a capacity furnishes its own motivation; K. Bühler[53] advanced the concept of "function pleasure"; and Diamond[61] held that stimulation was a basic requirement of the organism.

These concepts laid the groundwork for the development of a theory of exogenous motives, independent of visceral drives, which involve the efforts of the organism to both *control* and *predict* its environment. According to Seward ". . . an organism approaches and withdraws, explores and manipulates, as a function of specific differences between the present situation and the expectancies built into his schema of the world."

Earlier, White[170] in reviewing the status of motivation theory cited widespread discontent with theories based upon the concept of primary drives. Animal psychology, he reported, had found these theories insufficient in explaining exploratory and manipulative behaviors; psychoanalytic theorists found the theories inadequate in accounting for effective ego development. White advanced the concept of *competence* as a rubric, descriptive of behaviors with a common biological significance: they are all part of the process whereby the child or animal "learns to interact effectively with his environment." The behaviors leading to competence require more than instigation by drives. Competence receives major support from activities which, while they may be playful and exploratory, also are marked by "direction, selectivity, and persistence in interacting with the environment." These activities, White concludes, must be "motivated in their own right."

Psychoanalytic theorists[138] generally find the learning theories of academic psychologists too narrow, and believe that only a psychoanalytic theory could encompass all the factors necessary to consider in the learning process. Such a theory would have to include the drives, physical and social reality, autonomous ego functions, the processes of neutralization and automatization, the development of secondary thinking from the primary process, and the shift from the pleasure to the reality principle. This shift would require inclusion in the theory of the nature of gratification and frustration, factors that promote or inhibit identifications, and the roles played by anxiety, guilt, conflict, trauma, and active mastery. Along with these must be assumed also an autonomous, inborn mechanism of contact with reality, autonomously motivated. It seems clear that psychoanalytic theory is moving toward postulation of an innate ego apparatus with its own laws of development by maturation, along with an innate ego energy yielding pleasure of its own and providing a motivation for learning.

Seward's theory also takes into account the problem of stimulation, and thus most directly contradicts the tension-reduction model. Presupposing an optimal (or expressed) level of excitation, excessive stimulation produces emotional shock which diminishes arousal, whereas insufficient stimulation produces boredom which increases arousal.

The motive of excitation is especially significant in psychotherapy. Clinically one sees both over- and understimulated individuals. Establishing new levels of excitation expectancy appears to be possible through identification with the therapist, strengthening of ego functions, and corrective adjustment of superego demands.

Perhaps the most pertinent clinical observation is the phenomenon of autonomous improvement in the absence of further reinforcement from psychotherapy.

The critical examination of the tension-reduction model of learning and the widespread acceptance of behaviors that arise autonomously suggests that a single theory is not likely to explain all learned behavior. It is likely that there are several pathways to learning the same behavior, or that different behaviors may arise in the same way.

Some Practical Consequences of Learning Theory for Psychotherapy

Blundering inherent in the trial-and-error method may be expected in situations too difficult for the individual or those in which the individual's internal organization is inadequate because of lack in experience and motivation. Blundering may be resolved through teaching or the experience of doing, and certainly by a combination of these two forces. Psychotherapy essentially involves such a combination: The psychotherapist attempts to provide insight, and in the working-through process, to encourage the individual not only to reinforce the insight but also to acquire additional insight through experience. In effect, the psychotherapist provides insight and then encourages participation in situations in which the patient has an opportunity to test the significance of the insight and to provide himself with the opportunity for discovering other significant material.

The importance of motivation is stressed in all learning theory. Clearly, without motivation, learning is impossible. The early psychoanalytic observation of the perseverance of symptoms long after insight had been established supports this conclusion (e.g., secondary gain). Both punishment and reward have been used in learning experimentation, and are, as well, the basis of the establishment of patterns of socialization in children. Notably, the consensus of learning theorists is that motivation is most successful when it is positive. Drastic forms of punishment tend to spread effects over the entire learning situation which produce inhibition and unresponsiveness. This finding is of significance in psychotherapy where we rarely attempt alleviation of symptoms by appealing to the superego for punitive motivation, but rather to the ego for more positive, realistic satisfactions.

Rewards that result in immediate and complete release of painful tension are most effective in fixation of a response. In psychotherapy this obviously means that interventions that result in the ability to pursue and obtain certain satisfactions are most likely to remain with the individual. Interventions which only partially achieve these results will require additional effort.

The findings of conditioned-learning theory tell us that repetition alone is insufficient and that reinforcement is required to prevent the disintegration or extinction of a response. Pavlovian theory also indicates that learning must be adapted to the situation in which the behavior is to operate: Psychotherapy must be related to real life situations and problems. It is insufficient, therefore, to be content with the determination of genetic causations; the psychotherapist must proceed beyond this point to make sure that contemporaneous configurations are not only understood but are manageable.

Another finding of Pavlovian theory is that in the teaching of discriminations it is helpful to proceed from the coarse to the fine. A parallel theorem in the art of interpretation and in the explication of an individual's behavior to the individual is to proceed from concrete to abstract factors in observable configurations. Thus in interpretation one proceeds from examples of smaller scope to those of broader compass. This approximates a guide we obtain from Gestalt theory, that the learner be prepared to confront an all but complete figure. Insight into a pattern operative through both historical and contemporaneous life may be achieved more readily by reviewing the many smaller situations in which parts of the pattern can be observed.

The Gestalt school holds that blundering is an indication of improper motivation, a point of view which suggests that before learning may properly take place the subject must be in a state of anticipation or expectancy. A therapeutic task, therefore, is to assure that such a state exists. One technique is to identify and thus mobilize the elements which are already possessed by the patient so that expectancy will be operative. For example, in the treatment of passivity a readiness to learn activity can be generated by leading the patient through a review of the outcome and satisfaction derived from situations when he had been active. Psychotherapy has also discovered that much motivation lies dormant in the individual because of irrational unconscious fears of the consequences of behavior stemming from the motivation. In these cases motivation is mobilized when the fears are identified and worked through—a matter of unlearning before learning.

Gestaltists also have taught us that the control of configurational factors is essential in learning. Here they are referring to the presentation of the material to be learned in a configurational pattern which encourages visualization. This concept is easy to overdo; one may erroneously present configurations which are too wide, too sweeping, and possibly too confused for ready perception and understanding. The concept, however, is meaningful if one keeps in mind that the configuration and its visualization must be made meaningful to the patient by employing images that are appropriate to his intelligence, interests, experiences, and culture.

Learning by Identification

Psychoanalytic theory has made some unique contributions to learning theory. Significant examples are the discovery of levels of awareness, of the operation of primary-process thinking and its evolution into secondary modes of thinking, of the learning which takes place unconsciously, of phase-specific learning, or learning which is particularly effective if the "learned" material relates specifically to a current phase of biological development of the child—for example, phallic trauma in the phallic period. Perhaps most significant for our purpose here is the psychoanalytic concept of learning by identification. Identification with the therapist plays an important role in therapeutic learning in that, for instance, the less irrational superego of the therapist may restructure an archaic superego and a variety of other introjects may be acquired via the therapist. It is important to think of learning by both positive and negative identification in efforts to understand the configuration of a given individual's behavior. Learning may arise as a positive emulation of another individual or as the avoidance of specific modes of behavior related to a "bad" introject.

The concept of identification, as well as that of introjection, while much discussed, is still in need of better definition. For a general background, Scheidlinger's paper[144] is illuminating.

Introjection undoubtedly refers, among other meanings, to the simple fact that all apperception becomes part of the apperceptive mass which in turn becomes part of the structure of the personality (other parts of the structure are the biological, constitutional features). In this broad sense, psychoanalytic theory is built upon the perceptual school of Hume, Berkeley, and Herbart, tempered by biological knowledge thus superseding the simple ideas of the *tabula rasa* and *esse est percipi*.

More specifically, in the libido theory psychoanalysis provides a true timetable within which learning interacts with biological–psychological phases of development. It provides specific theories covering the most basic learning experiences, in a manner provided by no other theory. This includes the process of identification with parents and other significant figures.

Identification in that sense barely differs from introjection. What needs consideration is the degree of emotional investment of each introjected experience, and the adaptive and defensive fate of these experiences: emulation, denial, reaction formation, etc. Also to be considered is the degree of "regency" (to use Murray's term) which each of these incorporated experiences will have upon personality structure and future behavior.

The only other confusing usage of the term "identification" that needs mention here is the use of "primary identification" to mean a regressive phenomenon: In certain pathological conditions a person may identify himself entirely with another person—complete regency of one particular introject or identification object over the self—with dire consequences.

Insight Learning in Psychotherapy

Personality may be viewed as a structure acquired by a unique organism via learning experiences. Each person may be conceived as being the sum total and Gestalt of past perceptions and affects, plus a particular constitutional substratum; each new perception will serve as a base for accretion of the next perception, so that in effect the personality structure is the result of a series of superimposed data that merge with each other into configurations which in turn affect the apperceptions of future experiences. The psychotherapeutic process is an attempt to analyze the contemporary configurations into its parts (historical, constitutional) and to effect a restructuring of distorted apperceptions. Psychoanalysis and intensive psychotherapy are long processes because their goals require that the patient review a great mass of apperceptions for restructuring. In brief psychotherapy the task is to perceive the main problem the patient brings now, so that we may deal with the most crucial present learning problems, and intervene to restructure these. To repeat, the task in each psychotherapy is tied to the explicit question: How will this patient best unlearn, learn, relearn, or learn differently what he needs to learn? More specifically: How may he learn to lose certain symptoms, acquire functions, respond differently, and change aspects of his personality?

What therapeutic learning procedures are available to us? The most widely applied learning concept in psychotherapy undoubtedly is that of insight, which may be related to the Gestalt principle of closure. Almost always in psychotherapy, learning by insight must be reinforced by the process of working through genetic, contemporary, and transference experiences. In the working-through process, learning by conditioning undoubtedly plays a major role, in the sense that "correct" behavior is rewarded by freedom from anxiety, alleviation of troublesome symptoms, and by the ego satisfaction of achievement. "Wrong" (neurotic) behavior is "punished" by anxiety or other forms of neurotic pain. Both these approaches to psychotherapeutic learning are applicable to the brief therapeutic procedure. As we have indicated, learning by identification in which the analyst is made a new introject plays a role in long-term psychoanalysis, and may be employed in some specific ways in psychotherapy with those patients who require a long period of "holding" and ego mending. Essentially psychotherapy is rooted in learning by insight and by conditioning during the working-through process. Since insight is accomplished largely by interpretation during the "audible" part of the psychotherapeutic process, this approach to learning receives particular attention in the next chapter.

CRISIS RESOLUTION IN BRIEF THERAPY

Crises tax the resources and strengths of individuals and threaten their integrity. A crisis may traumatize by imposing conditions that are beyond the individual's capacities for adaptation.

But the crisis also may mobilize the person's resources, and above all his motivation for learning new ways of dealing with anxiety-inducing situations. This potentiality is enhanced when the therapist becomes allied with the person in crisis, thus adding the resources of psychotherapy to those of the individual.

Brief psychotherapy is an ideal intervention for facilitating the resolution of many crises. The person in crisis is pressed by the need for resolution; the need is so compellingly immediate that it usually cannot be postponed. Tension and anxiety are high and motivation born of discomfort is great. The person in crisis is in a state of precarious equilibrium in which a small input has the potential for effecting a change disproportionately greater than the input.

Crises may develop from sudden shifts in the social forces bearing upon the individual. These may involve alterations in role or status: the acquisition or loss of income or wealth imposing new modes of living and of relating to others; the acquisition or loss of titles or occupational roles requiring or removing responsibilities, and also altering ways of relating to others.

Crisis and Development

A more predictable series of crises are those developmental landmarks all humans traverse in the inexorable progress of the birth-to-death-life cycle. Many childhood and infant events may properly be identified as developmental crises (the ego development and the conflicts it provokes associated with the "terrible twos" as an example) where resolution is dependent upon the changes in or actions of another person, usually the mother and/or father. Other developmental crises arise from internal changes that press upon the individual in confrontation with the demands of society: leaving home and mother for school and teacher; the physiological changes of increasing strength and emerging genitality, and later the waning of these same forces; the shift from dependency to needs for independence; the role changes from child to adolescent, adult, spouse, parent, and grandparent. Often it may be the parent who is precipitated into crisis by the change or need for change in the child, for example, the necessity to control body limits or aggression. Adolescence is sometimes described as an implicit crisis through which the maturing personality must pass. For individual adolescents the crisis may involve the establishment of identity, a widening separation from parents and the dependent role, the growing supremacy of genitality, the pressure to select a life style, the preparation for vocational status, or negotiating deterence of peer and social pressures such as in the use of drugs and alcohol.

The successful adolescent will traverse these crises only to encounter those of later years: the decision to marry or not marry, to parent or not parent, possibly to divorce, and certainly to encounter the inexorable process of aging.

A frequently observed crisis that involves many forces including both social and individual changes is generated by the loss of a beloved or needed person. Often the primary task is to encourage grief and mourning and facilitate the discharge of burdensome affect. Oppressive shifts in economic status, anxiety-provoking removal of an anaclitic or symbiotic relationship, or other role changes of hazardous import for the survivor also may be involved.

Traumas

Though not usually treated as such in psychotherapeutic literature, the trauma may be conceptualized as a crisis of extraordinary emotional and personality impact, in which external stimulation or internal tension increases to an unmanageable degree. Fenichel[66] has observed that in the first case the individual's capacity for tolerating the stimulation is inadequate to its intensity. In the latter instance, because of a failure to discharge, tension is accumulated to such pressure that a usual or normal degree of stimulation may prove traumatic.

Fenichel describes two major responses to traumatization: an effort to discharge the accumulated tension by hyperactivity and hyperemotionality, and through repetitive dreams and fantasies, inactivity and rest. From these spontaneous efforts at restoration come the techniques available to psychotherapy: quieting procedures or active cathartic ventilation.

An ego-function approach to the treatment of traumas is inherent in Kardiner's[100] study of war-induced neuroses. In his schema, trauma results from the sudden loss of adaptive capacities in the face of overwhelming forces or threats such as the loss of a limb, the paralysis induced by exposure to a nearby bomb explosion, or injury or death of a friend or nearby peer. Civilian events to some degree may be compared in the occurrences of an automobile accident, an explosion in a building, an energy blackout, an earthquake, a flood, exposure to rape or mugging, or the decision to undergo an abortion. The inability to adapt to (function in) a new, threatening situation produces an overwhelming inhibition of the ego and its functions that increases the individual's sense of danger and impotence. Treatment is directed toward the encouragement of activity and the acquisition of techniques of mastery.

Thus the goals of brief therapy in crisis resolution are derived from knowledge of cause and effect. These goals may include facilitation of affective expression and experience, encouragement of assertive acts, selection among alternative courses, collection of information, or sometimes even postponement of choice or action. In any type of crisis the major goal is to prevent regression by encouraging utilization of the stronger, more intact ego functions.

The types and frequencies of crises that are encountered indicate both the necessity for and applicability of a brief psychotherapeutic method for their alleviation and resolution. The resolution of crises in practice also illuminates at least two bases for the successful application of a brief methodology. The degree of tension and motivation present in the personality facilitates effective response to a comparatively small order of input or effort from the outside. And, as stated earlier, knowledge of causes and effects, observable in crises of all kinds, effectively guides the selection and application of methods of resolution. Very often the crisis and its resolution provide a unique opportunity for new learning that leaves the personality more mature and possessing greater ego strengths than before the patient encountered and negotiated the crisis.

EXPECTATION THEORY

The forces associated with the theory of expectation and hope have teleological import: Present anticipation of the future influences or predicates future outcomes, and anticipation of the nature of the future may modify present behavior and affect. Expectation theory is indeed another element of time–experience upon which a brief psychotherapy is based. Positive expectation in future time contributes to the ability of the patient to accept and tolerate the loss of the therapist inherent in termination.

Frank[68] has studied and commented on the teleological force of expectation and hope in the therapeutic process. The expectation of change and of relief of tension, anxiety, or depression enables the individual to sacrifice the time and/or money and permit the invasion of privacy that therapy requires. Additionally, the individual's expectations influence the outcome of the therapeutic venture.

Frank reports studies in which tests and questionnaires administered by the therapist were as effective in achieving mood improvement and diminution of symptoms as a placebo pill also administered by the therapist. He concludes, with good reason, that any interaction between patient and therapist that creates in the patient the expectation that he will benefit will lead to positive changes. Frank also cites evidence from other studies that these beneficial changes derive more from the patient's perception of the therapist's assuring attitude than from the patient's belief in the efficacy of a pill.

Awareness of the influence of expectation on the outcome of therapy contributes to the reasonableness of a brief therapy, the technical considerations governing the early sessions, and the handling of transference manifestations both in early and later sessions. When personality pathology is not too severe, perception of cause and effect relationships usually makes the therapist optimistic about outcome. Communication of this understanding, without at the time elucidating it, contributes to optimism in the patient. Writing a contract at the beginning of treatment, in which the responsibilities of both therapist and patient are delineated and in which a prognosis is incorporated, also enhances the expectation that the patient will be helped within the prescribed time.[16] Most important to success in brief psychotherapy, the teleological pull of expectation underwrites the early establishment and subsequent maintenance of a positive transference relationship (see Chapter 4).

4
The Basic Processes of Brief Therapy

The wide range of individual differences makes hazardous the schematic ordering of any human interaction. Nonetheless, in the psychotherapeutic process certain basic steps can be established which apply to almost all individual situations. Within each of these occurs a wider range of variation. The major steps in brief psychotherapy may be viewed as proceeding from establishing "relation cues" and identification of the presenting problem to taking of a history, establishing the relations between symptom and history, selecting and applicating interventions, working through, and finally to the ending phase of treatment. These steps overlap with the three general aspects of psychotherapy: communication, insight (or other structural change), and working through.

THE ORGANIZATION OF FIVE-SESSION PSYCHOTHERAPY IN CAPSULE FORM

Above all in advocating five-session psychotherapy it must be kept in mind that this number is not meant to be rigidly followed. There is a certain rationale in choosing to speak of five-session psychotherapy because reliable statistical data have indicated that the majority of patients, especially those coming to out-patient clinics, attend about five times and then break off treatment. They may have a medical model in mind, expect very prompt relief, and may not be acquainted with the longer and in-depth psychotherapies such as psychoanalysis. In this case, it is more expedient to plan on psychotherapy within the framework of what the patient is willing to engage in, than to plan longer psychotherapy and have the patient break off after five sessions.

Aside from that rationale, it has been feasible in our experience of the last two decades to do a reasonably good job in five sessions with a large number of patients. In practice, therapy is more often six sessions: The patient is usually seen once a week for five weeks unless there are reasons to plan it differently—either more often because of the intensity of the condition, or less often for administrative reasons or because it is not indicated clinically that the patient be seen once a week. After the fifth session the patient is usually seen about a month later for an evaluation (sixth session), as we will discuss later.

It is important to plan the therapeutic process in terms of what one can expect in each of the five sessions, and especially at the end of the first session, to formulate some clear-cut plans with regard to the *areas of intervention,* the *methods of intervention,* and the *sequence of areas* and *methods of intervention.* In the *area of intervention,* as in the case of a depression, the therapist addresses the problem of lowered self-esteem, or the problem of aggression which in the presence of a severe superego has been turned into intra-aggression or feelings of disappointment and deception. For a *method of intervention* one might choose in this case support, interpretation, or catharsis. It must be kept in mind that if the problem of lowered self-esteem is to be approached in terms of gaining insight and relating the most recent precipitating event to common denominators in the previous life history, the *area* and *method of intervention* will be followed by a discussion of the person responsible for the lowered self-esteem in the precipitating situation. The unconscious relationship between that person and earlier persons in the patient's life should be investigated, with some cathartic interpretation of the anger aroused. At the same time the therapist will give some form of reassurance that a person with such a severe superego would not only not permit himself to act on such aggressive wishes, but doesn't even dare think them. As much as possible *the entire therapeutic process should be formulated over the five sessions in terms of areas of intervention, methods of intervention, and their sequence,* including transference interpretations. It must be clearly understood that a conceptualized plan is not something to be rigidly followed but will be flexible enough to be changed as new material emerges or as the patient's needs require.

The schematic ordering of the psychotherapeutic process is hazardous because there are often departures and variations from the schema, however cogent and conservative it may be, and however carefully common denominators are identified. The therapy of some individuals will follow the schema seemingly "by the numbers," as if the patient had cooperated in writing the plan. Others will skip over parts of the process, condensing or eliminating steps. Still others will remain rooted at a particular phase, from which no amount of prodding (interpretation or suggestion) or defensive strengthening (encouragement, support, reassurance) will budge them. We are reminded of the farmer who, when asked to identify the signs of coming rain, replied, "All signs fail in dry weather."

The first session: History is the present status of the past. When a patient is referred initially, an exhaustive history is essential. But that history must first be concerned with what hurts the patient now; that is, the present chief complaint and secondary complaints.

In the first session it is important to find out precisely *when* the symptoms started and to understand the *life situation within which they arose,* and then, precisely why the patient chose to come in on this particular day. Only then does the therapist ask for an entire life history. When the therapist begins taking a life history, there must be heavy emphasis on the concrete details of the patient's growing up: relationship to parents, siblings, living conditions, sleeping conditions, and as much of an understanding of the social, economic, cultural, and ethnic background as possible. Therefore, *the major part of the first session is spent on history taking.*

It is important to look repeatedly for other complaints since patients often either forget or are reluctant to enumerate them.

After about 35 or 40 minutes, the basic patterns about the dynamics and structure of the patient's problems, their assets and liabilities, should become clear. It may be useful in this initial evaluation to keep ego-function assessment in mind, as will be discussed.

Above all, the therapist should begin to *shape some plan* about the theme of the patient's problems, the area of intervention, and the method and sequence of intervention as therapy continues.

The therapist guides himself best in the choice of areas of intervention, methods of intervention, and their sequence from the dynamic understanding he derives from common denominators in the general life history of the patient; the socio-psychological structure of the onset of the chief complaint; and the shared common denominator with the most immediate reason for bringing the patient in on this rather than any other day. The crux—the economy—of five-session therapy lies in the fact that all behavior is an attempt at adaptation, and that the current maladaptation which brings the patient to us is predicated largely on earlier learned modes of adapting to similar problems. Thus someone reacting with a depression to a present loss probably has suffered earlier losses and reacted to them in a similar way. Someone suffering from a panic will have experienced other panics, which he may not have been aware of at the time, but that are likely to have had the same dynamic pattern.

The better one understands the current complaint in terms of common denominators in the patient's earlier experience—general life history—and upsetting events, the more precisely one can formulate the areas, methods and sequence of areas, and methods of intervention. This is the central guiding rationale of five-session therapy. The sequence and areas of intervention are dictated by a variety of clinical observations, such as the urgency of dealing with aggression and intra-aggression in someone suicidal, while leaving phobic problems to be dealt with at some later time.

After the therapist understands roughly what the problem is about, it is advisable to give the patient an overview, some ideas buttressed with examples. Pointing out *common denominators* between his current symptoms and some of his past experiences and reactions is often helpful in promoting the beginnings of insight. It is useful to take a few minutes to explain the basic process of psychotherapy, namely, understanding together what happens inside his mind without his knowledge and establishing a continuity between the past and present, the conscious and unconscious, and symptomatology. The patient must feel that we know what the problem is about, and that what ails him can be understood and probably remedied. This should lead up to establishing a *therapeutic alliance,* which might be put this way: "There is a healthy part of you and an upset part of you. It is important that the healthy part work with me as much as possible to understand and help the disturbed part."

Having established a *basic understanding* and a *therapeutic alliance,* it is now time to *formulate the contract,* without necessarily calling it that. The patient is told that five sessions will probably be sufficient to help him but that whatever happens we want to hear from him in a month. He can do this in person, by telephone, or even by letter. Of course if there are further problems, therapy will either be continued or resumed. But the chances are good that the five sessions will be enough.

The second session should begin with the question of what the patient thought, felt, and dreamt after the first session. This helps to maintain some continuity as part of the therapy technique. It is important to ask the patient for dreams and not be shy about it. Dreams following the session are likely to reveal a great deal about transference phenomena, among other things. If he reports not having any, ask him if he had a flash or a picture, even a feeling or a few words. Patients often come forth with a good deal of dreaming with such encouragement. We should not worry about indirectly suggesting that the patient dream, because his dreams will still be his own and reveal his problems, not someone else's. Otherwise the second session is used both for further exploration and the initial therapeutic intervention, whatever happens to be most urgent or appropriate. Obviously in suicidal depression one would concern oneself especially with aggression, superego, and the object from whom the aggression might be displaced toward the self. In other instances the therapist may have occasion to explore whatever area seems best, following the usual rule of dealing with relatively accessible and superficial problems first, and with the more submerged and highly defended ones later.

The same process goes on in *the third session,* when the patient is likely to show some improvement. This is also the time to work through any separation anxiety by mentioning again the *coming separation* and saying that this separation may possibly be so threatening as to make things worse again.

The fourth session often produces a patient who is feeling worse. Working through these feelings, the patient and therapist can cover previous material, the relationship to the therapist, and separation anxiety. The therapist should repeat again that he wants to hear from the patient and will be available to him if necessary.

The fifth session is a mopping-up operation. New material, any working through that can be done, summing up and reviewing information, and leaving the patient with a positive transference are all appropriate grounds to cover in this session. If for some reason the patient is not well enough for termination, one might now continue therapy with the idea of playing it by ear. When the therapist thinks the patient has reached a plateau, he might suggest starting again in three months.

At the end of the fifth session the patient is asked again to contact the therapist at least a month hence even if he feels perfectly well. In many circumstances it may be advisable to ask the patient to come for a follow-up session approximately a month later. This may be done, for instance, if the therapist is not sufficiently sure that the patient will be well enough or if he feels that other material needing work may still crop up. Thus, sometimes five-session therapy translates into six-session therapy, or, as will be made clear from at least one of the cases discussed later, even eight-session therapy or whatever the actual needs demand. Even with its apparent rigidity, the five-session therapy model has worked exceedingly well in the majority of cases. If and when variations are indicated, a clinician has to be flexible enough to make them.

THE ROLE OF THE DIAGNOSTIC FORMULATION

Dynamic Assessment

Formerly diagnosis was purely descriptive of a malfunction, but at our current level of knowledge it includes the determination of the relationship between the person we meet in the therapeutic situation and the past and contemporary events in his life. Diagnosis requires that we establish precisely the relationship between this patient and the events that, at different times, went into forming him. These events may pertain to people or to events in the cultural setting. The therapist must remain ever mindful of the organismic equipment of the individual as much as it can be discerned, as well as of the stage of development at which the patient had a given experience. The problem is complicated, because not only must individual events be evaluated, but also the effect of event Z in relationship to the fact that events X and Y preceded it. Thus, for example, the loss of a mother in the patient's childhood must be brought into relationship to the earlier advent of a sibling and the previous prolonged absence of the father from the home.

Not all personality factors can be related in a one-to-one relationship; separately experienced events not only affect subsequent events, but a variety of experiences may assume configurations which, in terms of Gestalt psychology, are more than the sum of the parts. They become newly emergent wholes, which have an effect as such on later experience. Nor is our task made easier by the reflection that we may no longer think in terms of the rigid determinism of the nineteenth century. We can only expect a diagnostic hypothesis to provide a guide to the most probable effects—that is, diagnosis must be cast in terms of probability. Fortunately, current psychoanalytic theory provides a sufficient framework to permit a useful and credible job when applied rationally and systematically.

By definition, brief psychotherapy involves intervention within the shortest possible period of time. The exigencies of the situation require, therefore, that the intervention be not haphazard but firmly rooted in definitive understanding, enabling us to ascribe the patient's complaint to the dynamics of the precipitating situation and in turn to historical factors. The result of the diagnosis should enable the therapist to identify the factors most susceptible to change and to select and apply methods for effecting the change. Thus if a patient complains of depersonalization in a particular setting, the task of diagnosis is to determine what goes on in that situation; what in the past has created the susceptibility to the current situation; what can be done about it; and how the intervention should be performed.

Stated in another way, the first task in diagnosis is to understand the symptom. Comprehension of symptomatology proceeds from the most general meaning to the most specific. Freud gave us the valuable insight that every symptom contains both a wish and a defense. Further, clinical experience has elucidated some general meanings for various symptoms. For example, a depression may develop as a result of loss of self-esteem, loss or threat of loss of a love object, or deflection of hostility against the self. But then the specific meaning (or meanings) of the symptom to the patient must be identified. This requires the most elaborate details of the present and the past. Consider a depressed woman of 60 whose present situation is that she must nurse her seriously ill husband, recently incapacitated. What is the wish and the defense inherent in her depression? Does her depression arise as a loss of self-esteem? Does it arise from the threat of the loss of her loved husband, replicating the loss of love experienced in the past? Or does it arise because she is angered by the necessity to serve as a nurse, thus experiencing deprivation in her social life, a deprivation possibly traceable to previous deprivations with comparable reactions?

A major guiding concept in diagnostic fomulation is that the dynamics of the present situation can be identified in the genetic and developmental history of the individual. Freud has said that an adult neurosis breaks out when a contemporary situation repeats a traumatic infantile situation. The present illness is understood if the precipitating situation can be clearly perceived as a pattern repetitive of an earlier one, and if the significance of each contemporary factor is clearly seen.

Diagnosis is the complex appraisal of disturbances. For that purpose the nature of the disturbance needs to be described as well as brought into relationship to the various time variables in question. Nosological description provides us with only the most general statements concerning disturbance. Psychoanalytic theory provides us with the tools for making a detailed survey of ego functions (and of the individual patterns of their disturbance) as a basis for a qualitative–quantitative assessment of the nature of disturbances. Psychoses, as a group, share the common denominator of relatively more severely disturbed ego functions, or of having more ego functions affected than in the neuroses or in the normal range. Relatively circumscribed profiles of disturbance constitute the different nosological groups, including the organic ones. Psychoanalytical dynamics provide us with an excellent set of propositions for understanding intermediary states and the changes from one clinical group into another, since it permits us to speak of forces which in some individuals, under some circumstances, may become stabilized into the classically known disease pictures, while remaining fluid in others. Use of an ego-function profile permits the ascribing of the complaint to the dynamics of the precipitating situation and to historical factors. At the same time, the ego-function profile enables the therapist to identify those factors most susceptible to change, and it points toward methods for changing them. The assessment of ego functions for diagnostic and therapeutic purposes will be more fully treated in later sections.

The diagnostic formulation, therefore, attempts to understand the complaint and the patient dynamically, and to establish a set of hypotheses concerning causality that must then be substantiated by historical data.

A frequently impressive and useful experiment consists of having the presenting clinician give only the life history of the patient and letting the rest of the group attempt to predict what the symptomatology is. At other times we do the reverse: The presenting clinician offers only the symptomatology that brought the patient in and the rest of the group attempts to *post*dict what the history might have been, and what events might have played a role in the history of the patient. Actually it is part of the elegance of the interlocking nature of psychoanalytic hypotheses concerning the theories of personality, psychopathology, and psycotherapy that should enable such tasks to be performed in systematic experimental fashion. This was done as part of a systematic study of the therapeutic process by Bellak and Smith[19] for classical psychoanalysis, and Bellak and Small, first edition of this volume, and Bellak with S. Rosenberg et al.[30] for brief psychotherapy.

As an example, consider a patient who comes into treatment in panic because he has experienced loss of sensation around the mouth. The patient is an intelligent individual in his early forties, professionally employed. He complains that he has been getting along poorly with his wife in recent years, that there is estrangement between them, and that he is upset about his situation. But he also communicates that he had comparable symptoms when he was on a field trip, an occasion that marked the first time that he was ever away from his home town for a significant period. These few bare facts permit the proposition that the patient has a strong dependency need and is prone to feelings of oral deprivation.

Then the patient communicates that he had experienced two love affairs prior to his marriage which had not worked out the way he had hoped. Rather long depression had followed these events. Further history revealed that he had been breast-fed until he was five years old. Clinical experience has taught us that getting too much of something may produce the same problems as getting too little. Thus we may hypothesize that this patient, having been given a great deal orally as a child, had had raised in him a high level of oral expectancy and established a predisposition to feelings of deprivation.

These hypotheses explain the location of his symptomatology in the perioral region. An additional hypothesis is necessary to explain the anesthesia of the lips. This can be understood as a negation, a denial of an intense wish to have the breast, and to be graphic, to have the breast in his mouth. The situation is intelligible dynamically then as an oral wish, ungratified, against which excessive defensiveness results in the production of a symptom. Clinical sophistication requires an additional hypothesis: Deprivation has produced an anger and hostility toward the depriving love object, in the immediate situation to his wife, in the past to his mother. Metapsychologically, therefore, there is a conflict between wish and censorship with the conflict resolved as a denial of the wish in the form of anesthesia. In terms of ego psychology, we perceive a repression of the drive, an intensification of the defense, and a disturbance in object relations. This case also illustrates the usefulness of looking for common denominators between past and present events (the long nursing, the relationship between the current upset, the perioral sensations, their previous occurrence at the time of the field trip, and the depressions when two love affairs didn't work out).

This approach[5] corresponds closely to what Small[156] conceptualizes as a psychodiagnostic approach intended to guide a therapist's thinking about a patient through the history-taking process from diagnosis to treatment and prognosis. His conceptualization embodies a series of *implicit* questions for which the therapist seeks answers as he takes a history and then proceeds with psychotherapy:

1. What is the complaint?
2. What is the precipitating cause of the complaint?

3. What are the antecedent analogues of the patient's present situation?
4. What do the symptoms mean? Historically? What are their generic and individual dynamics? Do they have other possible origins in physiological, endocrinological, neurological, genetic, or cultural determinants?
5. What is the state of the ego system? The condition—strength or weakness—of the different functions?
6. What dynamic changes are required to reestablish homeostasis?
7. What therapeutic interventions will most likely promote the desired changes?
8. What therapeutic allies are required? Which are available?
9. What shall be the procedure of this therapy with this patient?
10. What is the prognosis?
11. If the organismic and/or cultural factors have been identified as the primary or secondary determinants of the symptoms, how do these affect the ego? The choice of intervention? The prognosis?

With this formulation and guide as prelude we shall examine components of the process in detail.

Ego-Function Assessment (EFA): A Further Guide to the Diagnosis and Planning of Interventions

So far we have emphasized solely the dynamic basis for the diagnosis (and correlated treatment) of the patient—the dynamic understanding of common denominators and interpretations, and other kinds of interventions.

The sicker the patient, the more useful it is to attempt also a *structural* assessment in terms of ego functions, which permits a plan of therapy in terms of major liabilities and major assets.

A systematic attempt to study ego functions was undertaken by Bellak et al.[37] From this study of ego functions (see Table 1) in schizophrenics,

Table 1.
List of Ego Functions and their Components

Ego Function	Components
1. Reality testing	Distinction between inner and outer stimuli.
	Accuracy of perception.
	Reflective awareness and inner reality testing.
2. Judgment	Anticipation of consequences.
	Manifestation of this anticipation in behavior.
	Emotional appropriateness of this anticipation.

Table 1.
List of Ego Functions and their Components (continued)

Ego Function	Components
3. Sense of reality	Extent of derealization.
	Extent of depersonalization.
	Self-identity and self-esteem.
	Clarity of boundaries between self and world.
4. Regulation and control of drives, affects, and impulses	Directness of impulse expression.
	Effectiveness of delay mechanisms.
5. Object relations	Degree and kind of relatedness.
	Primitivity (narcissistic, attachment or symbiotic object choices) *vs.* maturity.
	Degree to which others are perceived independently of oneself.
	Object constancy.
6. Thought processes	Memory, concentration, and attention.
	Ability to conceptualize.
	Primary–secondary process.
7. Adaptive regression in the service of the ego (ARISE)	Regressive relaxation of cognitive acuity.
	New configurations.
8. Defensive functioning	Weakness or obtrusiveness of defenses.
	Success and failure of defenses.
9. Stimulus barrier	Threshold for stimuli.
	Effectiveness of management of excessive stimulus input.
10. Autonomous functioning	Degree of freedom from impairment of primary autonomy apparatuses.
	Degree of freedom from impairment of secondary autonomy.
11. Synthetic–integrative functioning	Degree of reconciliation of incongruities.
	Degree of active relating together of events.
12. Mastery–competence	Competence—how well a person performs in relation to his capacity to actively master and affect his environment.
	Subject's feeling of competence as measured by his expectations of success on actual performance.
	Discrepancy between actual competence and feeling of competence.

neurotics, and normals evolved a scheme (Figure 1) of 12 ego functions and their components, and a scale for rating them on a 7- or 13-point basis. Table 2 presents a detailed rating, which may not be necessary for the simple clinical checking of assets and liabilities in brief therapy.

Since the original work on ego functions, attempts also have been made to appraise ego functions for analyzability or treatability by Bellak and Meyers,[39] for following the analytic process by Ciompi et al.,[57] for the assessment of brief psychotherapy,[150] for drug therapy by Bellak et al.[35] and to discuss the broad scope of EFA generally by Bellak and Sheehy.[41]

EFA's primary role in brief psychotherapy, however, goes further than the diagnostic assessment of the overall structure and its liabilities.[39] EFA can also identify the areas which need most urgent attention, and the relatively intact areas or functions which may be used as a basis for the

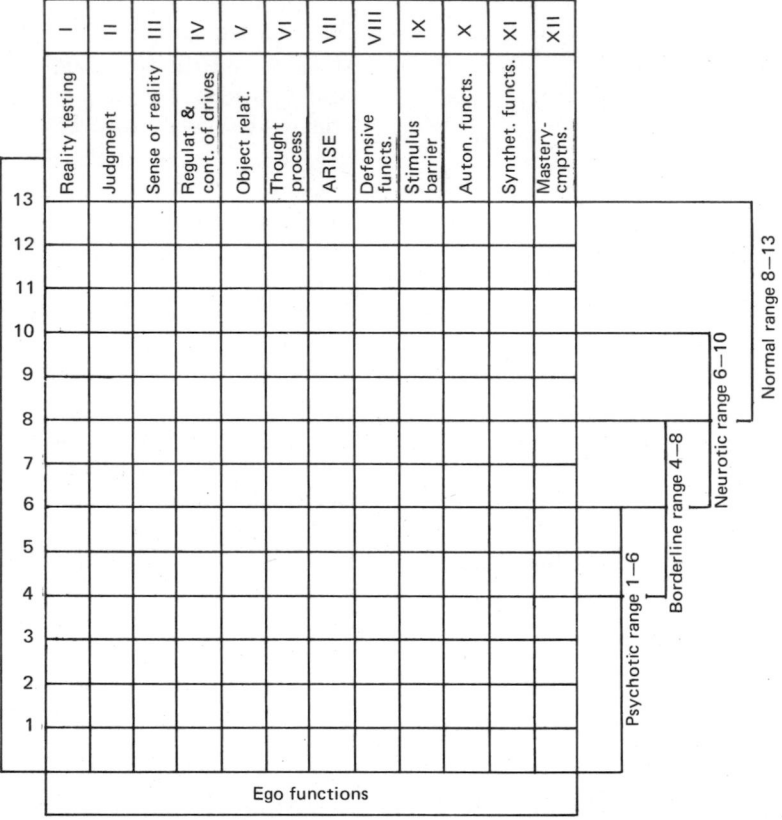

Fig. 1. Ego-function rating form, showing the approximate *ranges* of normality, neuroses (and equivalent character disorders), borderline conditions, and psychoses. (From Bellak, Hurvich, and Gediman, *Ego Functions in Schizophrenics, Neurotics, and Normals.* Copyright © 1973, by C.P.S., Inc. Reprinted by permission of John Wiley & Sons, Inc.)

Table 2.
Scoring of Reality Testing Component A: Distinction between Inner and Outer
Stimuli.*

	Maximal Impairment
Point 1.	Hallucinations and delusions pervade.
	There is minimal ability to distinguish events occurring in dreams from those occurring in waking life and between idea, image, and hallucination.
	Perceptual experience is grossly disturbed (e.g., moving things look still and vice versa).
Point 3.	Hallucinations and delusions are severe but limited to one or more content areas. Patient may show considerable doubt about whether an event really happened in his mind or in a dream.
Point 5.	Illusions are more likely than hallucinations to be found. Patient may be aware that he sees and hears things that are not there; he knows that others don't see or hear them.
Point 7.	Projection of inner states onto external reality is more likely than frank hallucinations or delusions. A "stimulus-bound" reality testing may occur at the cost of libidinal investments and gratifications.
Point 9.	Confusion about inner and outer states occurs mainly upon awakening, going to sleep, or under severe stress.
Point 11.	Inner and outer stimuli are well distinguished. Occasional denial of external reality in the service of adaptation.
	Optimal Functioning
Point 13.	Clear awareness of whether events occurred in dreams or waking life.
	Correct identification of the source of cognitive and/or perceptual content as being idea or image, and accurate identification of its source as internal or external.
	Distinction between outer and inner percepts hold up even under extreme stress.
	Checking one's perceptions against reality occurs with a very high degree of automaticity.

*The detailed scoring of ego functions is described in Bellak, Hurvich, and Gediman.[37] The table above might serve as a brief example of some score points.

therapeutic alliance and for other constructive purposes. A patient with very
poor impulse control, for example, might have excellent thought processes;
one could therefore use the vigorous interpretation of the acting-out process
as an attempt to prevent further impulsive behavior. At the same time this
assessment might indicate the need for phenothiazines to control the impulses. With a patient in whom the sense of self as part of the sense of reality
is especially poor, phenothiazines might be contra-indicated because they
often impair this ego function further. If any medication is needed aside from

the necessary psychotherapeutic interventions, usually diazepan (valium) or a simpler drug would be preferable.

In addition, ego-function assessment may be particularly useful for research in brief psychotherapy, as was detailed in Chapter 1.

Of course, people vary over time. For a more complex study, we have found it useful to assess current, characteristic (i.e., throughout life history), optimal, and lowest ego functions. Figure 2 is a graphic presentation of one patient assessed at the beginning of analysis by Sharp and Bellak.[150]

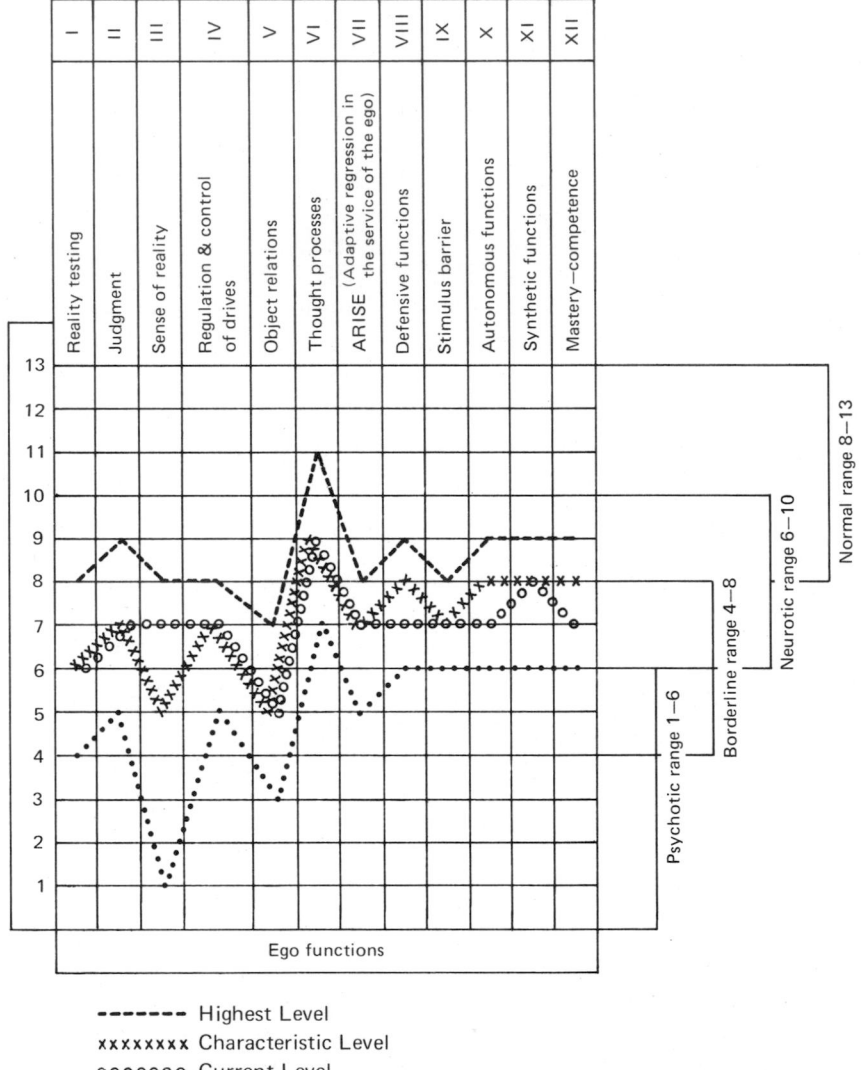

Fig. 2. Patient at onset of analysis.

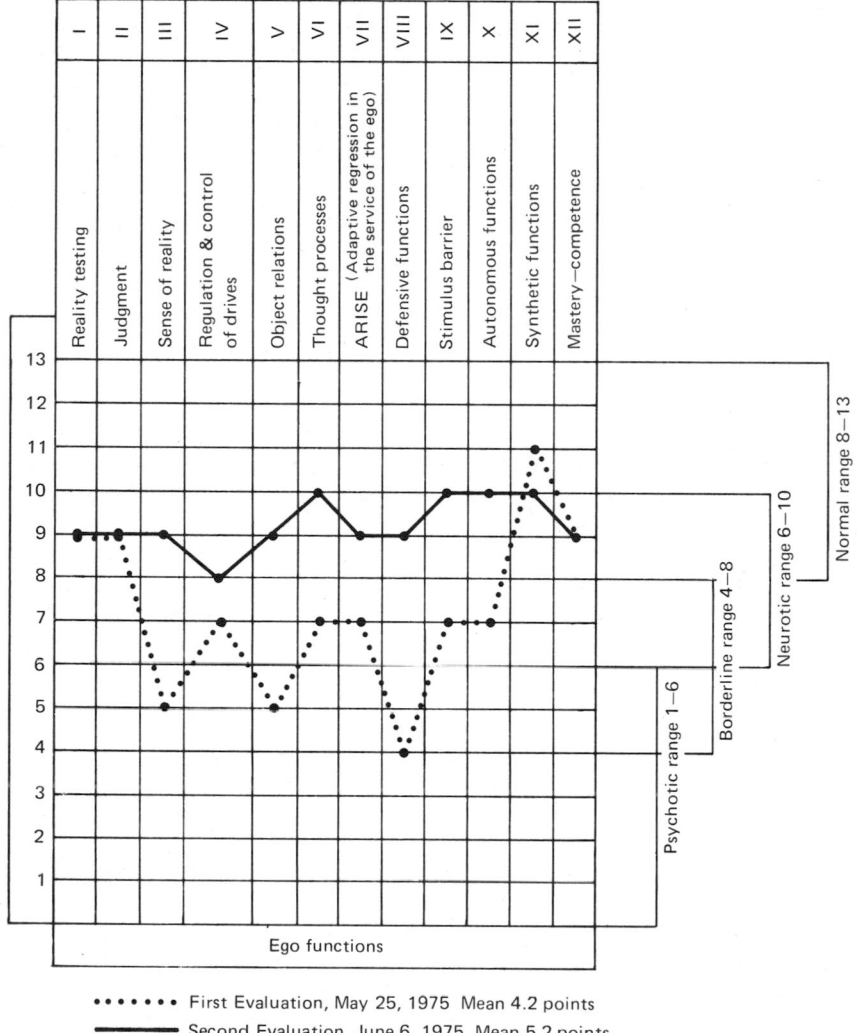

Fig. 3. Analytic patient Z.B. (Ciompi, et al. Reprinted by permission of the authors.)

A brief form of evaluating ego functions in 15 minutes of clinical evaluation also has been formulated by Ciompi et al.[57] The reliability of their procedure was tested by using two psychoanalysts as independent raters. Very satisfactory correlations in a sample of 100 patients were achieved by this technique; progress in psychoanalysis was demonstrated by comparing two ego-function assessment profiles taken a year apart (Figure 3). Clinicians discussing plans for brief psychotherapy might utilize a similar technique. Researchers could use it for follow-up assessment.

It was also shown (Bellak, Chassan, et al.[36]) that these ratings could be derived either from a two-hour standardized interview, or from regular sessions of psychoanalytic psychotherapy, and that the ratings correlated highly between these two sources. (See Figure 4.)

An informal inquiry of the 12 ego functions should suffice most therapists for a systematic appraisal of these ego functions in relation to brief psychotherapy. For those further interested in a systematic inquiry concerning ego functions, as well as in the rating manual, information is available in Bellak et al.[35]

THE HISTORY

The task of history taking is to secure the data illuminating the personal experiences of the patient, and thereby to permit a diagnostic formulation. The requirements of brief psychotherapy demand that most of the first session be devoted to the taking of a detailed history of the personality.

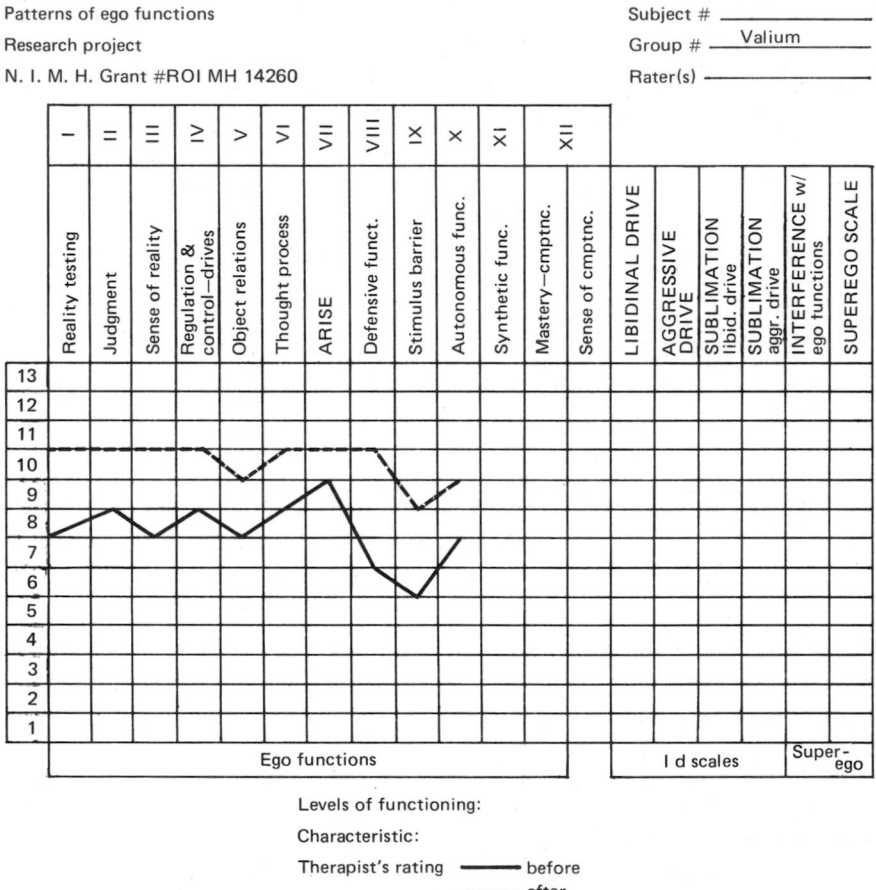

Fig. 4. Ego function ratings at beginning and end of treatment.

The first step is to obtain a history of the chief complaint, its description, and every available aspect of its onset. The aim of this segment of the inquiry is to gain a complete understanding of the precipitating factors and of the entire contemporary life situation. This requires then that the therapist, in addition to obtaining data concerning the complaint, also obtain the facts of the patient's present living arrangements, his relationships with other people, and his vocational and social situation. In many instances of emergency psychotherapy, for example, the availability of helping family and friends is extremely important.

The next requirement is an exhaustive developmental history. The purpose here is not to obtain data to be filed away and forgotten, but rather to understand the development of the patient in a given family environment: relationship to parents, to siblings according to relative ages and the impact upon each other, and the cultural and socioeconomic setting. We want to know the persons with whom the patient identified at different stages, the persons whom he loved and those by whom he was frustrated, whom he imitated, and with whom he competed. Ages and dates become an important aspect of the developmental history, but only when they can be related to pertinent facts. "In which month did you get your first tooth?" may be an event of little consequence. Not so insignificant is the age at which the patient experienced the arrival of a sibling; to the boy of six, a new-born sister creates a dynamically different experience from that which would occur at the age of two. *The history taking is complete only if, as a result of it, the onset of the present illness can be thoroughly understood in dynamic terms and related to preceding genetic, developmental, and cultural events.*

History taking, of course, also must include detailed attention to physical developments, illnesses, and any organic disorder possibly playing a role in the patient's complaints.

Model for History Taking

With some trepidation we present a model for basic inquiry in brief psychotherapy, realizing that any model offered will have gaps and will fail to meet many situations. The psychotherapist will need flexibility to modify and adapt his mode of inquiry and method of approach both to his own personality and to the personalities of his various patients. The objective, however, always remains the same—exhaustive, illuminating data that permit propositions as to dynamics and onset, and provide the groundwork for therapeutic interventions.

History taking begins with the patient's being permitted to present his complaint. He may then be asked to describe in detail its onset at the present time. When this has been done to the satisfaction of the therapist, the patient should be invited to supply a brief autobiography, and allowed to begin and develop it in any way he chooses.

As this information unfolds, the therapist is identifying and collating relevant data. At the same time he is observing omissions. Thus, for example, a patient in detailing his autobiography may omit any mention of his father. When queried about this, he may show some surprise and then launch immediately into an angry, bitter denunciation of his father, or a completely colorless statement.

The number of questions needed to obtain the required material will depend almost entirely upon the communicativeness of the patient.

Some degree of sophistication on the part of the patient is often helpful, but every patient, if communicative, will in his own language express important information; wanting to be helped, and the dynamic unconscious linking of cause and effect will push him to present the significantly related information of his present and past situations.

Often the job of the therapist in history taking is to supply the missing elements. Freud, in his elucidation of the obsessive–compulsive neurosis, stressed the omission, the elision, and how the meaning of the symptom becomes clear when the missing detail can be supplied. This may take the form of an actual omission in a situation where our clinical common sense tells us a certain affect must be present: We know that anger usually accompanies deprivation. Or the omission may take the form of an overelaboration of an ego-syntonic detail in order to obscure an ego-alien detail. Thus, a young man may extoll the virtues of his mother, elaborating on the fineness of her personality, the unselfishness of her giving. He describes her activities on behalf of other people, activities which kept her so preoccupied and so busy that she was out of the house all day long and far into the night. Our common sense tells us that what is being omitted here is both a sense of being deprived of his mother and of anger at her for so depriving him.

Certain forms of historical data are seldom volunteered by the patient during the initial history-taking hour, but an inquiry into their nature should be pursued by the psychotherapist. Early memories and dreams particularly yield psychodynamic information of value in establishing the meaning of present symptomatology. Dream information may be investigated by beginning with recollected childhood dreams: Dreams persisting in the memory over the years are usually pregnant with dynamic content. Repetitive dreams provide a unique opportunity for establishing patterns which have persisted. Recent dreams, of course, often shed considerable light upon the patient's unconscious reactions to the dynamics of the precipitating situation. To advance the brief therapy process we should feel free to encourage the patient to write his dream on awakening, even though some emotional dilution may take place as a result. We also should encourage the reporting of dream fragments; these, though sparse and incomplete, often allow the formulation or rounding out of dynamic propositions that otherwise may escape us.

Early memories will often produce information illuminating the nature of the patient's object relationships: memories of being fed, of the appearance of a sibling, of sadistic expressions, of being in a masochistic position. Often, too, early memories tend to contradict manifested attitudes toward central figures. A man of thirty professing great love for his mother and distaste for his father presented this memory: He was lying in his crib crying; his mother and father came in to him; they were both dressed in white. His mother took his diaper in which he had had a bowel movement and pushed it into his face; his father protected him from this maneuver and made the mother desist.

Masturbatory fantasies may be most productive of material illuminating object relations. Obviously inquiries of this nature must be appropriate to the situation of the patient and the relationship between patient and therapist. One would be unlikely to inquire of a sixty-year-old married woman whether she masturbates, even though there is the possibility that this situation may prevail. Certainly an inquiry into the sexual behavior of the individual is pertinent and relevant to the objectives of psychotherapy as, in the same fashion, are the patient's educational, vocational, and social history.

Employment history is an extremely important aspect of inquiry since the employment situation provides a ready field for transference phenomena to employers as parents, to co-workers as siblings. Quite typically we have found that the paranoid personality has a sporadic employment history, moving from job to job after relatively brief intervals, a situation reflecting the build-up of intolerable anxieties which are projected onto the employment situation.

THERAPEUTIC ASPECTS

History taking is not and certainly need not be traumatic. To the contrary, if accomplished tactfully, persistent and detailed questioning will afford the patient a degree of narcissistic gratification (indicating, as it were, the interest taken in him) and will increase his rapport with the therapist rather than upset him.

For many an individual the history taking becomes a cathartic experience, in the sense that it may be a first opportunity to tell someone what is really troubling him, information which he may have concealed from family and friends. In such a case, the opportunity to share with a professional person provides a lessening of burdens, with concomitant improvement of symptomatology and certainly with an improvement in optimism concerning the situation.

Having obtained a meaningful history, the psychotherapist should not hesitate to provide some therapeutic help for the patient at once. This may take the form of assurance that the patient's problem is understood and can be dealt with, or it may be a minor interpretation in which the patient's present situation and reactions are related to a past situation and reactions, showing him that he had some such experience before and managed to work his way out of it. We might conceive of 90 percent of the first session devoted to history taking and the remaining ten percent to some useful intervention.

TIME AND QUESTIONS

In taking the history of the patient for brief psychotherapy, the therapist obviously must chart a course somewhere between a free-flowing, unguided type of communication and a totally structured question-and-answer interview situation. Our experience is that most individuals are able to communicate sufficient information in a single history-taking session with a combination of structured stimulus from the inquirer and the opportunity for free response to each query.

For the most part questions should be of the open-end variety, which does not permit a yes or no response, but which compels the patient to reveal something of his preferences, aversions, attitudes, and responses. "Tell me about your parents" is preferred to "Tell me about your mother" or "Tell me about your father." The order of presentation in serial possibilities is almost always indicative of negative and positive valences (as in the Draw-A-Person Test, the sex of the first figure drawn is a clue to sexual identification).

There are other situations, however, where the therapist should pursue information by direct interrogation; for example, when it is essential to obtain precise chronology in the sequence of dynamically charged events.

There are some individuals whose history is so lengthy, complicated, or obscure that more than one session may be required. There are others from whom even additional sessions will not yield the necessary information unless the therapist resorts to adjunctive measures of communication.

FACILITATING COMMUNICATION

In psychotherapeutic communication, two conversations are usually going on, one beneath the other. The psychotherapist is accustomed to searching for the latent meaning contained in manifest content. Here the psychotherapist's knowledge of psychodynamics and psychoanalytic theory, especially as they relate to child development, provide him with what might be called "uncommon" sense. Without being cynical, the psychotherapist must operate somewhat as does the Napoleonic code of law: What the patient says manifestly must be suspect, and examined for its possible latent content.

A problem in discerning latent content is seldom encountered among people who communicate freely in a verbal way. Difficulties arise, however, when patients do not easily verbalize. Individuals of relatively low intelligence may find it difficult to communicate verbally. The same may be true of individuals from social or economic groups where verbal communication is neither valued nor encouraged. Other patients may not be accustomed to introspection or to verbalizing the consequences of their introspection. The individual may not have the vocabulary to describe what he feels or thinks, and above all, he may not be accustomed to telling another person about it. Facilitating communication, therefore, becomes an important responsibility of the psychotherapist, particularly when he has very little time.

Communications with some individuals may be facilitated by first requesting that the patient give the psychotherapist, in everyday terms, the details of contemporary events, either those surrounding the onset of the symptomatology or those which have taken place since the last visit. The psychotherapist must scan the details with the patient very carefully, soliciting affects and responses. Careful attention to the patient's appearance and manner is often helpful in this respect, provided that comment upon the manner or appearance is carefully phrased in a nonpunitive way, so that the patient does not suffer a narcissistic blow. Thus, the psychotherapist might say, "The way you walked in gave me the feeling that you were afraid that somebody would bite your head off," "You looked frightened," "You looked worried," or "You looked blue."

Elicitation of dreams is another device for facilitating communication, not only from those who find verbal communication difficult but also from others who speak more freely. As stated above, it should be a custom of the history-taking procedure to inquire about recent dreams, recurrent dreams, and childhood dreams which may have remained active in the patient's memory. Here again, the search is for the theme, the repeated common denominator, the latent content. The psychotherapist may say to the patient, "You have a recurrent dream that you are trying to call up somebody and you never get that person. The phone is busy or you just wake up before you get through. What do you think this is all about?"

In brief psychotherapy, it is wise to choose for interpretation only those portions of dreams which contain manifestly discernible features of a recurrent pattern. Thus, for example, a patient repeatedly dreams of herself as a little girl in her mother's house. This probably expresses her wish to be a little girl again and to be cared for instead of having to be a mother herself and to care for her own child. Communication of this inference may lay the groundwork for bringing out her oral longing and anger over its frustration, as well as anger directed at her child who demands attention and who may also be an identification figure for the patient's younger sibling who was the original rival.

In communication, the search for missing elements is imperative. Thus, for example, a woman had a recurrent dream in which she was always trying to reach a former boyfriend. In discussion it turned out that he was French. Later it became known that she had lived in France with her mother who died there when she was a child. In one way, therefore, her efforts to get in touch with the former French boyfriend on the telephone were really saying, "I want to talk to my mother; I want my mother back; I miss her; I was badly deserted then; I want to be taken care of."

ADJUNCT MEANS FOR FACILITATING COMMUNICATION

Very often the Thematic Apperception Test (T.A.T.) provides a channel for understanding patients not otherwise communicative. The main value of the T.A.T. lies in its capacity to reflect the actual dynamic picture of basic conflict patterns. Hence, it is of greatest use to therapists trained in psychodynamics and psychoanalysis.

The T.A.T. was originally developed by Henry A. Murray,[130] with the help of Christina Morgan in 1936, at the Harvard Psychological Clinic. A great number of pictures were tested for their ability to evoke fantasies of value in diagnosis and treatment. Twenty pictures were selected for the first series, and they remain the total number of pictures in the present third edition of the test. In standard procedure, the T.A.T. is given in two sessions on successive days, with ten pictures administered at each session. However, the psychologist customarily abbreviates the administration of the test and selects pictures which he expects will be particularly revealing with the specific patient. The subject is asked to tell some stories about the pictures he is shown, stating what is going on in each, what led up to the situation, and what the outcome will be. The subject is impressed with the necessity of making the story dramatic, involving all the sentiments and thoughts of the characters described.

The T.A.T. is an excellent way of studying both horizontal and vertical or genetic patterns, which are revealed particularly by the psychologically naive, without the subject's awareness of the implications of his stories. Valuable insight and cooperation frequently are gained when the patient first finds out to his surprise how he has reproduced unwittingly some of his most important problems.[15] An abundance of autobiographical material is revealed in the T.A.T., enabling the therapist to study some of the vertical patterns in the subject's behavior. Very often when denial interferes with communication and insight, reading back several stories may dramatically bring home to the patient the operation of denial. Two cards especially, one depicting a pregnant woman and the other a figure huddled by a couch with a gun on the floor, have been useful in such situations. Patients denying sexuality and/or hostility will often omit mention of the woman's pregnancy or of the gun; it is then relatively easy to show them how denial has caused them to exclude from their perception objects and circumstances of such high visibility. The operation of denial may then be interpreted in specific aspects of their real-life behavior, with great insight than otherwise would be forthcoming.

Many and diverse measures may be used to attain the goals of brief therapy, provided indications for such measures are clearly established in one's mind and are used within the total context of dynamic understanding. Among the measures to be employed with such caution, belongs the often controversial technique of hypnosis.

Obviously, there are many instances where the use of hypnosis is contraindicated: patients who are threatened by passivity, those who have excessive, passive needs to be taken care of, and patients who are likely to progress to dissociated states or paranoia.

On the other hand and in the absence of contraindications, hypnosis may be useful in obtaining repressed material from patients who can easily be induced. It sometimes happens that in the face of persisting amnesia we hypothesize that a significant episode took place at some point in childhood because many of the patient's memories and much circumstantial data direct us to such a conclusion. An hypnotic state may then be useful in relieving the amnesia and in discovering the presumably crucial event. Before attempting hypnosis, it is essential to explain to the patient the specific use to which hypnosis will be put, to elucidate some of the general principles of hypnosis, and to quiet, by anticipation, fears the patient may harbor (e.g., being helplessly in the power of another). It is essential also that the material recovered by means of hypnosis be reproduced to the fully awake ego, to permit us to synthesize the previously unconscious material and utilize the data in psychotherapy. One way to accomplish this is to obtain the patient's permission to tape-record the hypnotic session and later to play back whatever significant material might have emerged. This procedure will help make the material ego-syntonic to the patient. One must keep in mind that if the memory arouses a traumatic situation for the patient, he should be properly prepared for it, since the deep repression presumably served a necessary defensive purpose. If, for this reason or another, confrontation with the tape-recorded material is not desirable, it becomes important to relate the obtained material selectively to the patient so as to tie it in with the rest of his material. In this way the material can be made useful and ego-syntonic, and become part of the general dynamic therapeutic process.

Establishing Causal Relations: Overdetermination

The well-trained psychotherapist establishes a causal pattern automatically as he listens to the presenting complaint and takes the history. We have separated this topic for discussion only to emphasize its critical importance in the brief psychotherapeutic process. Establishing causal relations demands well-grounded training in psychoanalytic theory, a wide range of clinical experience. and all of the personal attributes we have set forth as necessary equipment. In brief, the perception of causal relations requires every bit of intellectual and emotional equipment the psychotherapist can muster. He must readily recognize the facile ability of the hysteric to displace, the overcontrolled rage of the obsessive-compulsive, and the myriad varieties of reaction formation. No unconscious process, no defensive reaction, no primitive quality in the human being can be alien to him.

Consider the possibilities for diverse causes of the same manifest symptoms. Sleeplessness is a particularly fascinating symptom, and its causes are highly diversified. Many people are afraid to fall asleep for fear of what they will dream. One woman we knew was afraid to fall asleep because she feared she might swallow her tongue. A man's sleeplessness was quickly illuminated when he revealed the hypnogogic fantasies that finally permitted him to fall asleep. Originally, his fantasy was that he was in some protective place; later, this became a blockhouse; later on it was surrounded with barbed wires; still later with land mines; and finally, machine gun nests were added. When he achieved this ultimate in protection, he was able to sleep. Another man could fall asleep only after he had wrapped himself tightly in his blanket so that no snakes might get in.

A woman complained of a series of curious pains in one spot on her head. On various occasions, she described the pains as stabbing or crushing. A thorough checkup revealed no organic causes; the psychogenic features were those of a hysterical disorder and it was possible to relate these pains to various details of her sexual history and fantasy.

The task in establishing causal relations is to understand how a symptom was precipitated by a particular event, and what the meaning of both the symptom and the event are in relation to the specific patient's history and structure.

A woman came for treatment complaining of acute panic. She had already taken tranquilizers but since these did not help, she consulted a psychotherapist. Her panic was not helped when her seven-year-old child developed a school phobia. A classmate had begun to vomit every morning, disgusting and upsetting the child, and she was reluctant to go to school anymore. It is reasonable and understandable that the mother was upset because her child had developed this school phobia, but it is not a cause for panic. She consulted the school authorities, including the psychologist. Arrangements were made for her to accompany the child to school each day, since they did not wish to encourage the phobia, and sought to make it possible for the child to continue to attend school. At this point, the mother's panic became acute. She described it as fear without parallel in her life. It was apparently a free-floating type of anxiety with no specific content that she could identify. The therapist then began to inquire: Was her panic a response to her child's school phobia? To the classmate's vomiting? To her need to attend school with her child? A careful history revealed some relevant features. She was married to a man several years older than herself. Her marriage, she said, was fine in every respect. But for the last ten years her mother-in-law had been very ill, and often required care at the patient's house or made a great many demands upon her husband, and by implication, upon her. The husband often would leave her to sleep at his mother's house in order to take care of her.

Another feature was that her youngest child had developed the phobia; one other child was now in adolescence and much more on his own. The woman, it was discovered, was quite gifted and had considerable artistic talent. She had been happily making plans to return to a part-time career, plans accompanied by a sense of freedom heightened by the recent death of her mother-in-law. It became clear that she had been resentful all the years her mother-in-law had been a burden and had required the catering attention of herself and her husband. In addition, she had always felt the job of bringing up her children to be a burden. She was from other evidence a fairly oral person and had evidently married her husband in her own mother's image. Under ordinary circumstances, this created no special problem; but just when she thought that she was to be free and use much of the day for the pursuit of her own interests, her child played her a "dirty trick" by developing a phobia that imprisoned her in the classroom. The primary meaning of her panic apparently was fear that her rage at her child would reach unbearable proportions and erupt. Her panic, therefore, was a danger signal. Secondarily, a fear of fainting accompanied her panic; she was now able to turn to her husband and say, "I am sick, I need to be taken care of. You must look after me the way you looked after your mother. You must look after me, rather than force me again to look after a little child."

Given this focus, it was possible to ask more intelligent questions about her history. It developed that she had had earlier experiences of anxiety. She was able to recall "flickers and flares" of anxiety in the past, none of which had ever reached the extreme she was now suffering. The content of these former situations resembled the present dynamic constellation; they involved rage and passivity comparable to the present circumstances.*

Overdetermination of a symptom is perhaps the most cogent argument in favor of the comprehensive history. Clinical sophistication demands not only that we recognize the individual genetic variations in relationship to symptomatology, but that we recognize as well that a given symptom in an individual may arise from more than one cause. In intensive psychotherapy overdetermination generally becomes apparent as treatment proceeds. In brief psychotherapy the therapist is dependent upon the comprehensive history in identifying an overdetermined system.

A highly successful businessman came to therapy with the alarming symptom, for him, of an elevator phobia. His livelihood depended upon his ability to visit buyers of his commodity whose offices were most often in the upper floors of skyscraper buildings in New York. His panic in elevators was massive and incapacitating; his real-life circumstances were adjusted to a level of expenditure that made his continued ability to earn a high income almost a matter of life and death for him. He had experienced another alarming situation. He had been able to go to Rome for a few days on a lark with the determination to "live it up a bit." His reasons for going to Rome without his wife were quite obvious, but instead of being able to enjoy himself there, he developed a panic and had to return to New York within 24 hours of landing in Rome. Upon his return, the elevator phobia appeared. At first thought, his wish for sexual adventure might seem to have precipitated the panic, thereafter symbolized by the elevator, which so often in dreams is an indicator of phallic excitement, with tumescence and detumescence being represented by its rise and fall. However, the patient pointed out with perfect reasonableness that his business trips had usually taken him about the country, and that on these trips he had been able to have sexual affairs without emotional consequence. However, his business traveling in the past had not taken him too far from New York City. The facts suggested that the risks of infidelity alone had not produced defensive panic and the elevator phobia, but that there was in the essence of travel to a foreign country a more significant dynamic meaning.

As his history unfolded, it became clear that he had an ambivalent attachment of great intensity to his mother, and that his wife played a similar role in his life. Being in

*The emergency psychotherapy for this patient involved some interpretation of the dynamics of the situation, and arrangements for her to sit in the school secretary's office where for the time being she could carry on with her own work while waiting for the child.

a foreign country apparently meant being far away from the mother figure, and he had responded with anxiety to the idea of being helpless if anything should happen to him (especially as punishment for sexual transgression).

The elevator phobia could be understood in the same terms. For this patient the affective meaning of the elevator was not phallic tumescence and detumescence, but rather a feeling of being closed in a small space and not being able to get out. Again, this was a feeling of being powerless, of losing mobility, a feeling which, for him, was related to his overpowering mother, and which represented another facet of his wish to be taken care of. Thus he feared being helpless, but also feared being overpowered by his wish to be helped.*

The consequences of his elevator phobia had to be considered. If it persisted, he would not be able to make a living; he would become dependent. Realistically and financially he would have suffered a ruinous experience, but apparently would have been satisfying the wish to be taken care of. It was determined that he also actually had a preconscious motivation not to have as much money as he had been earning: He was supplying large sums of money to a brother who was in a particularly needy situation; unconsciously he resented the demands of this sibling, whereas consciously he professed the most sympathetic concern.

Thus the history of this patient revealed several dynamic relationships between his Rome panic and the elevator phobia: phallic desires in conflict with a fear of being helpless, the wish to be taken care of which exposed him to the feeling of being overpowered and crushed, and the desire for dependency.

THE THERAPEUTIC CONTRACT, THE THERAPEUTIC ALLIANCE, AND THE TRANSFERENCE SITUATION

The concept of the therapeutic contract was first formulated by Karl Menninger in 1958.[125] Menninger anticipated consumerism in much later writing by speaking of treatment as one of the services the patient buys from a therapist. He specifies that part of the contract, however, must be an agreement on goals and time limits, and transactions involving adjunctive measures such as drugs or interaction with other people. The contract also involves agreement on time, fee, and whatever else may belong to the therapeutic interaction. It is as important that these be clarified in brief psychotherapy as in other forms of therapy.

The *therapeutic alliance* is akin to what Greenson[79] described as the "working alliance." It constitutes the patient's willingness to carry out

---

*The trip to Rome was the height of his attempt to be independent, far away, sexually free; when this aroused more anxiety than he could bear, a major regression took place which precipitated the elevator phobia with its prephallic conflicts. It is as if he had said, "As it seems to be dangerous to be a promiscuous male, I might as well be (I am afraid to be) a helpless child (in danger of being overpowered) who is taken care of rather than having to take care of others."

analytic procedures, to identify with and accept the analyst's attitudes and methods of work. The working alliance is between "... the patient's reasonable ego and the analyst's analyzing ego," a condition essential for the analysis and working through of the transference neurosis. The alliance enables the patient to transcend "an experiencing, subjective, irrational ego," in order to evaluate emotional reactions with "a reasonable, observing, analyzing ego."

The pursuit of a positive transference in brief psychotherapy seeks to establish something similar to Greenson's concept of a working alliance, and yet something considerably different, so we elect to call it a therapeutic alliance. While avoiding the development of a transference neurosis, the patient in the therapeutic alliance, as in the working alliance, is asked to look at irrationality with the intact, healthy, realistic portion of his ego. But additionally, in order to effect a change in a short interval as opposed to the relative timelessness of psychoanalysis, the therapeutic alliance encourages a sense of optimism about the change; the expectation that the therapist and the patient working cooperatively, in benign partnership, with understanding and candor, will effect that change; and that by working together they will ameliorate symptoms and bring the patient to a greater degree of comfort. The effort is not only to produce this sense of optimistic expectation, but to encourage participation by the patient, to combat passivity, to foster the development of competence, and to promote movement in the therapy.

The *transference* situation must be considered in brief psychotherapy as in all forms of therapy.* The psychotherapist must be alert to and in command of transference from the first moment of contact with the patient.

In fact, transference is understood here, by extension, to comprise the totality of the patient's relationship to the therapist: in stating that we regard a positive transference as essential to brief psychotherapy, we also mean that we hold it essential that the patient, at least after a little while, consider the therapist to be likeable, reliable, understanding, accepting. The patient

---

*Transference has varied technical meanings. In the classical sense, psychoanalysts use it in a short-hand manner to refer to the drives directed toward and sentiments held for the analyst that are aroused during the various phases of regression inherent in what is properly called the *transference neurosis:* that is, a brief recapitulation of earlier phases of conflict and development with sentiments projected onto the analyst which once were held for other figures, especially the parents.

Analysts themselves have used the term in a broader sense, often including ready sets of expectations brought to the analyst before actually meeting him, and any kind of projection. Transference is sometimes used almost synonomously with projection even outside therapeutic situations—a confusing and ill-advised use.

In the present dicussion, transference is used broadly as comprising all the nonrational sentiments of the patient toward the therapist including hopes, fears, likes, and dislikes. (It should hardly be necessary to remind one that many sentiments, including negative thoughts and expectations that the patient has toward the therapist, may be entirely reasonable).

should at least have a somewhat hopeful expectation that the therapist may be able to help him.

This type of relationship is a prerequisite for the motivation to learn and relearn in the short space of time available; sometimes it is essential because of the patient's limited frustration tolerance and ego strength.

While a generally positive relationship is necessary in brief psychotherapy, this does not mean that negative factors in the relationship should be ignored or left uninterpreted, especially if they either interfere with therapy or could constitute an essential part of therapy. For the hostile, suspicious patient who feels that "a clinic doctor" is probably ineffectual, it should be pointed out that he has this attitude in other situations. In brief psychotherapy it may even be permissible, if done tactfully and with a light touch, to indicate that the therapist has perfectly good qualifications.

Initially, many patients need help to ventilate, briefly, their feelings about "head shrinkers who are probably crazy thermselves" and similar sentiments.

All transference manifestations or all aspects of the patient–therapist relationship can be the subject of interpretation. However, in brief therapy we will not analyze defenses which are likely to arouse negative sentiments beyond that which can easily be dealt with immediately for constructive purposes. (When the patient behaves in an irritating way, one can immediately couple this behavior with a constructive statement that allies the therapist clearly with the patient.) As an overall goal, it simply must be remembered that a positive relationship is necessary for the learning involved in brief psychotherapy.

The emphasis in brief psychotherapy is thus to maintain the therapist as a benign, interested, helpful figure. This will also require, however, that the therapist be able to predict and then manage the positive transference in those patients who are prone to develop a clinging, overly dependent relationship. The therapist may elect to do this by lengthening the intervals between sessions to a matter of weeks rather than days. He may also attempt to guard against feelings of profound rejection by arranging for regular telephone contact at intervals after the brief therapeutic experience is terminated.

Because of the emphasis on positive transference, the selection of the proper therapist for each patient assumes great importance. The factors that may be involved include the therapist's age, sex, most comfortable role, and cultural suitability.

Something may be said about special situations in the development of positive transference. The therapist may be sure that a positive valence can usually be achieved by the combination of ordinary courtesy and a professionally oriented, helpful attitude—indeed by the very act of taking and recording a careful, thorough history. Certain situations, however, require modification of approach. In dealing with adolescents of either sex (and regardless of the sex of the therapist) any spatial proximity is best avoided, even the shaking of hands. If the therapist is a man and his patient an adolescent boy, the possibility of stimulating homosexual anxiety may be avoided by omitting the handshake; in the same way the implication of a sexual overture may be avoided with the adolescent girl. With an attractive, bright, flirtatious young woman, it is well for the therapist to maintain a polite, formal relationship, albeit an interested one. He may find it desirable not to permit himself even to smile, hard as this may be. However, he should be aware of her flirtatiousness, and seek data outside of the therapeutic relationship with which to interpret it. In contrast, an obsessively isolating woman with great reserve and inhibition may benefit from a direct, earthy approach. Following this the therapist will need to be alert to the emergence of a defensive posture which he can quite properly relate as her response to his behavior.

Depressed, angry patients may present special difficulties, because their hostile attitude may arouse a negative transference in the therapist. One is often rewarded with a turnaround of attitude by carefully maintaining a courteous, attentive, understanding posture and taking care not to respond in kind to the patient's angry, questioning, rejecting manner. Later, in the same or a subsequent session, the therapist usually will be able to return to the patient's initial mood, to interpret its roots and to show the patient how it serves as a self-fulfilling prophecy.

THE PRESENTING PROBLEM

Usually the presenting problem is quite clear. The patient suffers from anxiety, depersonalization, depression, doubt, confusion, or some other identifiable state. As we shall see, the nature of the presenting problem very often, in itself, serves as a guide to the psychotherapist in his search through the life history and contemporary situation for contributing factors, and beyond that begins at once to lay the groundwork for the formulations permitting hunches about etiology.

Difficulties arise in identifying the presenting problem when the complaint serves to conceal the actual situation. While everyone would immediately recognize that a husband's alcoholic problem is indeed a difficult situation for a woman, and could well lead to depression, anxiety, insecurity, and concern about the welfare of her children, the realistic nature of the complaint may obscure the only basis for psychotherapy with the woman who presents such a complaint: The treatable problem in such circumstances may actually be her contributions to her husband's alcoholism.

In any event, the problem as presented by the patient is the way in which the patient views his situation, and must therefore be treated with dignity and a willingness to understand. The therapist must start with the patient at the point where the patient is. However, the psychotherapist comprehends that dynamically there are factors beyond the immediate situation which the patient does not see.

Moreover, the patient's presenting problem initiates a set of formulations and conceptual expectations which the history confirms, modifies, or negates.

TREATMENT: THE CHOICE OF DYNAMIC INTERVENTIONS

Having determined the causes of symptoms, the therapist is led to the task of undoing. In brief psychotherapy specifically, he must establish those factors which require change or lend themselves most readily to it. These in turn lead to the choice of intervention, which may be verbal operations or selected from among the adjunctive measures available to the psychotherapist. In the case of panic described earlier in this chapter, the reader will note that both verbal and environmental interventions were employed.

In this section we shall describe the interventions based essentially upon oral communication between patient and therapist, and conclude with suggestions for the ego-function assessment as a guide to the choice of interventions. Of necessity, we shall allude here and there to adjunctive measures, but these await fuller description in the next chapter.

Imparting Insight—The Traditional Intervention

Traditionally, psychotherapy has sought to cure or ameliorate by conveying insight to the patient about the nature and cause of his fears and concerns, his impulses and his defenses against them, and his preconscious and unconscious motivations.

The rationale of this treatment approach rests upon the observable effect of insight, in many cases, of bringing about a dynamic realignment of the personality which results in a stronger ego and more effective ego functioning. With patients for whom psychoanalysis or intensive psychotherapy are suitable, insight therapy is the treatment of choice. The treatment of the psychotic, the person with a character disorder, the acting-out person, and the patient in an emergency situation require other interventions from the therapist's armamentarium. Insight therapy, however, remains a crucially important technique in brief psychotherapy; because of time limitations the therapist must use it judiciously here.

The therapist, through the interpretation, imparts insight which, along with the aptness of diagnostic formulation and choice of intervention, is one of his greatest skills.

THE INTERPRETATION

Success in psychotherapy usually requires simultaneous change in several vectors or variables. At the same time that a patient gains insight into the cause of his symptoms, he must develop a sense of alienation from them. In some circumstances the drive must be made ego-syntonic in one respect and ego-alien in another; intra-aggression in the depressed patient must often be converted into extra-aggression, while cautions are taken that the latter does not become excessive or inappropriate. With some patients, the task may involve de-emphasizing one defense and increasing reliance upon another, minimizing one role while encouraging another, fostering his hating one parent less and disliking the other more.

A first and major concern with interpretation, therefore, is that it avoid the danger of oversimplification through singleness of purpose. The therapist must try to predict the effect of his interpretation and build in safeguards if he judges them necessary. This requirement should prevent some widespread confusion about the imparting of insight through interpretation. Uncritically to pursue the uncovering of instinctual urges is a misapplication of psychoanalytic practice. Psychotherapy must simultaneously strengthen as it uncovers, if indeed, it must uncover. Another misapplication often arises from the time-tested observation that the insight which is accompanied by an affective change is most effective in achieving the desired therapeutic results. The danger arises from attempts to induce the most intense affect possible on the premise, no doubt, that if affect is good, the more the better. The unitary striving to uncover or produce affect leads to the device of "confrontation" in which the therapist directly, baldly, interprets the drive which the patient has been denying or repressing.

The least dangerous consequences of confrontation are increased denial or repression. More serious possibilities are the eruptions of panic, deep depression, serious acting-out, even suicide. Consider the treatment of symptoms arising from the repression of an aggressive impulse or drive. Confrontation in such cases may create havoc. The danger is that it will make the drive even less tolerable for the individual, increase intra-aggression, and result in a suicidal venture. The nature of the patient's symptoms very often is in itself a clue to the ego's ability to tolerate confrontation. Thus, in one instance an adolescent boy jumped out of a car which his father was driving, and quickly developed the delusion that he had destroyed the world. It became quite clear that he had wanted to kill his father, and had to jump out of the car to remove himself as a danger. By secondary elaboration it became acceptable to him that he had destroyed the world, rather than he had had an impulse to destroy his father. In confrontation, often mistaken for the cathartic interpretation, one might say, "Look, what really ails you is that you wanted to kill your father." This interpretation might lead immediately to a suicidal attempt.

Imparting insight through interpretation must take into account the patient's ability or readiness to accept and use the insight. To use the interpretation of an impulse properly, for example, the patient must be ready to accept the drive as a component of his personality, experience it, discharge it in a nondestructive fashion along with the anxiety and tension that have accompanied its repression, and achieve an active reorganization of his defenses with a resulting realignment of forces in his personality.

Therefore, we must guard against stressing the primitive qualities of a drive until, if ever, the patient is prepared through ego strengthening to accept them without feeling undue threat. Care must be taken to assure that the patient recognizes that he has adequate defenses against the drive to replace those more pathological defenses associated with his symptoms.

FACILITATING INSIGHT

We believe that many of the formal aspects of learning theory have been neglected in therapeutic application, and that their adoption would enhance psychotherapeutic learning.

Many therapists have commented upon the importance of timing of the interpretation in facilitating its acceptance. Couched in learning terms, timing involves the readiness or set of the patient. Thus, if the patient is concerned about some visible neglect on the part of the therapist, an interpretation that the patient is dependent and wishes to be supported is inappropriately timed. R. Löwenstein tells the story of the analyst who falls asleep and drops his cigar, which rolls into the patient's view. Looking behind him the patient remonstrates with the analyst, who then interprets, "You always want to be the center of attention." Löwenstein comments: the interpretation is correct, the timing is not.

Another important aspect in facilitating learning is economy in presentation of the interpretation. Short, direct, pithy statements are more effective than wordy, literary allusions. An amusing story illustrates the point. Hitler's car broke down in a small Polish village, and all the assembled Nazi big-wigs and engineers could not make it move again. Finally, a little old Polish mechanic was brought up. He took one look, struck part of the engine a hard blow, and the motor sprang to life. When the astonished Hitler asked how much he owed him, the man requested one thousand zloti. "One thousand zloti for one whack?" Hitler asked in astonishment. The mechanic shook his head, "Only ten zloti for the whack; 990 for knowing where to whack."

Colorful language has a heightening effect which will long be remembered by the patient, and subsequently continue to serve as a guide or example. It is more effective to say "You think he is a son-of-a-bitch" than "You are angry with him."

The use of stories with pregnant, vivid illustrations is an excellent means of fostering learning through verbal communication. The great teachers used parables for good reasons! As an example, we have found the following gentle story particularly useful in helping patients overcome feelings of passivity and in encouraging self-assertion. The story concerns a discussion of the emotional aspects of juvenile delinquency with a group which ranged in experience from young, eager teachers to older, more sophisticated, somewhat disillusioned principals of schools. The lecturer took the point of view that the delinquent was a disturbed individual who required psychotherapy. One of the young teachers protested, "But, Doctor, what do you do when a boy tells you to go to hell?" While the lecturer fumbled for an appropriate response, one of the older men spoke up. "Don't go," he said. There is greater likelihood that the patient will remember this story, and perhaps even repeat it socially, so that it will serve as an ongoing guide for him, more so than some abstract advice from the therapist to the effect that he does not have to do what people tell him to.

Another formal aspect of learning methodology applicable in psychotherapy is the dictum that active learning is more effective than passive learning. At one level this would mean that the patient should discover for himself as many of the necessary insights as he can. In brief psychotherapy this is seldom possible, but the patient may be encouraged to learn actively. He may then be asked to formulate certain propositions, to repeat them, and to integrate them with other facets under consideration.

Switching roles in the session may facilitate insight with some patients. One patient may be asked, "Pretend you are the therapist. A man tells you he is always finding a repelling blemish, even in the most beautiful woman—her teeth are a little crooked, she has a mole on her cheek, her jokes fall flat. What would you say is bothering him?" It is well to start with some uncomplicated dynamic not likely to arouse resistance, or even one taken from the life of another patient.

An established principle of learning theory involves spacing or dispersal of training. Periods of learning interrupted by pauses are often more effective than a continuous effort. The concept of "silent learning" has been used as an explanation for this phenomenon. Very often the regressive effect of the therapy itself and the secondary gains from dependency upon the therapist may be minimized by spacing of treatment. In addition, this allows for "silent" integration and working through during the intervals between treatment sessions. The experience of the plateau, typical for every learning curve, often has a retarding effect on the psychotherapeutic process, if not an altogether disruptive one. A hiatus in treatment may prove more fruitful than prolonged and discouraging efforts to work through "resistance." We shall return to this principle in a further discussion of working through.

Learning by repetition is perhaps the most widely understood of the formal applications of learning theory. In psychotherapy repetition is utilized when a dynamic is interpreted in various aspects and time phases of a patient's life.

The Thematic Apperception Test may be used in application of the repetition and the active learning principles. The therapist may take the stories which the patient has given in response to the pictures and read them back to him. Then the patient may be asked, "Well, what do you think the stories were about?" This procedure often has the effect of increasing the patient's awareness, especially of preconscious feelings and thoughts.

The psychotropic drugs have permitted us to carry on learning by insight with many patients who would otherwise not be amendable to the process. Overwhelming anxiety or lack of frustration tolerance and of impulse control sometimes make the therapeutic process unbearable. Drugs have helped to ameloriate these aspects so that the learning process may establish a new structure well enough automatized and integrated so as not to require prolonged use of the drugs. The psychotropic drugs resemble the aid which supportive physiological measures give during a surgical intervention, in the sense that they seem able to increase the synthetic functioning of the ego Dissociation seems decreased and learning becomes possible in cases where without the drugs the primary process abounds to the extent that secondary-process activity is disrupted.

OBSTACLES TO INSIGHT LEARNING

Repression and denial, involved as they are in symptom formation, are the most widely encountered obstacles to the learning effects of interpretation. The presence of repression, however, does not mean that the brief intervention is predictably inadequate. Continued repression naturally implies that the therapeutic process must go on for a longer period of time. Denial, like all other human behavior, is observable along a continuum. Essentially, it is a preconscious process which means that we are dealing with variables which can relatively easily be made conscious, in contrast to those resulting from repression.

Insight may be impossible for some patients because they do not have the logical equipment for the syllogistic thinking required. This may be due to a failure to acquire enough of the secondary process and of the hierarchal relationships of cause and effect, time, place, and person.

Overconcreteness of thinking is another problem. Verbal therapy and the use of interpretation and insight may be impossible in some such instances, though Arieti has suggested ways of dealing with this problem.[6]

In these situations particularly, adjunctive measures are of critical importance when brief psychotherapy is attempted.

Increasing Self-Esteem

One technique which has a role in the psychotherapy of nearly all patients who come for treatment, especially in emergency situations, is that of strengthening the ego by increasing the patient's self-esteem. Counteracting the traumatic impact of the very necessity to seek help for an emtoional or mental problem is often indicated. For many people, the need for psychotherapy is a blow to self-esteem and a stigma. The patient feels that he must be seriously deficient, and this notion adds to the feeling of lowered self-esteem. In addition, there are associated feelings of rejection and failure. The positive features in his life must be pointed out to such a patient, who, in addition, may suffer feelings of oral derpivation, projection, and regressive phenomena. The therapist must express recognition that the patient has accomplished something, that he has been able to tolerate many difficulties, and especially that he has been willing to do something rational about his condition. One must impart to the patient the feeling that his situation is understood and that he can be helped because of this understanding.

Being on fairly familiar terms with the patient (contrary to usual psychotherapeutic practice) may be useful in order to increase his feelings of self-worth. Although the therapist is necessarily the authority, the patient must be led to feel that he is on the same level with the therapist and that the therapist has no contempt for him. The patient should be helped to see that all human beings suffer from the same things, that there is nothing small or mean about the patient, or especially large and awesome about the therapist, and that both of them can talk over things together.

Yet above all, one must be careful not to overdo this approach, or to be insincere in its application. The therapist may choose to personalize the situation by bringing himself into the picture, indicating that he, too, at one time was in a situation comparable to the patient's, or had feelings comparable to the patient's. Here we should repeat that this approach to raising self-esteem must have a realistic basis, and not arise either out of the therapist's own anxieties, unitary approach, or simple desire to be kind and helpful to a distressed person.

Catharsis

The cathartic interpretation concerns itself with transposing an unconscious drive or thought into consciousness. All of the cautions necessary in the interpretation of a drive must be exercised. In effect, the cathartic interpretation may be best defined as confrontation with optimal safeguards practiced, which derive either from the patient's present ego strength, from a therapeutic process of ego-strengthening, or from modifications of the cathartic interpretations.

The exercise of caution in the use of the cathartic interpretation is similar in some respects to the care taken in making the usual psychoanalytic interpretation, but differs considerably in the type or method of caution employed and, of course, in the time interval available for the deployment of cautious preparation. In analysis the material to be interpreted usually has become preconscious if not conscious; the patient is ready for the insight, and indeed may arrive at it without the interpretation being offered. In brief therapy the time needed for this type of preparatory process is not generally available, so that the cautions exercised derive from estimates of the patient's ego strengths, lending the patient the therapist's ego, or from modifications of the interpretation itself.

With a reasonably strong personality suffering a neurotic disturbance, the therapist may go directly to the core of the symbolic content (aggressive, sexual, exhibitionistic, etc.) of the disturbing sentiment. Consider, for example, the relatively intact adolescent who suffers panic accompanied by a fear of having an epileptic seizure. His concept of the seizure is that one becomes excited, loses control, and behaves in a wild, animalistic fashion. In the absence of neurological findings, the seizure symbolizes an aggressive sexual act. This conceptualization is reinforced when the boy relates that the fear of seizure is with him particularly on dates. He has never had a sexual experience and doesn't know what really happens during intercourse. His fantasy is that the quantity of excitement during intercourse is uniquely greater than during masturbation or petting. One might say to this boy: "You must have felt an impulse to grab this girl and really let yourself go. You were afraid of what you might do because you don't know really what happens in sex between a man and a woman. You were afraid you might lose control, hurt her, and hurt yourself. In other words, you were afraid you would behave like an epileptic." Following this, real information would be necessary to replace his distorted notion about sexual behavior.

As intensive psychotherapy proceeds, the opportuneness of the cathartic interpretation increases: With time the patient gains gradual insight and acquires greater ego strength. Obviously in brief psychotherapy, this long, slow conditioning process is not available; consequently, the interpretation and its effects must be geared to the prevailing circumstances. Modifications of the cathartic interpretation are required to protect the patient from the full impact of repressed drives and ideas. As a rule, except for the truly "ready" patient, in brief psychotherapy it is best to err on the side of caution and to dilute the cathartic interpretation.

"Mediate" Catharsis

The desired effect of the interpretation in mediate catharsis may be:

1. To temper its uncovering potential;
2. To offer reassurance along with the uncovering;
3. To provide an acceptable outlet for the drive so that it will not be dammed up;
4. To alienate the patient from the drive at the same time as it is made more ego-syntonic;
5. To "lend" the patient the ego strength of the therapist for combatting his own punitive superego.

In tempering the uncovering effect of an interpretation we substitute more "civilized" words for primitive ones: "That made you *damned* angry,'' or ''You must have thought he was a bastard,'' rather than ''You must have wanted to *kill* him.'' The words used are usually geared to be somewhat stronger than the patient would use in social exchange, hence pungent and carrying some affective charge.

Reassurance may be offered along with uncovering for the mediating effect: ''You are so *damned* angry at your sister that you wish she would *drop dead* (note: *not kill*). But because you are so conscientious that you couldn't harm a fly this idea upset you very much. You were really angry at yourself for having such a thought and that is how you became depressed.''

Too often a therapist attempts to convince a patient that all his troubles will be ended if the patient will only permit himself to experience the rage which the therapist correctly perceives is unconsciously seething in the patient. If the therapist is successful, the patient is left with an open cauldron of hate against which he has little defense, and which spreads through all his object relations, alienating family and friends and leaving the patient with overwhelming feelings of isolation and danger. The borderline paranoid psychotic is a notable example: The unwitting therapist may find intensely disturbing phobic symptoms emerging as he pushes the patient to a presumably cathartic experience of anger. Yet—since even without the pressure from the therapist the patient is uncomfortably angry much of the time—the drive must somehow be recognized and mitigated. The patient feels endangered because the impulse is ego-alien, yet the danger is that interpretation will make it ego-syntonic. The therapeutic task is to steer a middle course that seeks simultaneously to make the drive more syntonic and yet preserve the ego's feeling of alienation. This multiple goal will seem less contradictory when we realize that the patient's anxiety about the impulse is derived from the superego pressures upon the ego; hence, the task becomes one of simultaneously lessening superego pressures and increasing the ego's capacity for both recognizing the impulse as an acceptable human feeling and realizing that its expression must be limited.

A young woman very clearly displays a borderline paranoid personality. A highly competent factory worker, she is ceaselessly moving from job to job. At first on a job she is content, but soon dissatisfaction and anger with peers and supervisors emerge. With this, and usually preceding the anger, she experiences disturbing phobic reactions to vermin (in her dynamics, siblings). She has been maintained in yearly brief contacts by mediate catharsis. First efforts are made to achieve acceptance of her rage with colleagues and bosses by recognizing it, discussing it around the specific issues she perceives as being at stake, and by identifying her angry response as a rather universal one that most people in her situation experience. Then come efforts to preserve alienation: All people get angry in such situations but accept it as part of the job; her anger often arises from fear that a criticism or correction will lead to her dismissal so she quits rather than be fired; her fear of dismissal is somewhat exaggerated, other workers in the department are criticized and corrected without dismissal.

The ego-strengthening effects of mediate catharsis are often facilitated and reinforced by ''lending'' the therapist's ego to the patient: ''If I were in your place I would be furious,'' then, ''. . . *but* I'd clear the air by talking it over with her,'' or ''*but* I'd decide that's just her way of doing things and I'd get used to it,'' or ''*but* I'd decide I needed my job more right now than to rub her face in the dirt.''

When, in brief psychotherapy, cathartic insight into an impulse is desired, the brevity of the therapeutic contacts dictates that mediate catharsis be the approach of choice. The patient cannot be left ''holding the bag,'' or holding an open Pandora's box of much impulse and little defense.

Drive Repression and Restraint

With many patients the necessity to restrain or repress a drive becomes the important therapeutic task. A patient, under pressure from his peer culture, may be engaging in sex, stealing, or destructive behavior that is resulting in extreme anxiety or depression. A wife and mother may be leading a promiscuous life without feeling any concern for the effects of her behavior upon her children and marriage. A husband and wife may engage in savage battles in the presence of their two-year-old child without thought or perception of the child's reactions. A young man may be struggling with powerful but latent homosexual impulses that appear repeatedly in dreams that awake him and make him fearful of sleep.

To interpret the impulse or drive in many such cases may produce increased anxiety and psychotic regression (as with the latent homosexual) where the ego is weak, or an attitude of ''So what do you think I've been after?'' (as with the philandering wife) where the supergo is lax. In some cases, the task is to increase the operative force of the superego, in others to strengthen the ego, and in still others to increase both simultaneously.

One might delineate for the quarreling husband and wife the predictable and dire consequences for their child. We could appeal to the philandering wife's narcissism by the threat of venereal disease, her unfavorable position in a divorce action, and the effect of both these upon her children. With the young adult or adolescent we may appeal to reason and judgment in suggesting delay of gratification until such time as he is more mature and can permit himself libidinal gratification under more sanctioned circumstances. At the same time, predicting future effects of present behavior can reinforce the suggestion of delay.

Where drive repression is the effort in therapy, repeated dreams may nonetheless keep pressure upon the patient and threaten to emerge into consciousness. The therapist cannot ignore these dreams; he must deal with them therapeutically. He may decide to work only with the manifest content and relate it only to contemporaneous events in the patient's life—a quarrel with the boss over the work schedule rather that the patient's wish for a sexual connection with his father. Or he may choose to deal with fear of the counterdrive rather than with the wish for gratification of the pressuring drive. Thus one might stress the fear of aggressivity rather than the wish for passivity.

Another technique is to encourage defenses against the eruption of a drive. One may detect in a patient's history the former operation of a moderate obsessive-compulsive component and elect to encourage its return by praise for this kind of behavior, while at the same time showing the patient areas of his life where it may be applied. A young man was successfully encouraged to devote his evenings to compiling statistics about stocks instead of spending them in depressed isolation in bars. By way of additional benefit, his research led to careful investments, and his increased income permitted him libidinal discharge in travel.

Still another approach is to provide substitute or sublimated outlets. An angry, hostile man may be encouraged to punch bags, sculpt stone, or chop wood. A mild, passive person may be supported in his feminine attitude without danger by encouraging him to contribute his services to the care of the elderly.

Reality Testing

Even among neurotic patients perception both of the external world and internal strivings may be distorted or warded off in order to avoid painful wishes and fears. Denial, as in children, of unpleasant realities may be the defense employed. Projection of internal wishes and reactions may be resorted to by others. The mild paranoid reaction, often in the service of masochism, is found in many people who are not psychotic.

Memory and learning are fundamental to the development of reality testing, and become the techniques in the treatment of impaired functioning in this area. Memory of former, more appropriate responses may be elicited and contrasted with the present maladaptive distortion. The therapist may teach reality testing by suggesting outcomes of behavior, alternative interpretations of a situation, or a third person's comments, or by ascribing alternative motivations to the behavior of another that the patient may be misinterpreting.

Many people have simply not learned the appropriate pressures upon or emanating from a role, position, or status they occupy. A youth, newly employed, may not know that it is appropriate for him to be sent out for coffee by the older workers, or that he in turn may request another to do something.

Sensitization to Signals

Perception of both internal and external signals might well be classified under the rubric of reality testing but merit special comment as a therapeutic intervention. Pointing out to patients that they have not been heeding warning signals from themselves or others is often helpful. We are reminded of a young girl who broke into tears of shame when her date proposed sexual intercourse, and to his amazement and hers then blurted, "Mary told me you would do this if I went out with you."

Requesting a patient to go over a situation or event in minute detail often supplies the data needed to show the patient that he had indeed received a signal but ignored it. This intervention may then provide the necessary receptiveness for an insight interpretation.

Intellectualization

The development of psychoanalytic practice has resulted in a degree of condescension toward the use of intellectualization as a therapeutic device, if not outright disapproval of it. The emphasis upon the cathartic experience, with insight accompanied by affective changes, undoubtedly is responsible for intellectualization being relegated to a position of disrepute. Nonetheless, as a practical matter, if the development of a defense, previously slightly used by the patient, results in a decrease in use of a more pathological defense, then a psychotherapeutic change has been brought about. The effect of intellectualization, therefore, has a proper place in the practice of psychotherapy. Knowledge where there has been misinformation, reality where there has been fantasy, often go a long way toward relieving the anxiety patients experience as a result of lack of information. Every psychotherapist has had the experience of immediate amelioration of anxiety when a patient has learned that his symptoms are, for example, not unique, but are rather widely experienced. Combatting distortions attendant to masturbation are perhaps a prime example. In cases where anger is generated in a relationship, we have effectively stated that many people respond with anger to situations in which they actually experience fear. This idea has been helpful in enabling the patient to contain the reaction based on rage, while intellectually he searches for those aspects of the relationship which may be generating anxiety. The effect of intellectualization is often the cutting through of denial, to assist in making that which is preconscious conscious, in turn permitting eventually a more insightful type of learning.

Much of the pain of anxiety and other symptoms derives from the feeling of helplessness vis-à-vis the symptoms. The patient feels attacked by an unseen antagonist or force. Intellectual presentation of the cause of depression, of displacement and somatization in hysteria, for example, can impart optimism and motivation to cooperate in psychotherapy.

Intellectualization is most useful in giving the patient a new way of looking at his behavior. It provides a start on a new approach to his problems, an approach that might never occur to him spontaneously.

Reassurance and Support

The psychotherapeutic technique of reassurance lends either implicit or explicit support to the patient. A good example of implicit support and reassurance is a therapist's statement of his availability 24 hours a day to the panicky or suicidal patient. Through this statement of availability, which, of course, must be substantiated in practice, the therapist tells the patient: You are not alone; I am here as a source of help whenever you might need me. Most patients use this offer judiciously; some even must be reassured several times that the offer is a sincere one. They come to a therapeutic session reporting panic in a sharply conflicting situation which occurred in the interim between sessions; they had not called upon the therapist by telephone. In these circumstances, a therapist should repeat his offer and indicate how it might have helped. A very small number of patients exploit the offer of availability, either to test the therapist's sincerity or perhaps to tax him to the point where he is inclined to withdraw the offer, therefore proving the patient's contention that he is rejected by everyone. These latter patients can often be helped by interpreting their testing of the therapist or their excessive passive needs. Still others can be helped by preventive predictive measures, indicating that sometimes the offer may seem so tempting that the patient will invent a conflict situation in order to justify his use of the therapist's assistance; then, abuse of the offer must be clearly delineated.

Implicit support and reassurance may also involve feeding the patient a variety of possible oral gifts: cigarettes, coffee, cookies, fruit, etc. This technique fosters the incorporation of the therapist as a benign introject and is a useful approach with the "depleted" personality observable in depressions, especially those of a depth which involves suicidal risks.

Explicit support and reassurance are manifest in expressions by the therapist of approval or of his own identification with the patient's emotions, utterances, and behavior. In these statements, the therapist is, in effect, lending the patient his own stronger ego and less severe superego. Thus, he may say to the patient, "If I were in your position, I would have been angry too." Or, "You were right to be angry." The therapist may support and reassure the patient in requesting a raise in salary, in standing up to an overbearing parent, in moving away from the family home, and through a host of similar and related situations. Many patients need support and reassurance through what might be called "vestibule" anxiety; anxiety experienced on the threshold of a new situation but which the therapist is reasonably sure will disappear, or be mitigated once the patient has acted. This is often true of patients who need support while they are being pushed into involvement with a phobic situation.

On the other hand, in some situations the patient must be supported and reassured against certain feelings he experiences. Perhaps most prominent in clinical experience are those feelings which terrify a patient because he feels that they mean he is crazy or homosexual. With such patients, the therapist may offer direct reassurance, indicating that in his opinion they are neither crazy nor homosexual. He may also generalize or universalize the feelings, indicating that the patient is not unique in having experienced them, that they are phenomena characteristic of large numbers of people.

Counseling and Guidance

Counseling and guidance techniques are employed when the patient should be moved along a path of behavior which, the therapist has determined dynamically, will be beneficial for the patient. Directions for behavior may be required in the patient's interpersonal relationships, but most often will require use of environmental intervention which are treated more fully in Chapter 5.

The therapist may be nondirective, in a sense, in his approach to counseling and guidance with patients who he feels have sufficient capacity for insight and reality perception to make their own decisions on the basis of data which he provides. In these situations, the therapist's statements usually fall short of being recommendations; they more often are posed as alternatives to a situation with predictions of the consequences involved in the alternatives. On the basis of these, some patients may be expected to arrive at decisions which foster the progress of their therapy.

With the acting-out patient the therapist may find it necessary to make a flat, direct statement of desired action. With a very few such patients, adherence to or compliance with the recommendations may sometimes be a necessary concomitant of the therapist's willingness to assume or continue therapeutic responsibility.

Conjoint Consultation

Conjoint family therapy as developed especially by Jackson[89] may also facilitate learning. In our usage, this procedure might be more appropriately termed conjoint consultation: When the dynamics of a patient are well understood, the therapist may decide that desired changes will come about best, not by a single relationship between him and the patient, but by a joint facing of problems which involve both the patient and the figure or figures with whom he is most in conflict.

This procedure will be totally inadequate and seriously disruptive if the therapist does not have a specific idea of what he wishes to accomplish by the conjoint consultation. It can be a useful device only if the therapist has clearly determined its purpose in advance. He must first understand the whole problem in terms of the history. Then he must understand what goes on between the two or more people, so that when they are brought together he has a clear-cut idea of how he wants the interview to proceed, and is able to steer it in the direction which will add something of help to the patient. By and large, the therapist in conjoint consultation seeks to help the patient solve a conflict or alter a relationship with the conflicting figure. Following the conjoint meeting, the patient must be seen alone for an analysis of what took place during the meeting.

The conjoint meeting may be particularly useful with spouses where the outstanding feature is a sado-masochistic relationship. A remarkable feature of such relationships is that the partners usually are not aware of how long the sado-masochism has gone on. They are always aware of the most recent incident, but they lose perspective in a view of the past 20 years. The therapist may point out, "Look, you were fighting about X, but actually what you are fighting about does not make any difference from what I gather. You have been fighting for the past 20 years about several hundred different things. There is something in the situation between you that apparently makes you fight. Now, what is it about?" The effort is to make them aware that their quarreling is not episodic but is a part of their characters, and that it has been going on for a long time.

People often are not aware of how miserable they make themselves. Denial, of course, is involved and the emotion of the immediate situation tends to obscure their own participation. One couple, both in their sixties, had been fighting with each other for more than three decades. They were told, "Look, how much longer do you think you will live? You are not going to live forever, you know. You are now in your mid-sixties so that you have perhaps ten years. You have a choice: You can drive yourselves crazy for the next ten years, or you might look at what you have been doing. You might look at how you are doing it, and you might make an attempt to at least change now and live pleasantly together for the rest of your lives." On the surface this is a cruel thing to say, but the psychotherapist must not be afraid of presenting cold, hard reality if he knows why he is doing it, and if he is able to offer an alternative. This presentation was obviously a shock to the couple, but it ameliorated the situation between them enough so that they were able to continue more amicably thereafter.

With their permission each one's individual history was explored, showing them how they had acquired sado-masochistic behavior and mannerisms with the father, mother, or an older sibling. They were shown how they both came into the marriage with this pre-existing sado-masochistic set. They were able to see that there was much unrealistic expectation in their mistreatment of each other which went beyond the immediate realistic issues they fought about. They were given some information about cues in meeting each other.

An explanation of role playing in response to the cues presented by others is often helpful in such situations. A good example involves department store sales personnel. The same salesperson may react quite differently to different customers in succession. One customer may speak in a squeaky, shaky voice that says in effect, "Excuse me, please, for living, but could you tell me . . ." The salesperson, perhaps fed-up with his work by this time, will be happy to be nasty. Another customer, however, may come in like a battleship and the same salesperson will act quite meekly. The task very often is to point out that the original cues were presented years before, and that the two people have been reacting ever since on the same basis.

With a child particularly (and here we mean a child of any age), seeing him with the parent is often helpful. With the therapist present to give support he may be able to express something to the parent which he could not alone. The goal is not to have the child call the parent names, but rather to state a point simply, "Look, this is what *you* have been doing. You won't let me grow up." The therapist must then explain how many parents do not easily realize that their children have come of age. One can be half-flattering and half-realistic in pointing out to a father that he feels he is self-made, has come up the hard way, and therefore has a good deal of contempt for his son whom he employs. There is the story about an elder Rothchild to whom someone said, "Look, you are only giving me a dime. Your son always gives me a quarter." Rothchild replied, "Well, he has it easier; he has a rich father." We may tell the father that he is contemptuous of his son for not being self-made, that he will neither train him for responsibility nor let him go out on his own. Highlighting a bit of the most obvious, if not the most conflicting factors in the situation, can produce some change in the relationship immediately, and may provide a start for further changes. It may not accomplish all one seeks to, but the patient can be worked with further in individual therapy and helped to develop a different attitude toward his antagonist.

Kaffman[98] has reported upon the use of brief conjoint consultation in family treatment in Israel. His study indicates some basic concurrences with the approaches presented in this book. The approach used in his clinic actually appears to combine percepts of both brief psychotherapy and conjoint consultation in treating both individuals in the family and the family as a unit.

Kaffman indicates that we are or should be searching for new psychotherapeutic tools which allow treatment of large masses of people. He feels that the simple fact that a large proportion of emotional disturbances both in children and adults can be dealt with satisfactorily without resorting to prolonged methods of treatment cannot be denied. This is usually true for the vast majority of reactive emotional disorders and for acute and crisis situations leading to a breakdown of previous apparently "normal" beahvior. Well-timed assistance can help restore emotional homeostasis and prevent further impact of disorganizing anxiety which could determine progressive maladjustment, disintegration, and serious psychopathology. However, clinical experience has shown repeatedly that even long-established emotional disturbances might improve following short-term psychotherapy.

Kaffman makes the interesting observation that shared expectations about the length of treatment as perceived by both the therapist and the patient may determine much of the outcome of treatment. Patients of the lower social class usually cannot accept the fact recognized by the more sophisticated that emotional disturbances, unlike the usual physical complaints, require prolonged and intensive care. Members of the lower social class become suspicious and uncooperative if the prospect of long-term psychotherapy is mentioned. The sophisticated patient, on the other hand, is disappointed, skeptical, and uncooperative if short-term psychotherapy is offered instead of intensive treatment.

Kaffman's paper reports a study of brief family treatment at two children's clinics in Israel. Individual pathology cannot be separated, particularly in the case of a child, from family group psychopathology. Clinical evidence shows that changes in family dynamics may alleviate individual disturbances even in the absence of systematic individual therapy. On the other hand, successful individual treatment of a child may fail to elicit clinical improvement because of the absence of parallel changes in family psychopathology. Therefore, their approach was neither child centered nor parent centered but focused on the integrated family reaction.

The author comments on the "snowball phenomenon." The beginning of healthy changes in behavior and attitude, both on the part of the child and the parent, induces further mutual shifts in the parent–child relationship with additional positive achievement: Therapy has broken a vicious circle and from then on clinical changes do not run parellel to the intensity of treatment.

In the selection of cases, the following categories were excluded:

1. Long-standing psychoses;
2. Sociopathic personalities or cases in which institutional care is indicated;
3. Established neurological damage and mental deficiency as the essential clinical problem;
4. Chronic severe psychopathology in which the symptoms are highly structured and unchanged for several years.

On the parental side they required the presence of a minimal amount of positive family ties and excluded from study the totally rejected, abandoned child. Complete lack of motivation on the part of both parents was also seen as counterindication.

Suitable cases embraced all forms of child psychopathology up to the age of 16, provided that the emotional conflict was not totally internalized, and that the child had enough ego strength and anxiety to feel motivated in establishing a meaningful object relationship with the therapist.

They view history taking as a crucial part of the clinical procedure, inasmuch as previous knowledge of significant data helps the therapist assume an efficient leadership role. The intake interview is conducted by a psychiatric social worker who meets with both parents.

The clinics use a single therapist as opposed to the team approach, believing the single-therapist approach allows for significant saving in time and effort, a cohesive view of the family dynamics, and consequently a consistent and uniform therapeutic intervention.

The first interview is a joint family one, attended by both parents and the child and often other significant members of the family. It is a prolonged interview, lasting from two to three hours. The purpose of the interview is to help everyone, including the child, to reach a clear view and definition of their most distressing problem. No fixed formula is established for subsequent interviews. Different members of the family may be seen separately in the course of the same initial interview. Individual short meetings with the child may then take place. Sometimes the need for such interviews is not appreciated and treatment continues on an indivisible family basis. In most instances, the initial interview embraces four meetings: the whole family interview, the child alone, the parents, and again, the entire family. At the end, the therapist summarizes in a clear and concise way to all members of the family whatever has become evident about the basic problems which are under discussion. He will add specific suggestions and recommendations if they are necessary. Subsequent interviews follow the same flexible adjustment to group and individual interview needs.

For all members of the family, each interview usually includes: redefinition of the problems, summary of what has been established during preceding sessions, analysis of recent events, further scrutiny of factors determining failures in accomplishment in the treatment, realistic appraisal of the situation and expectations of the treatment, and specific acknowledgement of gains and improvements. In more than 75 per cent of 29 families in the study, a remarkable improvement was obtained, as shown by the disappearance of the central symptoms and referral problems.

Group Therapy

Group psychotherapy may be considered as an aid to psychotherapeutic learning to follow or to run concomitantly with individual therapy. The unlearning and relearning acquired in individual therapy may have to be supplemented by, or in the first instance attained by more concrete or often repeated experiences of a certain kind. Group therapy involves the learning of the consequences of "wrong behavior," and reward by the group for "right behavior." This may help build impulse control and achieve other restructurings unattainable by verbal abstractions in the very best of individual therapy.

THE CHOICE OF SOME STRUCTURAL INTERVENTIONS: BRIEF SYSTEMATIC SUGGESTIONS FOR THE TREATMENT OF EGO-FUNCTION DEFICITS*

The more disturbed the patient, the more relevant are the schematic suggestions below.

---

*This material is treated more extensively in Bellak, L., Hurvich, M., and Gediman, H. *Ego Functions in Schizophrenics, Neurotics, and Normals.* New York: John Wiley & Sons, 1973.

Treatment of Disturbances of Reality Testing

Whatever the severity of disturbance of reality testing, the therapist's role is to a certain extent that of an *auxiliary ego*.

If the disturbance of reality testing is severe (e.g., if the patient lives primarily in a world of delusions and hallucinations), a number of preliminary steps are necessary: entering into the patient's world, establishing understanding on a primary-process level, gaining the patient's confidence. Letting the patient know that he is being understood decreases his secondary terror (about his strange world) and makes possible some bridging of the gap between the psychotic world and reality.

Interpretation of some of the distortions is then possible. There may be cathartic interpretations of feared drive impulses (best exemplified by John Rosen's technique), of defenses, or of the superego factors, *judiciously paced*.

Therapy may have to include *sensitizing* the patient to the perception of *internal reality;* for example, getting him to recognize anger or anxiety before they are translated into major or minor projections. Prediction of possible distortion of emerging events will play a major role in the patient's avoiding the distortion and helping him recognize traumatic situations. This holds true particularly for defects in judgment, as seen in various degrees of acting out.

Education may play a role if some of the defects in reality testing are exacerbated by inadequate information (e.g., a fear of becoming pregnant from a kiss).

Drugs may play a major role in the control of excess drives responsible for the distortion of reality. Psychotropic drugs, for example, can improve reality testing indirectly, and the phenothiazines may have an effect on the synthetic function, thereby improving the quality of thinking and, in turn, reality testing.

Group psychotherapy, like a rehabilitation-workshop setting, may provide feedback for reality testing: If the patient behaves or talks unrealistically, the group or workshop personnel lets him know. Inasmuch as faulty reality testing in such settings leads not to dire consequences but to therapeutic intervention, they are "settings of self-correcting reality."

Id and superego are actively involved in reality testing. For instance, unrealistic guilt feelings may be at the root of self-harming, masochistic behavior. Excessive sexual push (e.g., in involutional disorders) may lead specifically to grossly sexual delusions and hallucinations. In such cases, the whole therapeutic armamentarium, from interpretations to achieve insight to drug therapy, is appropriate in the service of improved reality testing.

Treatment of Disturbances of Judgment

It is entirely possible to be able to test reality adequately and yet be insufficiently aware of the probable consequences of ill-considered action. A common example of such a situation is acting out, which spans normal, neurotic, and psychotic behavior. Persons given to acting out can, if queried about the details of reality, offer perfectly accurate accounts. Because of the impulses motivating their behavior, however, they engage in acts that, obviously to everybody else, show poor judgment. Even eminent scientists and outstanding statesmen make such mistakes. A scientist of great repute, who certainly must ordinarily have excellent judgment, nearly came to grief when he and his son, neither of whom could swim, went sailing on the ocean. A highly placed government figure of ascetic personality, in accepting a relatively minor gift, ruined his career with a presumably single instance of poor judgment.

On the other hand, the superego may also interfere with good judgment, in neurotics and normals as well as in psychotics. Some feel, for instance, that John Foster Dulles's diplomacy was sometimes adversely affected by his evaluation of other nations according to his own moral standards.

Psychotic defects in judgment are most likely to be rooted in firm delusional systems, particularly of a paranoid nature; very intelligent patients are especially likely to use exquisite reality testing as a basis for acts showing poor judgment.

Defects in judgment may occur with some degree of independence from reality testing, since judgment involves a proper matching of perceived reality with memory material regarding social, physical, and other factors. Apparently, the process of matching may be interfered with in minor or major ways by fatigue, disruptive impulses, undue superego pressure, or failure either of superego functioning or of signal anxiety. A businessman who is perfectly capable of judging contemporary reality may permit himself undue optimism and buy a trainload of lumber when a small truckload would do. Conversely, depression may color judgment so as to cause unduly pessimistic anticipations from relatively correctly perceived reality. Anxiety may so affect one's anticipation of consequences from a relatively correctly perceived reality as to lead to disastrous and even psychotic decisions.

In the majority of psychotics (particularly in cases of affective disturbances and of the schizophrenic syndrome with affective features), defects in judgment occur relatively independent of reality testing.

Although defects in judgment may be relatively independent of reality testing, they are usually fused with defects in reality testing and are often combined with problems of impulse control and/or disturbances of defenses and other ego functions.

Treatment of poor judgment is largely treatment of the factors underlying it: that is of elation, depression, anxiety, or defective reality testing, poor impulse control, projection, and other disturbances of the defenses. Disruption of the stimulus barrier is sometimes serious enough to lead to poor judgment.

Patients who habitually use poor judgment need constant review of cause and effect. Sometimes prediction of poor judgment in specified circumstances will help to prevent it.[25] Another important strategy for preventing acts based upon poor judgment is to have the patient agree to a delay of the action—for instance, an ill-advised marriage or business deal. Homicidal, suicidal, or delusional acts may lose their motivation if the patient can be made to agree to postpone action. He will then retain freedom of choice, except for a delay. Delay interferes with the pleasure of immediate impulse discharge, thus obviating the act.

Frequently, an outstanding part of the treatment is to increase the patient's "signal awareness" or anticipation of mental sets or reality circumstances that are particularly likely to trigger poor judgment.

Treatment of Disturbances of Sense of Reality, of the World and of the Self

Disturbances in the sense of self are closely allied to disturbances of the sense of identity. The concepts of identity crisis and loss of identity are at present in wide use (from Erikson, Edith Jacobson, and Rosenfeld, to Laing and Sartre). Freeman, Cameron, and McGhie[69] have placed a disturbance in the sense of self at the center of the schizophrenic disorder. In this they closely follow Federn's[63] conception of an underlying disorder of self-boundaries, which he described primarily in terms of shifts of cathexis depleting healthy ego cathexis. On the other hand, Freud spoke primarily of a libidinal withdrawal from object cathexis onto the self. Federn, and Freeman et al., put the emphasis upon the loss of what are best called self-boundaries rather than ego boundaries. Varying degrees of disturbance in the sense of self may in fact be caused by a variety of factors, and therefore treatment also varies a great deal.[27]

In some persons, the sense of self may never have developed well because of autistic or symbiotic relations with the maternal figure by virtue of poor, inconsistent introjects. A crucial factor in a poor sense of self lies in a conflict between two parts of the self, which results in an increase in the self-observing function of the ego. Withdrawal of libidinal energy from outside subjects may also play a role in a poor sense of self. On quite a different level, hysterical focusing on the distance when looking at near objects may also produce depersonalization and so may hyperventilation, with subsequent dizziness and changes in proprioception. Perceptual isolation, fatigue, and drugs (a paradoxical, anxiety-arousing effect of sedatives, for instance) may cause it. More than ordinary awareness of usually automatic functions, such as walking (onto a stage, for instance), may lead to what Simon[153] calls the deautomatizing effect of consciousness and of special effort.

Aside from interpretation of relevant dynamic aspects, depersonalization may be treated by drugs if it is caused by panic or if it is caused either by overbreathing or by nuchal rigidity.

In severe psychotic disturbances of the sense of self, the work of Federn[64] and Sechehaye[148] and Freeman and associates[69] needs to be consulted. Sechehaye painstakingly restored a sense of self-boundaries in individual patients by body contact and interpretation. May and associates'[121] Body Ego Technic (first developed by Salkan and Schoop) permits patients to relearn through rhythmical movements, proprioception, and so on. Gindler's technique of muscle reeducation is also very useful, especially for minor disturbances of body image, as described in Meyer.[126]

The more disturbed the patient, the more active the therapist has to be in helping him build (or rebuild) self-esteem and in helping him structure his life, at least temporarily, so as to avoid experiences that destroy self-esteem: Do not let him take on a larger task than he is likely to be able to manage. Specific self-concepts need analyzing. Concretization of the self as something dirty, dangerous, and loathsome is frequent and needs great attention.

A few joint consultations with the patient and the important figures in his life may be very helpful if there are specific disturbances of role perception, especially in relation to one or more of these significant people.

Mintz[127] has suggested ways to strengthen the sense of self by helping the patient become more aware of aspects of his body image; she suggests improvement of reality testing in borderline patients by increasing their awareness of cause and effect and by strengthening their time sense. She sees this therapeutic intervention as different from influencing the patient directly through guidance and encouragement. Other techniques are discussed earlier in this chapter.

Treatment of Disturbances of Regulation and Control of Drive, Affect, and Impulse

Poor regulation and control of drives is probably the most frequent cause for hospitalization of psychotics. It causes more social disruption than most other ego-function disturbances and is generally perceived as a threat. Historically, unenlightened response to psychotic behavior primarily entailed an interference with freedom by chains and incarceration. When a person was said to be possessed by the devil, reference was almost always to his loss of regulation and control of drives and impulses.

The more recent traditional forms of dealing with severe disturbances of drive regulation and control were restraining sheets, wet packs, various other hydrotherapeutic procedures, camisoles, and locked doors. These means of dealing with psychotic disturbances of control have been almost entirely replaced by chemical restraints, psychotropic drugs, and reform of hospital wards into therapeutic communities with patient government, nurses out of uniform, and open doors. Among the latest psychotropic drugs, lithium carbonate as a specific treatment of manic excitement is particularly relevant to the control of excessive drive.

Drugs play a crucial role not only generally in the treatment of psychotics but also in psychotherapy and in the classical analysis of patients suffering extreme disturbances in drive regulation and control. In Ostow's[134] hands, psychoanalysis of schizophrenics is made possible by a sort of "drug sandwich": Drugs of the phenothiazine variety are used to put a ceiling on the patient's drives, and stimulants, energizers, and antidepressants are used to establish a bottom. (Something akin to titration establishes the most useful midpoint between excessive control and lack of control within which to carry on the analytic process.)

The strictly psychotherapeutic treatment of a lack of drive regulation and control still has a large role to play. Cathartic interpretation, as practiced especially by John Rosen,[142] may be very useful for diminishing uncontrolled behavior or interfering with excessive control (catatonic or depressed). A strengthening of the superego, as well as a decrease of the drives, by interpretation, is often an important stragety.[35] Typically, the superego of the very disturbed person is inconsistent; in part too severe and in part too lenient. The appropriate psychotherapeutic operations strive toward greater consistency by strengthening some parts and weakening others. In all grades of severity of acting out, it is important to cstablish continuity for the patient in place of the discontinuity that exists through his use of denial, magical thinking, and other distortions. In addition, repeated prediction of the consequences of acting out is a useful therapeutic strategy.[25] Excessive aggressive behavior may, of course, be a denial of fear of passivity. Recent studies suggest that if delusions of grandeur used as a means of inflating self-esteem are interfered with, violent actions, including homicide, are easily precipitated.

Very often a lack of regulation and control in an adult is caused by a lack of education, as well as by early overstimulation of aggressive and sexual drives. In such cases, the building of controls and the decrease of stimulation necessitates a long, drawn-out therapeutic effort that strongly resembles education. Interpretation of apperceptive distortions (which incite excessive response from the patient) is a traditionally helpful intervention. If it is difficult to modify an inconsistent superego psychotherapeutically, it is even more difficult to bring about a progression of drive from pregenital to genital orientation, neutralization, and sublimation. Where strictly psychotherapeutic means do not suffice, active changes of the environment may be necessary: A patient whose sadism is excessively stimulated in a butcher shop or whose homosexuality is excessively aroused in a barber shop needs to be helped to change his occupation.

Above all, the patient needs to be helped to develop better signal functions of the ego, awareness of both a dangerous buildup of drive and the lack of an appropriate response before it becomes excessive.

Very general measures for tension reduction and drive reduction, such as vigorous exercise (especially in the presence of an excessive aggressive drive), may temporarily play a very useful role.

Treatment of Disturbances of Object Relations

The readmission rate within five years for first-admission schizophrenics is 15 to 25 percent in the United States, but only five percent in Denmark and Finland.[146] This difference is ascribed to the attention that the Scandinavians pay to the psychosocial aspects in the overall treatment program. The disturbance of object relations is one that will probably remain in the area of psychodynamic treatment (via transference) regardless of what future developments there are in drugs or in the etiology and pathogenesis of severe disturbances of object relations. Drugs may help those for whom object relations are very conflict-ridden and tension-arousing, but they cannot help a person *develop* object relationships that are not there.

Sechehaye's[148] accounts of the painstaking development of object relations via the transference relationship are especially dramatic. Both Rosenfeld[143] and Searles[147] are particularly concerned with the schizophrenic's fear of being destroyed or of destroying the object.

Group-therapy settings and rehabilitation workshops like Altro[17] attempt to help the patient learn object relationships in group settings and permit corrections in object relationships without the great penalties, such as total rejection, which might occur elsewhere. The workshop may help the person to develop an optimal distance or closeness to other people, as well as to learn to tolerate what is for him an optimal number of object relationships. Except by the sociometrists, rather little attention has been paid so far to proximity and distance or to the different number of relationships and tolerance for them in different people called the Porcupine Index.[32]*

Treatment of Disturbances of Thought Processes

Disturbances of thought processes have played a major role in the conception of schizophrenia since Bleuler first described them as being primarily characterized by "loose associations." The specific types of thought disorders have been the subject of much controversy and experimentation.

The close interconnection of thought processes with other ego functions has been emphasized by many. Cameron,[55] one of the earliest investigators, suggested that normal adult thinking is the result of repeated social communication and that disorganized schizophrenics have never developed adequate role-taking skill. Disturbances of communication patterns[154] and the double-bind concept of Bateson and Jackson[11] continue to play important roles. These conceptualizations all imply a close relationship between object relations and thought processes. It is evident that if schizophrenic thought disorder is caused by the failure of persons to develop, among other things, syllogistic thinking because of poor object relations or disturbed

---

*Paradoxically, the treatment of object relation disturbances is discussed so briefly here because it lies at the core of treatment and there already exists an enormous amount of literature on the topic.

communication patterns with other people, particularly parents with whom they grew up, the establishment of thought processes via good object relations in individual therapy, group therapy, or rehabilitation workshop plays a major role. Investigators as diverse as Mednick and Arieti agree that anxiety and other emotions may interfere with thought processes and lead to a regression, developmentally speaking, from secondary-process to primary-process thinking. Mednick[122] sees thought disorder in terms of conditioned avoidance; Arieti,[6] from the psychoanalytic point of view, sees it as a defense. On either hypothesis, it is obvious that treatment of thought disorder must often address itself to anxiety and other disturbing affects. This may be done by drugs, by psychotherapy, or by a combination of the two. A study by Bellak and Chassan[29] suggested that Librium and psychotherapy are able to reduce primary-process thinking; the phenothiazines are well known to be especially able to produce this change in the severely disturbed. Such changes can be attained relatively easily if good secondary-process thinking has ever been attained by the patient. Constant review of events for the patient may decrease dissociation and show him logical relationships between one mood and another.

Evidence of the Valium effect and clinical evidence from psychotherapy suggest that any therapeutic intervention—drug or psychotherapy—that reduces anxiety improves all ego functions and, specifically, thought processes. Anyone who has ever witnessed the effect of cathartic interpretations on psychotic patients will have observed a similar improvement in thought processes almost instantly. What is more, intravenous sodium amytal or pentothal dramatically transformed catatonics into almost normally behaving people while the drug lasted. The drug also brought about dramatic, if temporary, improvement in the verbal productions and thought processes of a good many patients who had appeared hebephrenic. Nobody would claim that barbiturates have a specific antipsychotic effect. It is doubtful, therefore, that the phenothiazines have anything but a secondary effect on thinking, by virtue of improving drive control and decreasing anxiety. However, they are as a class (including the many commercial variations) the most effective "antipsychotic" drugs.

If one becomes aware of actual gaps in the patient's thinking, it is important to illustrate them to him repeatedly—that is, sometimes thought processes are discontinuous because the patient is simply too narcissistic to engage in the role playing that Cameron considers essential to good thought processes, and to pay enough attention to whether the thoughts expressed are intelligible to the listener. If the patient reveals overinclusive thinking, which so many consider the most frequent and basic disorder in schizophrenic thinking, again it is important to illustrate this to him and to interpret the reasons for his doing it.

In other instances, one has to enter the extremely disturbed schizophrenic's world by thinking in "schizophrenese." One woman, for instance, thought that she was able to understand and talk to the birds. It was necessary to understand the ellipses in her thinking to enter into meaningful communication with her. In principle, this is more difficult than to interpolate into the thoughts of the manic patient. As Lewin has pointed out, the manic patient's thinking is centrifugal.[111] His primary defense mechanism is denial; his thoughts rush away from what troubles him, but one can infer what it is from listening to the centrifugal trend.

Disturbed thinking is much more difficult to treat if the patient has never acquired much secondary-process thinking. Then the patient must virtually be trained in syllogisms and in the logical hierarchy of socially acceptable thought. Concrete thinking is a particular problem, especially in patients suffering from somatic delusions. In others, cathartic interpretations, practiced especially by John Rosen,[142] may be necessary—for instance, "You are holding your hand in this particular way because you want to hit your father." One patient, a man who apparently complained only of constipation the way many people do, in fact had a thinly disguised somatic delusion that some living organism was interfering with the function of his intestines and needed to be taken out. His delusion that an embryo was in there had to be interpreted very directly to deal with the disorganization of thought processes that occurred whenever this conflictual topic came up. The use of syllogistic interpretations is almost entirely without effect in such patients until they have much improved.

Paranoid delusions and thought disorders can be very tightly organized, as they represent attempts at solutions of extremely painful conflicts that may show great resistance to change. It is in such circumstances that the use of LSD to bring about a disorganization of a too well-formed paranoid system may possibly be useful: After the disorganization, it may be possible to help the patient attain better compromise formations than the paranoid ones.

Treatment of Disturbances of ARISE

Unlike work with other ego functions, a relative *reduction* of creativity (ARISE, or adaptive regression in the service of the ego) in the therapy of psychotics may play a desirable and important part in the increase of defenses against the emergence of primary-process material. Therefore, plans for improvement in that area in some patients should be very carefully weighed, since the price may be too high to pay. Sometimes, as a relatively desperate measure, a decrease of ARISE may be a therapeutic goal precisely in the attempt to stem an influx of overwhelming psychotic thought. If nothing else will help, some therapists have suggested not only noninterference with, but the active encouragement of fads, "obsessive" occupations, or interest in religious ritual, as forms of defense at the cost of ARISE. Parenthetically, it may be remarked that rather healthy siblings of psychotics often suffer from constriction and loss of ARISE because they are afraid "to be crazy" like their brother or sister, in essence, a phobic defense.

Dynamic psychotherapy may be affected by a disturbance of ARISE, because a lack of tolerance of ambiguity is involved. Syllogisms, which are the basis for all dynamic interpretation, are impossible for the patient to engage in. In the extreme, concrete thinking is present. Patients with disturbances of ARISE, even if not psychotic, cannot possibly tell a story about a T.A.T. card other than the merest description. In such patients it is the first phase of the oscillating process that is disturbed. No decrease in perceptual acuity is permitted. In the workaday world there are many borderline psychotics who function by virtue of doing the same thing in the same way every day of their lives, and those in contact with them soon discover the futility of any attempt to get them to react adaptively to a change in circumstances.

A psychotherapeutic attempt to change this rigidity can sometimes be predicated on illustrating to them that other people see things differently or see different things in the Rorschach and other tests, or have different stories to tell for the T.A.T. pictures. Long ago Bellak suggested that barbiturates (sometimes mixed with stimulants) may help produce the first phase of ARISE in the psychotherapeutic session and provide an avenue for further work.[12] Interpretation of extremely rigid defenses may be helpful. In patients given to very concrete thinking, decreasing the equation of a thought with an act will also decrease anxiety and produce more adaptive ability.

Extreme disturbance of the first phase of the oscillating process necessary for ARISE is more often seen in people best diagnosed as psychotic characters than in obsessive characters.

An extreme ability to regress in the first phase combined with insufficient ability to return to adaptive structural functioning in the second phase characterizes psychotics in their artistic productions as well as in their other activities. Such people often appear to be gifted not only artistically but in many other ways. Structurally or educationally, however, they do not have enough adaptive potential for their efforts to lead to any fruition. Psychotherapy to strengthen reality testing and drive control is necessary. There are probably exceptional people in whom a disturbance in the second phase of ARISE coexists with congenital ability or acquired structural and adaptive characteristics of such strength that, although they are psychotic for all other purposes, their productions are still artistic in the sense of communicating powerfully (rather than having only private meaning). In such instances, strengthening of the adaptive functions by psychotherapy, training (for instance, learning the craft aspects of their art), and drugs are indicated.

Treatment of Disturbances of Defensive Functioning

The treatment of the disturbance of the defensive functions preeminently involves, of course, insight psychotherapy of the primary impulses, the apperceptive distortions, and the inappropriate defenses. In part it parallels the treatment for loss of drive control—for example, manipulation of the environment to decrease stimulus, changes in vocation, living place, and habits. Drugs are useful. The therapist must assess dynamics quickly and, if the patient is psychotic, insist upon even drastic changes rather than stay aloof from decisions that involve reality.

In taking an ego-function approach to therapy the importance of general dynamic understanding must be stressed. This includes the likelihood that the decreased effectiveness of ego functions is the result of a defensive attempt to avoid anxiety. Thus, in psychotherapy, attempts to improve the adaptiveness of a given ego function include interpreting to the patient the defensive aspect of his symptoms and interpreting what was being defended against.

Interference with ego functions as a result of defensive reactions must be distinguished from secondary interference resulting from regression of another ego function; for example, poor memory will secondarily affect problem solving and other ego functions.

Treatment of Disturbances of Stimulus Barrier

The stimulus barrier has not usually been treated as an ego function. The argument against doing so has been based on the idea that the stimulus barrier is congenitally given, rather than a result of development or experience.

It is questionable whether stimulus barrier is more of a congenitally given factor than some other autonomous ego functions. Certainly, stimulus barrier may also be the result of infantile and even later experiences. Excessive stimulation of infants and cramped, noisy quarters probably raise both the stimulus barrier and the arousal level; such people may be in a higher state of arousal and need more stimulation (stimulus hunger)[33] but at the same time have a higher barrier against input.

It is, however, likely that some children are born with a relatively low stimulus barrier and others with a relatively high one. If low stimulus barrier is diagnosed early enough, it would appear rational to try to decrease the amount of perceptual input for such children, as extreme overloading may be responsible for the development of some schizophrenic conditions. Such children are likely to overreact to physiological events, such as teething, fatigue, and the auditory, visual, and tactile stimulations of everyday life. On the other hand, some autistic-appearing children may be suffering primarily from a high stimulus barrier, and in such cases greater efforts to communicate with them must be made. Systematic attempts to stimulate their sensory capacities may be appropriate and necessary for optimal maturation (similar both to the Montessori methods and to those used in Luria's Institute of Defectology in Moscow).

It is conceivable that a low stimulus barrier coexists with a disturbed electroencephalogram in *some* cases, for which drugs to correct the electrical functioning of the brain may be useful.

Some physiological states, such as premenstrual water retention and changes in the electrolyte balance, lower the stimulus barrier and are probably primarily responsible for many marital conflicts. Conversely, dehydrating drugs frequently upset the electrolyte balance, which may in turn seriously affect the normal stimulus barrier.

Certain social conditions, such as the sharing of one room day and night by a large number of impoverished people, may result in such tremendous aggressive, sexual, and other overstimulation as to cause a lack or loss of control and certainly interfere with optimal development. Only socioeconomic changes are likely to solve those problems.

Therapeutically, one may have to take advantage of whatever environmental changes are possible. Changes in living conditions are sometimes possible. Changes in vocation or daily routine designed to avoid an "overload" may be essential for the prevention of further ego disorganization.

Tranquilizers may in part have their effect by increasing the stimulus barrier. The effect of lithium on manic states has been ascribed by some to its slowing down the processing of information. Lithium does not seem to have that effect on schizophrenics, but its effect on manics suggests that a similar drug for schizophrenics may be found. Overideational states, as well as catatonic excitement, might then be more amenable to a drug approach. There is some clinical evidence that catatonic stupor is, among other things, an attempt to decrease stimulus input (as well as to control affect); if so, such a drug would more specifically affect that condition than do the phenothiazines.

Treatment of Disturbances of Autonomous Functioning

The need for relative intactness of autonomous functions for the work of classical psychoanalysis has been pointed out by Loewenstein;[114, 115, 116] his broad definition of autonomous functions includes reality testing, anticipation, and self-observation.

In psychotics, the primary autonomous functions, such as memory, intention, movement, and language, may be severely afflicted. Nevertheless, within impaired areas some aspects of secondary autonomy may remain remarkably intact. A patient who stood around in a frozen catatonic state could play rapid and brilliant ping-pong once he was positioned to receive the ball at the end of the table. A kind of automatized function seemed to take over. As soon as the ball dropped from the table, by his or his opponent's doing, he froze back into a catatonic stance. Continued attempts to play ping-pong with him led to an increasing continuity of movement within the table-tennis setting and later to an abandonment of catatonic rigidity in other situations.

Special skills other than motor ones often resist psychotic impairment. Many a person with severe defects in reality testing, judgment, and control of impulses remains a skilled worker and retains special information—even several foreign languages—or professional competence. In such cases the still intact functions are most important, as they may be used in an attempt to improve the defective functions. In a rehabilitation workshop, a skilled mechanic may improve his object relations[23] while engaged in productive work. Any situation that helps to neutralize and sublimate drives, such as occupational therapy, music therapy, or athletics, is likely to improve autonomous functions.

In certain circumstances, very specific drugs may ameliorate psychotic afflictions of primary autonomous functions. Estrogens may be useful in the treatment of paranoid conditions, such as may be present in a woman of involutional age where olfactory delusions are frequent. The primary disturbance in these cases is probably a change in the mucous membranes of the nose (and sometimes, when fear of being poisoned is a preoccupation, of the mouth), caused in turn by endocrine changes. The correctly perceived subjective changes in perception are then misinterpreted in the form of hallucinations and delusions (for instance, that enemies are producing evil smells by spreading manure).

Treatment of Disturbances of Synthetic-Integrative Functioning

The treatment of disturbed synthetic function may proceed by strengthening other ego functions and by dealing with drive disturbances impairing the synthetic function. Drugs may also be useful. It may be necessary to advise the patient to decrease his burdens, at least temporarily. In such a case the decrease in demands serves like the splinting of a broken limb and permits the synthetic function to improve again almost spontaneously. In patients who have particular difficulty in synthesizing affect and thought, it is essential to establish continuity where they experience discontinuity.

It is very likely that perceptual–motor disturbances, to which increasing attention is being paid in connection with dyslexia and other learning difficulties, are related to some problems of synthetic functioning in the young and that educational help is necessary. In some such children, because of a primary lack of synthesis or perhaps a secondary continued frustration over their inability to perform routine motor and perceptual tasks, emotional explosiveness may also be part of a failure of the synthetic function.

Inconsistent upbringing is certainly likely to impede the maturation of synthetic functioning, and prevention of disturbances will have to be the ultimate treatment.

Treatment of Disturbances of Mastery–Competence

A feeling of impotence toward the forces of life, of an inability to master or alter them, seems characteristic of modern man, particularly in the post-World War II period and the atomic age. Existentialism (philosophical and literary) concerns itself primarily with man's relation to powerful forces. Camus's literary characters are helpless, confused, and at the mercy of both their drives and fate. Laing,[109] who is probably the most widely known latter-day exponent of the existential viewpoint in psychiatry, deals specifically with the schizophrenic living in today's world.

An improvement of object relations or impulse control, of reality testing or judgment, is bound to have an indirect effect upon mastery and competence. Self-esteem is of course related to the *sense* of competence. Many outstanding psychotic delusions and hallucinations are the direct result of disturbances in self-esteem, in objective competence, and in the subjective feeling of competence. Classically, delusions of grandeur—frequently encountered in schizophrenic patients with paranoid and/or manic disturbances—both defend against, and are intricately interwoven with, a deep feeling of impotence. A schizophrenic, especially one with manic tendencies, may well imagine himself to be an exalted personage. This easily leads to paranoid delusions—for example, that because he is so important, not only are many people interested in him but many are also inimical to him and eager to put him out of the way. At the heart of these grandiose feelings and the paranoid ones are feelings of smallness and passivity. One could well say that the psychotic makes himself so big because he feels so small; he feels so powerful and conceives of such powerful enemies because he feels so weak and helpless when it comes to *affecting* himself and his world.

Central to the treatment of disturbances of mastery and competence, therefore, is the treatment of low self-esteem. Such therapy may involve interpreting the pathological means of inflating or otherwise regulating self-esteem and then dealing with whatever precipitated the particular instance of lowered self-esteem. For example a patient's delusion of being extremely wealthy may have started with a business failure of objectively rather small proportions but of great importance to him in terms of his actual and subjective sense of mastery–competence.

WORKING THROUGH

We have already indicated that the process of working through is the application of learning to contemporary, transference, and genetic experiences. Learning theory has some particular applications here: We are first of all concerned with the problem of making permanent the learning which takes place in the psychotherapeutic situation. Clinically, we speak of avoiding relapses. In brief psychotherapy not much time is allowed for the working-through process, with the emphasis necessarily upon immediate learning. Here the formal aspect of learning theory which involves spacing or dispersal of learning is particularly applicable. The patient is often invited in brief psychotherapy to return at widely spaced periods for an additional session or two, or even to maintain telephone contact with the psychotherapist.

The problem in working through is to achieve reinforcement of learning of new behavior and the extinction of neurotic modes of adjustment. As in intensive psychotherapy, when a plateau has been reached and persists, cessation of therapy for a time has been found to remove the individual from the dependency inherent in the psychotherapeutic process and to permit him both to apply learning in real-life situations or to learn that he has additional problems. These experiences may have the effect of convincing the patient that he has adequately learned a new mode of behavior, or that his learning has been inadequate. The result in both cases is that psychotherapeutic learning has been heightened by the actual life experience.

ENDING TREATMENT

In brief psychotherapy, the patient must be left with a carefully cultivated positive transference and a clear understanding that he is welcome to return. The maintenance of the positive transference avoids a sense of rejection in the terminating process and permits the patient to retain the therapist as a benign, introjected figure. This has its effects on the whole personality and maintains motivation to do well for the sake of the therapist. These are forces similar to children's renunciation of primitive modes of behavior predicated upon the love and approbation of the parents as motivating factors until autonomy takes over.

The availability of the therapist to the patient should be stressed. At the same time, he should be urged to apply himself to the lessons which have evolved during the brief psychotherapeutic procedure. The patient should be told that he has been helped because he has, with the therapist's aid, begun to understand his problems. He should be cautioned to get in touch with the therapist before any future problems become unmanageable.

In ending treatment, it is, perhaps, most helpful to reinforce the learning which has been accomplished by helping the patient to anticipate future problems which may arise as a result of patterns of behavior which have been discerned in the patient. Anticipation of this order often has a preventive effect.

A definite motivating force, which helps maintain both the positive transference and reassures the patient of the availability of the therapist, is to ask for periodic follow-up reports from the patient. These can be made by letter or by telephone, depending upon the individual circumstances.

5
Adjuncts to Brief Psychotherapy

DRUGS AS ADJUNCTS TO BRIEF AND EMERGENCY PSYCHOTHERAPY

The Clinical Rationale

The clinical rationale is the most frequent one for combining pharmacotherapy and psychotherapy. In the broadest sense one could say that often the psychotropic drugs play the same role for the therapist as anesthesia plays for the surgeon: They provide the *enabling conditions* for performing the psychotherapeutic operations. Drugs are often necessary because psychotherapy might not be possible without them, at least not on an ambulatory basis and not outside the hospital.

This rationale holds true for the extremely panicky neurotic, the depressed, and the schizophrenic patient. The panicky patient can stay at work and home with the help of the so-called minor tranquilizers, or anxiolytic drugs such as diazepam, meprobamate or diazepoxide and others. The drug may enable him to talk about subject matter which he might otherwise avoid because of "approach anxiety."

The depressed patient who was relatively immobile and inarticulate prior to drug treatment can be helped with antidepressants—the tricyclics or monoaminoxydase inhibitors or others—to talk about his complaint.

Many schizophrenic patients might not be able to stay home at all, or they might be so disturbed by hallucinations or delusions that communication would be difficult to establish, except for the use of phenothiazines and their relatives. Though the psychotropic drugs do not offer a cure per se, they often promote the crucial means which enable the dynamic psychotherapy that would otherwise be at best difficult, and occasionally impossible.

Two case histories illustrate the combined use of psychotherapy and pharmacotherapy.

A college student was admitted to the clinic for brief therapy because of anxiety attacks before and during certain classes. It was close to examination time, and his inability to attend these classes put him in danger of losing credit for the whole school year.

The dynamics of the situation became clear in the first session and had to do with voyeuristic and exhibitionistic wishes. In his circumstances even five weeks of psychotherapy were too long to wait for remediation. He therefore was given 25 mg. of diazepoxide to be taken one-and-a-half hours before each class. He was told to take the drug this early in the hope that it would prevent the development of *anticipatory* anxiety which in turn would be likely to escalate.

Meanwhile, the phobia could be treated psychotherapeutically and etiologically—something which the drug alone could not do. Since the therapeutic timetable was affected by the reality of examinations, somewhat more than the usual five sessions were needed to deal with the phobia. A few additional sessions were used, sometimes several months apart, when anxiety-producing situations arose again. At times diazepoxide was used, again with the explanation to the patient that each instance of anxiety he mastered would constitute a valuable form of deconditioning, in addition to the gains made by insight. Two years later in a phonecall he informed the therapist that he had successfully graduated from college and accepted his first position of employment.

Another case, while not strictly an example of the use of pharmacotherapy combined with brief therapy, is an excellent illustration of the use of drugs to provide enabling conditions to carry on any kind of psychotherapy.

It involved a young man seen in consultation, who was already in therapy with someone else for a severe compulsion neurosis. It quickly became apparent that extensive hour-long toilet behavior either caused him to be at least a half-hour late for his psychotherapy appointment or to miss it altogether.

The recommendation was that he take 50 mg. chlorpromazine with 50 mg. imipramine HS. The considerations were dynamic. We know that aggression plays a marked role in compulsive urges. We know also, from experiments with artificially aroused primates, that chlorpromazine controls aggression; therefore chlorpromazine was prescribed. The imipramine, on the other hand, was necessary to counteract the soporific, energy-sapping effect of the chlorpromazine and also to counteract the depressive features that coexisted with the compulsion neurosis.

In this case the immediate reason for the pharmacotherapy was strictly clinical: one can't treat a patient who isn't there.

Of course, similar considerations as in the previous case history hold true for the many depressed patients who may not be able to get out of bed, or come too late to psychotherapeutic appointments, or suffer excessively from psychomotor retardation and are therefore unable to verbalize optimally. The use of antidepressants facilitates: The patient gets to his appointment and can communicate, so that even brief psychotherapy often may be promptly effective. Because imipramine and amitriptyline may take more than a week to become effective, methylphenidate is sometimes combined with imipramine or amitriptyline for its immediate antidepressant effect. The methylphenidate can be stopped as soon as the imipramine or amitriptyline becomes effective. To date no one treated by us has shown any tendency toward addiction or habituation to methylphenidate. It must be noted that these patients were not only carefully selected, but relatively closely supervised. In many drug clinics the patient is seen for a few minutes, at best, before being handed a prescription. In psychotherapy the patient is carefully evaluated prior to prescribing a drug or drugs. The subsequent therapeutic interviews provide the opportunity to monitor the patient's reactions to his prescription. He is further offered the support of the psychotherapeutic relationship and the emerging support from the tricyclic drugs, and almost immediately taken off the methylphenidate. Young people, or people coming from a culture promoting drug abuse, are excluded from medication by methylphenidate.

Thus, unless selectivity, caution, and supervision are used, it is better to combine only tricyclics with psychotherapy.

Some practitioners prefer MAO inhibitors for acute depressions because they take effect more quickly. The MAO inhibitors are generally less in favor because several foods, such as cheese, tend to produce violent allergic reactions.

In the treatment of affective disorders, lithium carbonate plays a special role, particularly in the care of hypomanics and manics. Since the therapeutic dose is close to the toxic dose, careful monitoring of lithium serum levels is necessary. The combination of lithium therapy and brief therapy facilitates both understanding the precipitating events, and attempts to work through the dynamics, thus decreasing the chances of a recurrence of similar circumstances and similar manic reactions, biochemically and psychodynamically.

Other Considerations

Drugs also may be used in psychotherapy on the basis of *structural* as well as *psychodynamic* and *metapsychological* rationales. The assessment of ego functions may be a basis for the metapsychological rationale. For example, if regulation and control of drives are poor, chlorpromazine may be indicated until something can presumably be done psychotherapeutically about impulsive acting out. Brief psychotherapy of an acutely exacerbated chronic psychosis may be greatly facilitated by a phenothiazine that improves the nature of the thought processes enough so that this combination is more helpful than chlorpromazine alone. Ego-function assessment (see Chapter 4), is useful as a guide when considering which combination of drugs to use during psychotherapy.

Ostow's suggestion for the use of a mixture of tranquilizers and stimulants[134] is basically related to an *economic* point of view. He hypothesizes that stimulants increase the available ego–libido while tranquilizers reduce it. On that basis he suggests a process similar to chemical titration, in which attempts by trial-and-error are made to find the optimal combination of the two drugs. Whether or not the theory underlying his suggestion is valid, clinically the judicious mixture of these two classes of drugs is successful, thus providing what may be termed a therapeutic validation.

An important indicator for the use of drugs combined with brief therapy may exist when a patient has so much *secondary gain* from the symptoms that he is unwilling to give them up. This may happen with people after long, chronic physical illness or with people on welfare, who have taken some pleasure in the passivity afforded them under the circumstances. A stimulant drug, given for just a few days, will enable them to get past this point to where they can again derive more pleasure from activity than passivity, and gain some realistic advantages and an increase in self-esteem.

Dynamically, it would be desirable to have a drug that could weaken superego forces. While the superego may be dissolved in alcohol, the process is neither reliable nor practical.

A *psychobiological* basis for using drugs in psychotherapy is inherent in the catecholamine hypothesis and in other theories conceptualizing the etiology and pathogenesis of the psychoses in biochemical terms. There is little doubt that a continuous interaction exists between experience and a broad spectrum of biochemical processes, including cortisol and growth hormone excretion. Diurnal variation of secretions almost certainly has an effect on cognition; eventually drugs and psychotherapy related to these biochemical changes will likely become especially efficacious.

Similarly, neurophysiological factors in disturbances such as minimal brain dysfunction need special medication to optimize the ability to communicate in psychotherapy and to control impulses, concept formation, and anxiety.[42]

Drugs may also be used for their oral significance as a placebo. Sometimes even a soft drink, coffee, weak alcoholic beverage, fruit, or cookies may play this role in psychotherapy. Their use with some patients helps to establish a therapeutic alliance, a rapport, a friendly atmosphere. The patient's response to these offerings or to an inactive drug will test whether a placebo effect is being obtained. If it is, the therapist may elect to continue this procedure or to use an active drug for both the placebo response and the physiological effect of the chemical agent.

Cautionary Remarks

Naturally, the use of drugs creates as well as solves some problems. As in all cases, advantages have to be weighed against disadvantages and risks. It must be kept in mind that, in a very simple way merely administering drugs introduces parameters in the therapeutic relationship and the transference relationship. Giving drugs may constitute unconsiously a feeding or a poisoning to the patient. It may mean a vote of no confidence. It may induce a fear of loss of control. Giving too much of an anxiolytic or antidepressant drug may seriously decrease the patient's motivation for dynamic work and insight, and prevent the basic restructuring that only psychotherapy can provide.

It is therefore important for the patient to understand that in most instances the drugs as part of the therapeutic alliance are merely auxiliary measures and not curative by themselves. It is also important to remember that at times the best drugs have a variety of disturbing side effects. The fear of loss of control may produce paradoxical anxiety on a strictly psychological basis. On a somatic basis, many of the drugs produce cognitive changes and at times effect the muscles so as to change proprioception; in such cases patients complain about feelings of depersonalization and derealization, of feeling "spaced out." It is well known that many of the major tranquilizers have a long list of side effects. The most frequent and innocuous of these are dryness of the mouth, some blurring of vision, and some soporific effect. A more serious potential effect on the nervous system are Parkinsonian-like symptoms. Some of the antidepressants can produce paranoid ideation or precipitate manic attacks. The therapist using drugs should thoroughly familiarize himself with them and instruct the patient carefully in their use.

Despite their possibly undesirable aspects, psychotropic drugs are important, sometimes by themselves, and often as adjuncts in the hands of the skilled psychotherapist.

ENVIRONMENTAL INTERVENTION

Psychotherapy is not bound by the psychoanalytic injunctions against intervening in the patient's life or permitting fundamental changes in the living pattern of the patient, such as marriage or conception, during therapy. Brief psychotherapy particularly sanctions both a scanning of the patient's modes of living, working, socializing, recreating, and an intervention where helpful.

The decision to attempt to intervene in the patient's life or environment and the choice of the intervention are based upon two prime considerations:

a dynamic diagnostic formulation of the patient's situation; and his actual life circumstances. Here are some examples of dynamic situations that may lead the therapist to attempt a modification of the environment:

1. A child is sleeping in the parent's bedroom and is subjected thereby to sexual overstimulation.
2. A severely obsessive–compulsive individual is essentially unresponsive to psychotherapy, and his present work requires quick decisions and actions which he is incapable of making.
3. A young man having difficulty with self-assertion is daily struggling with the overwhelming personality of an aggressive, perhaps sadistic father, with whom he works.
4. A patient is unable to find acceptable outlets for aggressive impulses with the result that he suffers constant intense anxiety and is developing obsessive–compulsive symptoms.

In such situations, the task may be to remove or modify the disruptive conflictual element, or to introduce into the patient's life an opportunity for sublimative outlets that he has been unable to invent or find on his own.

We must be alert to any actual life circumstance of the patient which is not modifiable through psychotherapy, and which in itself cannot be altered through psychotherapeutic change in the patient. A physically handicapped individual may not achieve full utilization of himself by psychotherapy alone, however well it dealt with the emotional impact of his disability. His full utilization may well depend upon the application of rehabilitation techniques. Problems due to the massive economic responsibilities of a husband and father will never disappear in the one-to-one talking relationship of psychotherapy. He may need help in finding financial relief, in caring for a sick wife, in providing dental care for a child. The unemployed person may need a job or job training. The physically ill person will need medical treatment. The widowed father may need help in caring for his children.

All of the foregoing implies the role of the social worker as a valuable adjunct to brief psychotherapy. Manipulation of the environment with the aid of the social worker may be carried on concurrently with psychotherapy, or, depending upon the situation, may be designed to operate subsequent or prior to it. In addition to a knowledge of the capability of social work service, the psychotherapist himself should have a wide knowledge and comprehension of the community services available for helping people in trouble. Most modern American cities provide a wide variety of such services through both public and private agencies. In addition to hospitals, clinic facilities, and general family casework agencies, certain services specialize in the care of children, the physically ill, mentally ill, parentless, or homeless; others specialize in the provision of vocational training, in vocational guidance, in the placement of individuals upon jobs; still other services provide free loan arrangements, vacations for children and families, or help for the inexperienced in traveling from one part of the country to another or to another part of the world.

Family and Friends

To ignore the familial and social relations of the patient is to consider him in a therapeutic vacuum. The patient does not live with the therapist or work or play with him. In a preceding section on conjoint consultation we have dealt with the occasional necessity to involve members of the family in the therapeutic process in order to relieve conflictual tension. In many cases, the treatment of a family is not required to bring about dynamic changes in the patient: The simple prescription ordering of changes in family customs and behavior may produce desirable results. Recommendations about privacy, dressing and undressing procedures, the use of the bathroom among family members, the cessation of sexually charged behavior by parents, are among those that may have to be made.

The therapist must not assume that identification of a source of conflict and disruption in the family calls immediately for the removal of that source. Thus hospitalization of a psychotic mother may not necessarily be best for her child. One must attempt to predict: Is it better for this child to have no mother or to be reared by this psychotic mother. Such considerations provide the realistic limits within which the therapist must exercise judgment.

In a similar vein, we cannot assume that sibling rivalry means that there is no love, consequently no support, provided between siblings. Close examination of a family disrupted by severely ill parents often reveals that older children have taken over parental roles in relationship to younger siblings. Encouragèment of these ties between younger and older siblings, and improvement of communication between them may facilitate the development of a feeling of connection and support in an individual who otherwise feels isolated and alone in the world because of the remoteness of his parents.

Relationships between patient and family must be carefully scrutinized for the operation of secondary neurotic gains; these must be actively interfered with if therapeutic gain is to be achieved. The husband who is totally accepting of and compliant with the fears of his phobic wife may be prolonging her illness because he is giving her no external reason for change.

All of the foregoing applies to relationships with friends as well as with members of the family. Particularly with suicidal risks, the utilization of family and friends as protection becomes important. Both family and friends may have to be called upon as guardians against the patient's tendency toward intra-aggression, particularly during periods of therapeutic stress. The utilization of drugs producing deep and prolonged slumber may be contraindicated unless friends or family are available to protect the patient from somnambulistic injury during the drug treatment.

The guiding principles in the adjunctive utilization of family and friends in brief psychotherapy are: the identification of both healthy and conflictual aspects in these relationships; the control or modification of the conflicts; and the encouragement, strengthening, and utilization of the healthy aspects.

Jobs and Job Training

It was Karl Menninger who observed that next to the choice of a mate the selection of an occupation is the most important decision in an individual's life. There are both tragic and comical aspects in the observation that individuals may respond to both marriage and occupational commitment in similar vein, ranging between feelings of entrapment to those of freedom for libidinal expression, vigorous activity, personality growth, and general happiness. Psychoanalytic investigators early recognized that work and work relationships satisfy object-libidinal desires, fulfill sadistic and aggressive drives, and involve a continuous adaptation to reality. Where these conditions are met, work may be said to serve an integrative function for the personality. The therapeutic task is to identify any conditions in the patient's work situation that are disintegrative to his personality. These may include such varied aspects as lack of self-esteem, monotony, fatigue, isolation, the absence of goals, insecurity and anxiety, a host of frustrations, work demands that challenge the defensive structure of the individual, conditions of noise, dirt, activity, decision making, mobility, or lack of mobility.

Whatever his theoretical orientation to personality, the therapist must perceive the relationship between the individual's dynamics and the influences of his job and job situation upon these dynamics. The role of work in the life of an individual begins with the simple assumption that the ability to earn one's living is fundamental to a sense of independence, optimism, and self-esteem. Beyond that we need to understand the particular needs of the patient in relationship to opportunity for his satisfaction.[155] Lack of opportunity for satisfaction of needs (autonomy, dependence, isolation, object relations, physical movement, compulsivity, dirt, etc.) may produce frustrations, mounting aggression, feelings of entrapment and depression. Some special job circumstances may threaten personality defenses directly or endanger them through overstimulation of primary impulses. The role of work in mental health cannot be overstressed. When one considers the many varieties of work activities and environments, one readily sees that, by careful selection, work type and work environment can be matched with individual dynamic needs. Work may take place in isolation, or may require human contact. Such contact may vary in frequency, or in intensity. An individual may work in such a large group that object relations are vastly diluted. Work can be constructive or destructive. It can tap compulsive qualities, or anal expressive qualities. Work can provide responsibility for the individual who thrives on this demand; other work permits the passivity a dependent person needs.

A person may remain frozen in one job long after he is ready to move ahead by virtue of experience and skill. Helping him through a change of occupation with increments, however slight, of income, status, prestige, responsibility, or some change of activity may in a short time produce more improvement in feelings of self-confidence than hours of psychotherapy. At the other extreme, the ability to tolerate one employment for a sustained period of time may considerably reduce anxiety and improve capacity for object relations in a borderline paranoid psychotic. Encouragment of higher-level or totally different job training may often be the therapeutic key. Such training may not only help the patient's employment problem directly, but for some—that is, the socially shy—may also provide the exposure to peers that they would not otherwise be able to tolerate. Thus a woman might be more readily encouraged into a wider range of social contact through a job-training course than by attending a public dance.

Rehabilitation

Rehabilitation techniques and services have been extended from the chronically physically ill and disabled to the mentally ill. One readily sees the applicability of rehabilitation techniques to the man who has suffered a cardiac attack: Shaken emotionally by his brush with death, he is helped psychotherapeutically to confront and deal with his anxieties, but he must also be taught concretely that all work will not kill him, and, in many instances, that he can be trained for an occupational activity that will not exacerbate his cardiac condition.[18]

Among individuals who have suffered a psychosis, those who were functioning well prior to onset, who suffered an acute onset and a rapid recovery, are generally able to return to their former level of functioning without too much difficulty. More frequently, the formerly psychotic person is plagued with doubts and anxieties about his ability to sustain the demands of a work schedule. He may fear that his emotional problems will be apparent to his fellow employees, that the noise of factory machinery will exacerbate his already taut nervous condition, that his hallucinations will return if a supervisor reprimands him or a fellow employee taunts him.

The extension of rehabilitation services to this group of patients has been found useful in returning the bulk of them to self-sustaining employment. The Altro Health and Rehabilitation Services in New York City[23, 50] have been providing such services to posthospitalized schizophrenics since 1954, with multiple casework and medical and psychiatric services as adjunctive resources. The mainstay of the process is the workshop—a graduated program of work exposure in a modern factory under conditons of regular employment. Here the patient learns more than a skill; he learns object relations, reality testing, and impulse control. Many learn to tolerate their symptoms (even delusions and hallucinations) while continuing to work successfully. Having learned that they can work without relapse, they move out to former occupations, to new occupations learned at the workshop, or to advanced training courses elsewhere in the city. The rehabilitation treatment essentially is a learning process developed in a work situation with work motivations and goals.

These patients, like all the mentally ill, suffer from damaged ego functions which are repaired or strengthened in the rehabilitation experience. Altro has identified another group of psychotics who benefit from the rehabilitation learning experience, the people whose egos never progressed sufficiently in developing the functions necessary for independent living and self-supporting activity.

Of interest is Altro's program in introducing rehabilitation services while the patient is still residing at the hospital. The patient continues to sleep and receive treatment at the hospital while spending a work day at the shop. Hospital staff have reported particularly a more rapid improvement in reality testing and obect relations among these patients.

Sublimative Activities

Excessive quantities of aggression always present a problem to the psychotherapist. Some patients, who have their aggressive instincts unfettered in the therapeutic process as pathological defenses are weakened, must actively be directed into socially accepted outlets for this aggression. Others come into treatment with an already excessive charge of aggression that must be diverted into acceptable outlets in order to minimize acting-out propensities. The active sports provide such outlets, particularly those which require vigorous use of the whole body and muscular movements equivalent to striking and smashing. It is obviously better for a man to "murder" his opponent on the tennis court than in fact.

Care must be exercised that one's recommendations, however, do not create conflict on the one hand while seeking to ameliorate conflict on the other. Thus a man with latent homosexual problems had best not be advised into swimming programs where he would be exposed in locker room and pool to homosexual stimulation. In a similar fashion, the patient's tolerance for body contact must be considered in recommending athletic activities. In any event, the therapist can probably start from the safe side and advise noncontact activities such as tennis, badminton, squash, shotput, discus, and javelin throwing.

Body mechanics and dancing courses are also of value. Tightly inhibited individuals will benefit from the ability to use their body in a more freely moving fashion than they otherwise might permit. Some acting-out individuals also benefit from the acquisition of control over their body musculature acquired in this type of training. Again, care must be exercised that men who may associate femininity with such activities will not feel endangered.

Painting, ceramics, and music frequently provide involvements and outlets that are helpful when recommended on what might be considered a prescription basis, that is, recommendations that have bearing for the patient's dynamics. The presence of some degree of aptitude and talent is essential to avoid loss of self-esteem. One readily thinks of the sublimative possibilities for the anal character in getting his hands into wet clay, or for the hostile personality in hammering out the Warsaw Concerto. We should keep in mind that these activities may be ego strengthening, not only because they provide a sublimatory outlet, but because they enhance the ego through the acquisition of skills that develop a sense of mastery.

Recommendation of volunteer social service may be indicated for some individuals, providing an outlet for tender, effeminate emotions, or opportunity for a reaction formation for aggressive individuals.

Any of the activities discussed here also are useful in filling the hours for individuals who spend their time in isolation or in brooding. This consideration is especially pertinent for the increasing number of people who are being retired at an age when they are still vigorous and who suffer depressions both from loss of self-esteem and from the damming up of aggressive outlets that were ordinarily provided by their everyday work behavior. Women of the upper economic strata have traditionally utilized volunteer social service and philanthropic activities as a means of increasing their sense of worthiness and as an outlet for aggressive drives. Many women whose children have grown, who find themselves idle and feel their worthiness is no longer demonstrated in their role of mothering infants and children, can benefit from being encouraged into such activities or, often better still, into paid employment.

Educational Techniques

Education of the patient to the nature of certain physiological and perceptual processes is helpful in allaying anxiety. The very anxious patient, for example, may be taught to observe that the hyperventilation accompanying his anxiety produces feelings of dizziness which in turn lead to increased anxiety about the dizziness and even feelings of depersonalization. Teaching the patient to be aware of this physiological process and to regulate his breathing is the technique of treatment in such situations.

In similar fashion, extremely tense individuals may often have backaches relieved by understanding the simple causal connection between their tight musculature and the experienced pain.

Patients suffering from depersonalization may sometimes be helped by demonstrating to them that feelings of unreality are widely experienced as a result of perceptual disturbances. This can be demonstrated by having the patient look at a near object without focusing, showing the patient that the perceptual change may give one a changed feeling about the perceived object.

Travel and Vacations

The traditional recommendation of the general practitioner when presented with emotional problems by his patients may have merit in some situations when the ability to take vacations or to travel is economically feasible.

"Getting away from it all" enables the patient to sever contact with a conflictual situation or person. The interval may serve to end the upward spiraling intensity of the conflict, which if allowed to go on would produce serious rupture, to provide a furlough that fosters ego mending—or it may serve an implicit warning upon both parties to the conflict, that loss as a consequence is inherent in their conflict.

Another dynamic consideration in the use of vacations and travel is that they sanction a structured regression and, when prescribed by the therapist, may restore "depleted" persons who, on their own, cannot permit themselves such gratification. Usually, masochistic reactions to the experience of pleasure and regression can be forestalled by preventive predictions of such reactions, demonstrable by recalling preceding responses of the patient.

RELAXATION TECHNIQUES

Recent decades have witnessed numerous behavioral modification techniques whereby an individual is conditioned against tension and anxiety in what were formerly tension and anxiety-producing situations. These techniques are based largely on a process of gradual approach, accompanied by concentration on pleasant associations or mental representations.

The literature presents claims of success in the treatment of many diverse conditions, including eneuresis and smoking addiction. Our impression is that the most success has been in the treatment of anxiety and tension conditions. This consistency has prompted us to regard some behavioral-related approaches as valuable adjuncts in brief psychotherapy.

Parallel to the development and use of behavioral modification techniques has been the somewhat slower and more limited development of biofeedback procedures in which physiological processes are made visible and/or audible by standard laboratory monitoring devices—sphygmomanometer, the EEG, the EKG, the GSR, as examples—and the subject is instructed in a desirable pattern in contrast to an undesirable one. Some startling successes in modifying even epileptic seizure patterns have been reported.[164] Modification of physiological states results in changes in emotional tonality as well as reduction of hypertension.

Related but less scientifically oriented phenomena are sometimes observed in the diverse, sometimes rather bizarre, and often mystical, if not religious procedures of Zen, Yoga, and Transcendental Meditation.

The significant common denominator in all of these procedures has been isolated and described by Benson,[44] who also enumerates a set of easily applied, relaxation-inducing procedures that are ideally applicable as an adjunct procedure for both brief and lengthy psychotherapy. Their virtue rests in their brevity, simplicity, and teachability, and their ability to modify the physiological components of tension, such as respiration rate, pulse rate, and muscle contraction. Moreover, they are not burdened with mystical implications, but rest upon a sound physiological rationale. We have been able to use these techniques in therapy to reduce tension and anxiety in a number of patients who did not respond well to insight, and in other patients who had no tolerance for psychotropic medication. In still other patients a reduction of their medication intake was made possible by the use of Benson's relaxation procedures. They are not any more a *panacea* than other psychotherapeutic interventions; we have found that there are some persons who appear unable to practice the technique sufficiently to reduce their tension state, even when that state may not be severe.

Benson's common denominator techniques are simple:

1. The environment should be quiet and preferably dark.
2. Sit in an upright position in a comfortable chair, with hands resting on the thighs, palms downward.
3. Breathe slowly, deliberately, and deeply. Concentrate upon the experience of *exhalation*. While so doing, silently repeat any one-syllable word of choice. Benson favors the use of the word "one."
4. Adopt a passive attitude to the process. If one's mind wanders, as it is almost certain to do, accept that fact with the knowledge that one can and will return to the observation of respiration and the concentration on exhalation.

Practice is essential in acquiring and applying this technique. Benson recommends that it be practiced at least twice a day for ten-minute periods. The effects of the practice are to reduce chronic tension and to make the technique readily available when acute episodes arise.

ELECTROCONVULSIVE THERAPY

In a narrow range of situations, electroconvulsive therapy becomes either the principal treatment of choice or an adjunct with psychotherapy: where the suicidal danger is too great to risk drug therapy or psychotherapy alone, or where they are ineffective and the depression or catatonic state is so deep as to make communication impossible. In cases of such extreme exigency, psychotherapy is often best restricted to suggestions of environmental changes that are advisable on the basis of dynamic insight, or to directive help for the patient in dealing with immediate problems. In some instances, if memory defects are not prominent, insight psychotherapy can be carried on even during the course of ECT.

The entire subject of ECT has been greatly eclipsed by pharmacotherapy. Much controversy and publicity have arisen concerning the possible lasting effects of ECT on memory. On the other hand, some psychiatrists have recently formed an association to support the validity of ECT as a therapy at least as safe and effective as drug therapy, and, in their opinion, at times preferable to drug therapy.

THE BRIEF HOSPITALIZATION

Situations arise in the brief and emergency treatment of both suicidal or borderline psychotic patients where out-patient treatment cannot proceed safely. A period of hospitalization in a general hospital provides both the required protection of the patient and the conditions of safety and scrutiny which permit the psychotherapist to make vigorous in-depth interpretations, producing both catharsis and ego mending as a result. Acute delusional states of recent precipitation may also be treatable under such circumstances.

Every clinician and facility using emergency psychotherapy should have easy access to a hospital for admitting a patient who may suddenly need hospitalization. It is equally desirable, though more difficult to arrange especially with university-affiliated hospitals, that the clinician be permitted to continue emergency therapy with the patient during his hospitalization; the patient is often particularly amenable to active treatment in this protected environment.

Equally important is the ability to keep the hospitalization short and to have the patient promptly discharged. Therapeutically speaking, many patients in emergency therapy may decompensate quickly but also reconstitute promptly. Prolonged hospitalization often produces unnecessary and undesirable regression.

Though the above recommendations are simple and basic—ease of admission, continuing therapy in the hospital by the primary and original therapist, and ease of discharge—they often are difficult to arrange. Institutional red tape, professional rivalries, insurance coverage, and other problems often interfere with this optimal arrangement.

In the out-patient clinics of hospitals providing emergency psychotherapy an even simpler device is desirable: the arrangement of two or three beds in a room adjoining the clinic where some patients might be kept 12 to 24 hours, to help them bridge a specific crisis. Because of the scarcity of space in most hospitals and clinics, even this modest variation of emergency psychotherapy often runs into difficulties.

PART II

Some Clinical Syndromes

6
Depression

CLINICAL FEATURES

In severe depression, the clinical features include a psychomotor slow-down of speech, walking, and gestures, along with the typically depressed face. The patient will state that he feels life is not worthwhile, he may not want to go on living, nothing gives him pleasure, he himself is a bad person who doesn't deserve to live. In less severe depression, the manifest picture will be simply a complaint of feeling depressed and unhappy; usually the patient will report that this sentiment is worse in the morning. A number of features associated with depression at times exist without a clear-cut subjective complaint of depression; these might be characterized as *depressive equivalents*. They include a general feeling of fatigue, at times perhaps associated with restlessness, as classically seen in the agitated depression; difficulty in making decisions; ruminations having more or less obsessive qualities; lack of appetite; insomnia; constipation.

Among the special diagnostic observations, it is especially useful to observe the patient closely during the first moment he is seen in the waiting room. One may then be able to note the droop of the face or posture, and the slowness of movement before the patient feels that he is being observed. Once the patient has risen and entered a social situation with the doctor, he may replace this typical expression with a more appropriate social demeanor.

The next chance for diagnostic observation occurs during the short walk the patient takes from the waiting room to the seat beside the doctor's desk. The doctor sees so many patients take that walk every day that he has a ready baseline for comparison.

These impressions will coincide with other symptoms. The depressed patient will engage in generalized complaints such as, "It's a tough life." He often reacts more markedly to cold than other people, as if he were transposing his feelings of emotional coldness, barrenness, and unhappiness to the environment.

Depressive equivalents (inertia, poor appetite, insomnia, etc.) may be associated with other psychogenic or with medical syndromes, but one should always bear in mind that they may be consistent with the diagnosis of depression. Hypochondriasis is often found to be associated with depression; the patient will complain not about depression but about somatic ailments.

The literature abounds in efforts to differentiate between varieties of depressions: endogenous and reactive depression; psychotic and neurotic depressions; the involutional depression; and the depressions associated with pregnancy. Dynamically, there is probably no difference between these various forms of depression except in the degrees of intensity, degrees of severity of ego impairment, degrees of regression accompanying the depression, and variations in the observability of precipitating factors.

The psychotic depression particularly involves regression to an infantile mode of behavior, accompanied by somatic manifestations, and alterations in reality testing and ego identifications.

The involutional depressions usually are associated with the onset or the process of menopause and are characterized by a variety of attending features: hot flashes, ache in the back of the head, paresthesias, peculiar taste and smell sensations, and sometimes paranoid ideation, especially with sexual connotations of being spied upon and looked at in embarrassing situations. The precipitating factors in involutional and senile depressions have certain specific features: loss of self-esteem in the female, or the loss of potency in a male, in the former case; and a loss of self-esteem with the loss of function in old age in the latter case. Not yet established is that the senile arteriosclerotic changes themselves relate specifically to the depressed features. It is likely, however, that a general weakening of the ego, brought about either by the physiological effects of the involution or the circulatory or biochemical changes in old age, may constitute a greater liability to the precipitation of depression.

Some clinicians insist that one can clearly differentiate so called "endogenous" depression from "exogenous" or reactive depression. Fenichel[65] could see no gain in the effort to distinguish between endogenous and reactive depressions, believing that the effort to do so overlooks the operation of the unconscious. Fenichel believed that every depression is to some extent reactive, though the provoking cause may not always be apparent. To the best of our knowledge, endogenous depression simply constitutes a greater tendency to react depressively to sometimes virtually subliminal precipitating factors, whereas in the reactive exogenous depression, the precipitating features can be clearly seen or even verbalized by the patient. The difference is likely to be more a quantitative than a truly qualitative one; some people may have more of a congenital, or possibly even a familial tendency, to react depressively. Some clinicians make the diagnostic point that only in endogenous depressions do the patients clearly report feeling worse in the morning. In our experience this holds true for practically all depressions.

A great deal of biological work has been done in the field of depression, especially in biochemistry. The role of catecholamine metabolism has been examined especially, and while drug responses tend to support these hypotheses, there is neither general agreement nor definitive proof for a causal role of catecholamine* or any other factor at this point.

Nevertheless, a biological factor is likely to play a role in *some*[33] depressions and drug treatment will be especially important in these cases.

A continuum may be conceived, moving from a minimum of external precipitating factors to a maximum of such factors. Everything else being equal, prognosis is better as the importance of the external factors increases; the person who required a realistic blow to react with depression probably had a better premorbid personality than the one who reacted to a minimal situation. However, the sicker a person is, the easier he will find situations frustrating and traumatically repetitive of the original disappointment by the parental figure. Thus the endogenous depressive is a person with such an unstable and ambivalent object relationship that the slightest frustration is a pathogenic stimulus.

A distinction should be made between depression and grief or mourning. The latter is a natural reaction that when not appropriately present must be encouraged (see Chapter 13) so that pathological symptoms do not develop. Of course, depression may complicate the mourning process, extending and intensifying it unduly.

Depressions associated with pregnancy and the postpartum period are widely encountered. Clinical features are comparable to those found in other kinds of depression. Important here is the recognition that the puerperal process carries dynamic significance for women. Sexual shame may be experienced by women of strict superegos in whom the pregnancy represents a punishment for sexual misbehavior. Some women experience narcissistic damage to their feelings of being attractive, which in turn generates hostility for the child. The child may be perceived as a rival for the husband's affection, thus casting the child in the position of a sibling. Some women may feel

---

*This point was agreed to in personal correspondence between Dr. Leopold Bellak and Dr. Julius Axelrod, who received the Nobel Prize (Medicine, 1970) for his contributions to the understanding of catecholamine metabolism when he presented a series of lectures on this subject. (1972 Salmon Lectures, N.Y. Academy of Medicine. *Biomedical studies on catecholamine and their impact on psychiatry.* Presented at the Institute of Living, Hartford, Conn.)

themselves bound into an unsatisfactory marriage by the presence of a child who must be cared for and reared. Still others see pregnancy and mother-hood as the end of their own carefree youth. Most obviously the first child particularly involves a serious change of role from that of young woman to the more serious role of mother.

PSYCHODYNAMIC CONSIDERATIONS

E. Bibring[49] emphasized the important role that the loss of self-esteem plays in the depressions. The loss of self-esteem usually proceeds from either the real or imagined loss of status, function, capacity, or affection. Thus the patient may have lost a job or been rejected by a spouse or experienced sexual failure or have felt some loss of importance in the family as, for example, when a younger sibling is born.

The role of disappointment in the psychogenesis of depression has been described by Jacobson.[90] She relates disappointment to the feeling of being deceived. Very frequently depressed patients have had a childhood experience of feeling deceived and disappointed by a loved person, reacting to this experience with depression; they are likely to react again with depression later in life when a similar dynamic constellation of deception and disappointment occurs.

Lowered self-esteem and/or disappointment may lead to a narcissistic overinvestment of the self. It is as if the hurt person says, "Since I can't trust anybody else and I'm being disappointed by everybody else and don't have much satisfaction in my life, I might as well focus on myself as much as possible and be interested in myself as much as possible." The hypochon-driacal features so frequently associated with the depressive syndrome can be easily understood in these circumstances: The patient is playing mother to himself and takes loving care of himself, checks upon himself con-stantly and worries about himself, all in response to a lack of gratification. Narcissistic overinvestment of the self is something like a hurt with-drawal into oneself, accompanied by a decrease of emotional investment in others.

A great deal of anger or aggression usually accompanies disappoint-ment, the feeling of deception, the lowering of self-esteem, and narcissistic withdrawal—anger over disappointment, over the deception, over the loss of love, etc. The anger and hostility thus generated are usually not acceptable to the patient's superego and they are therefore contained as intra-aggression.

Thus a severe superego is characteristically typical in the depressive constellation. The patient feels a great deal of hostility but is unable to express it in the direction of the object or situation which has aroused it, and has the tendency therefore to direct it against himself: Intra-aggression is an outstanding feature of depression. The careful history will reveal usually that the hostility currently felt but not expressed with regard to a certain person closely resembles the constellation that existed earlier in life when hostility was felt toward a genetically important person in a similar situation.

The aggression and hostility characteristic of the depressive constellation is usually or particularly of an oral aggressive nature, in which the wish to devour plays a major role (Lewin,[111] Abraham[1]). Lewin related the wish to devour as part of an oral triad which also includes the wish to be devoured and the wish to sleep—to be generally passive. The wish to be passive in relationship to general oral receptive tendencies needs to be taken into dynamic consideration with every depressed patient.

In some depressions, the specific idiosyncratic factors that operate must be identified, in addition to the standard classical features of depression. These include depressions which follow severe somatic illness, disabilities, major surgery and pregnancies, and the depression associated with senility. Thus it is important to be able to determine that for one patient an amputation may mean a loss of masculinity whereas to another it may imply punishment for sexual misbehavior. Postpartum depressions, particularly, illustrate the wide variety of idiosyncratic dynamics: the loss may be a loss of a clear-cut feminine function such as being pregnant, a role which had been emphasized in the patient's culture; on an underlying level it may mean the loss of a phallus. The hostility which is usually identifiable may be directed toward the child who must be taken care of, or toward the husband who has impregnated the patient, or toward the patient's mother who is expected to punish her daughter for her sexual misbehavior. With depressions associated with pregnancy, it is particularly important to keep in mind that the physiological condition may be related to the depressive picture— the marked change in endocrine function and the sometimes mildly toxic factors which are present.

THERAPEUTIC PROCEDURES

1. Addressing oneself to the lowered self-esteem of the patient is often the first step in the psychotherapy of depression. The therapist should recognize that the patient's need to come for treatment at all is a further blow to his self-esteem, since he may consider himself to be now too weak to handle his own problems. Point out explicitly to these patients that coming for help is more a sign of wisdom than of weakness.

2. Reassurance which can be evolved realistically from the patient's assets and ego strengths is a procedure closely allied to the increasing of self-esteem. But in turn such reassurance may be also dynamically related to decreasing the onslaught of intra-aggression, particularly where the patient is punishing himself because of the impulse toward extra-aggression. Such patients, where possible, should have pointed out to them that they never in the past acted upon these extra-aggressive im-

pulses, that they have shown excellent ability to tolerate tne thought without acting upon it.

3. Reversal of intra-aggression is perhaps the key maneuver in the psychotherapy of the depression. Catharsis will be a tempting procedure here, but since caution is important, mediate catharsis is the technique of choice. The reader will recall that with this technique the patient is not expected to express his feelings himself, but rather has them expressed for him by the therapist. Under these circumstances the therapist may choose particularly coarse language such as, "I guess you wish that the son-of-a-bitch would drop dead." With mediate catharsis one has the advantage that the patient is not required to take responsibility for the hostility expressed. Also the expression by the therapist, a respected person, makes the hostility more acceptable and potentially more ego-syntonic.

4. Wherever possible understanding of dynamic features should be associated with both the precipitating situation and earlier genetic situations in the patient's life. However, the brief intervention does not usually permit the emergence of a transference neurosis. It is, therefore, important to be able to illustrate dynamic features in relationship to a contemporary figure in the patient's life.

5. Transference manifestations must be dealt with promptly and clearly. Negative manifestations particularly should be interpreted if the patient does not express them, or participated in by the therapist if the patient expresses them in a tangential fashion. In such interpretations the therapist puts himself in the patient's place and reacts to the therapist— that is, to himself. For example, "You must have thought that I was a bastard for keeping you waiting."

6. Support through the expressed availability of the therapist *at any time* may be an important therapeutic maneuver, particularly in suicidal risks and in severely depressed patients.

7. Guidance can play a role in the treatment of depressions, and may be particularly urgent where there is suicidal danger. If the patient is clearly in a situation which furthers lowered self-esteem, the experiencing of disappointments, and the generation of hostility, it may be necessary to remove the patient from the setting or to alter the setting if possible. To help channelize hostility, encouraging violent physical activity (bag punching, bowling, etc.) may be recommended. For some patients, symbolic aggression such as chess is sufficient, whereas with others, more *concrete* expressions such as knocking over bowling pins is appropriate.

8. Drug therapy, of course, plays a major role in the management of depression (see Chapter 5). One problem in using these drugs is that they generally take from one to two weeks before they become fully effective, so that the therapist must be on guard to protect the patient fully during the period before the drugs take effect. Another difficulty may

arise from the fact that these drugs can have bad effects of both a somatic and psychological nature; if we are dealing with a schizoid–affective disorder, the energizing drugs may precipitate a schizophrenic picture.

In the management of agitated depressions, a mixture of sedatives and stimulants, tranquilizers and mood elevators or energizers, may be indicated.

9. Electroconvulsive therapy still has a definite role to play in the treatment of acute depressions, especially if the suicidal danger is great. In some situations the depression is too deep and the suicidal danger too great to wait for either the effect of drugs or psychotherapy. In many instances only a few electric treatments are indicated. Very frequently not more than seven are necessary. When this is the case, the effects of the shock on memory and on the integrative function of the ego are not so marked as to preclude psychotherapy as a follow-up procedure after a desirable symptomatic improvement has been achieved with the electroconvulsive therapy.

THE SPECIAL PROBLEM OF SUICIDE

The diagnostic appraisal of suicidal liability is among the most difficult, yet the most important tasks in the treatment of depression. For some time suicide problems stimulated such interest that a suicidology branch was created at the National Institute of Mental Health, and a Journal of Suicidology published. The most recent review of relevant problems can be found in an issue of The Psychiatric Annals (6:11, 1976), where a number of statistical findings are also reported.

The rate of suicide for children under ten is negligible, though adolescents are generally considered to be the second highest risk group. When sex and race distinctions are not made, suicide is statistically more common in older age groups. The peak age level for suicide varies according to population. For white males, suicide is most likely to occur after age 75. In white females, the highest risk period is 50 to 54. The peak period varies for nonwhites, although the highest rate is likely to be found in males over age 60, which is similar to the finding for white males. For nonwhite females, no general consistent pattern is discernible. Generally the suicide rate is two to seven times higher for males than for females.

Clues to the Suicidal Patient

Shneidman and Farberow[151] have published the tentative results of an experimental approach to the investigation of psychological factors in suicide. They found almost impossible the identification of the potentially suicidal patient from the details of his case history alone, however disturbed or traumatic that history had been. They also noted that most successful suicide victims had attempted or threatened suicide previously. Thus the suicidal gesture must not be taken lightly. Of extreme importance is the finding that almost half of the individuals who committed suicide did so within three months after having passed an emotional crisis and after they seemed to be on the way to recovery. It is important to remember that the degree of suicidal danger is not necessarily related to the degree of depression. Superficially stated, only when the patient has improved somewhat does he develop enough energy to harm himself. Therefore the patient who has been suicidal and appears to be improving must continue under careful watch by therapist and relatives for some period of time after the episode.

These authors discovered that psychological tests indicate that the person who has threatened suicide is more emotionally disturbed than the person who has attempted suicide. The authors also compared genuine suicide note writers with nonsuicidal simulated note writers. The genuine note writer is able apparently to actually imagine his absence. He therefore instructs and admonishes in his note as though he had reached a final decision and has accepted the fact that soon he will no longer be around. The discomfort statements in the genuine notes are characterized by deeper, more intense feelings of hatred, vengeance, demand, and self-blame.

A more recent study[105] of 211 unsuccessful attempts at suicide (71 had stated their intention to kill themselves; 140 had not communicated their intent) utilized the Suicidal Intent Scale after two separate interviews. The authors conclude that there is no justification for regarding "verbal communication, final acts, and previous suicide attempts" as reliable predictors of the intent to kill oneself, and that verbalization of thoughts of suicide or intent has little correlation with the intensity of the wish to die that is experienced at the time of the attempt. Suicidal ideas may be expressed without the wish or the intent to die; the converse is also true. Finally, the authors indicate their belief that communication or noncommunication of suicidal intent is more a matter of personal style than of despair or of concealed determination. However, they warn that the significance of communication should not be disparaged by their findings; rather, they stress the need for further examination.

It would thus seem that apart from a suicidal attempt in the history, the potentially suicidal patient cannot be differentiated successfully from another depressed patient. Given a clinical picture of depression, which may involve insomnia, fearfulness, fatigue, irritability, loss of interest, loss of appetite, weight loss, and feelings of self-depreciation, the therapist must not hesitate to ask the patient if he feels like killing himself. The direct inquiry may make the suicidal ideation conscious long before it becomes so in the ordinary course of events; left to his own devices the patient usually harbors suicidal ideas for a long time before giving conscious thought to them. During this lengthy period the feeling of depression, inadequacy, shame, and guilt have been gnawing at his autonomic nervous system and at such control points as the hypothalamus and the sleep center.

Given the state of the art, the therapist must rely upon clinical acumen acquired through experience. We have found that the Thematic Apperception Test is invaluable as an adjunct to the diagnostic process. Depressed patients often are unable to communicate dynamically significant content because of the oppressive weight upon cognitive functions. The test pictures provide a stimulus to which they can react at least to some degree, in contrast to the difficulty they experience in replying to the therapist's questions, however open-ended or provocative. Some depressed patients consciously resist responding to queries, and may respond more readily to the pictures without awareness of what they are communicating unconsciously. The test is useful for assessing the extent of denial; for identifying a wish for peace, sleep, and quiet associated with death; for revealing intra-aggression; for indicating the punitiveness of the superego; and for evaluating the degree to which suicidal ideas, if present, are ego-alien or ego-syntonic.

Psychodynamics of Suicide

It is not easy to differentiate the psychodynamics of suicide from those we understand to be involved in all depressions. The expression of the wish to die is most often an oral wish to sleep without cares, as Lewin has pointed out. Oral wishes such as these are widespread in the population and are probably responsible for the frequency of suicidal thoughts in the general population, especially among adolescents. When such *oral wishes,* however, are accompanied by a *great deal of hostility* in people with little ego strength and with a severe superego, the therapist then has much reason for worry. Understanding the specific dynamics of the suicidal impulse becomes important. Among those which may be operating are: the wish to expiate a real or imagined crime; a desire for revenge; the wish for reunion with a deceased mate or lover; the desire to force love from other people.

Thus the motivations that may result in a suicidal act do not always follow the same pattern, although the element of depression is common to most of them.

In any event, we must recognize that the suicidal gesture, the suicidal ideation, in fact the depression itself, is almost always a call for help, and the therapist must respond to this call.

Psychotherapeutic Procedures

The therapeutic procedures in the treatment of suicidal risks are essentially the same as those outlined above for the treatment of depressions. But since a suicidal risk presents a special urgency, several special points must be made, or rather remade.

1. While some studies dispute this, suicidal attempts are generally accepted to be equivalent to a demand for help. With this in mind, the

rapist necessarily must be willing to be available at all hours to the ient. This availability plays an important role in minimizing suicidal danger.

Witness to the crucial role of immediate availability of help is the proliferation of "hot lines" across the country in urban, rural, and suburban areas. These emergency centers provide counseling and information, and are accessible to anyone for discussion of any kind of problem. Often staffed by lay volunteers trained and supervised by professionals, many offer round-the-clock availability. Centers are based in diverse settings—churches, local store fronts, college campuses, and volunteer fire departments, among others. Many calls are received from depressed and suicidal persons asking where they can get help, how they can prevent themselves from taking their own lives, why they should not kill themselves. The patient in one-to-one or group therapy should be made aware of these local centers should the therapist be unavailable during an emergency.

2. Insightful work with the problem of aggression in a cautious but at the same time thorough manner is especially important in cases of suicidal danger. Extremely important is unearthing any existing suicidal fantasy to find out to whom they are addressed, either consciously or unconsciously. Where there is a conscious fantasy it must be analyzed. If there is no conscious fantasy the therapist must discover for whom the aggression is intended, and these sentiments must be vigorously brought out. The concept of "self-harm to harm another" must be dramatically illustrated for the patient.

3. Since to a certain extent suicide may be seen as a special form of acting out, gaining time is crucial, as with all acting out. Thus the patient may be told that there is always time to kill oneself, and that for the present the therapist may strive simply for postponement. This maneuver may provide the opportunity for further insight on the part of the therapist which can then lead to more vigorous psychotherapy.

4. Brief hospitalization may be especially pertinent with the suicidal risk, in order to provide the safeguards of nursing care while one is conducting vigorous psychotherapy and/or waiting for the effect of energizers to take hold.

5. As we pointed out earlier, the use of electroconvulsive therapy may be important in the treatment of the suicidal patient.

ILLUSTRATIVE CASE HISTORIES

Depression with Suicidal Rumination

This patient was seen three times in the hospital clinic. She was just under 50 years old, had a part-time job, had had no high-school education, was married and had five children.

First Interview.   The patient began a rambling discourse as soon as she was met in the waiting room and continued it as she was escorted to the consulting room. She spoke of death at an early age, nightmares, hospitalization, two marriages, a common-law relationship, abortions, and an out-of-wedlock child, the importance of religion and positive thinking. She was smiling. She was certainly using the mechanism of denial and her affect may have been inappropriate.

She was able to settle down and speak more coherently. For some time she had been having ego-alien thoughts of suicide. Tall buildings frightened her, she fantasized that she would jump off them and was thrown into a panic. The same thing happened at home when she saw razor blades. However, she was always able to remove herself from the scene when she became too frightened; she had never been close to killing herself, and on many occasions used razor blades in her household chores.

Inquiry yielded no data about events that may have precipitated her seeking help at the clinic. However, she had been suffering premenstrual tension for three days, and was probably menopausal. The therapist suspected that sexual guilt and loss of sexual prowess was involved in her symptomatology.

He assured her that though she had been frightened by her thoughts, she had always had the sense and strength to get away before anything crucial happened, and that she would be able to go on showing this kind of strength was likely. However, he added, it would be important for them to look into why she had these thoughts and to try to make them less severe. She appeared relieved and welcomed the therapeutic effort.

He then told her that her thoughts of suicide could mean that she felt she should be severely punished. Many people go around feeling they are bad, that they deserve punishment, and want to kill themselves. In her case, she wasn't aware of feeling bad, she thought only of punishing herself—that is, of committing suicide.

She admitted that she tried to forget the feelings of being bad, that what he said made sense to her. He then suggested that since it was time to stop, that at their next meeting they look into her past life and try to figure out what was making her feel guilty. She was placed on a regimen of Stelazine and Parnate.

Second Interview.   She revealed that she had been married for the first time some 25 years ago. During this marriage she became pregnant by another man. Separating from her husband, she lived with a third man, suffered a miscarriage, and finally had a child by him. The child continued to live with her. They broke up when her common-law husband was sent to jail. Following this, she had a number of affairs and finally married her present husband. She thought that thoughts about these past events always preceded her thoughts of suicide. She could see the self-punishment that was involved.

The therapist inquired about her present marital relationship. Her husband was very strict and domineering, very much like her father had been. He had suffered a heart attack which resulted in diminished sexual activity between them. At this point the therapist reasoned to himself that this was probably the chief precipitating event. He reasoned that her husband had served to curb her sexual acting-out by his sternness and his own virility. His heart attack weakened him in her eyes as a superego, as a male ego-ideal, and as a lover; her thoughts returned to earlier modes of accommodation, to other men. Her menopausal condition probably heightened her need for sexual gratification. She probably also had death wishes for her husband. As he was thinking these private thoughts, the patient told him that she had recently stood up to her husband in an argument for the first time, that occasionally in sex play she now bit him, and at times felt like really hurting him.

The therapist interpreted portions of his thoughts to her, accompanied by supportive statements: since your husband became less active sexually, you very naturally had thoughts about other men; this panicked you because you feared that you would return to the kind of life you had led earlier; you felt guilty and your anger for your husband made you feel even guiltier. So you thought of suicide as a way of punishing yourself, of ending these thoughts. Most women would turn to thoughts of other men in your situation.

The patient responded with thoughts of how she might make herself more attractive to her husband; perhaps she would buy a sexy negligee. She felt calmer; she felt that the therapist had helped her.

Third Interview.   The patient was obviously more cheerful. She was smiling and reported that she continued to feel better, that she was able to sleep well at night, the butterflies in her stomach had subsided, the tightness in her throat was gone. The suicidal thoughts remained but did not panic her.

Her relationship with her husband was gone over again, much in the same vein. She had begun to work full time and was not able to come back to the clinic for the time being. The therapist suggested that she might be able to work on her problems by herself as they had done together, and repeated the dynamics. He cautioned her that if she reached a point where she felt she needed his help, then she must not hesitate to return to the clinic.

Brief Therapy of a Reactive Depression

The brief therapy of depression can become particularly challenging and rewarding where one deals with a patient who has compelling realistic reasons for the depression—for instance, when there has been a death in a family.

A middle-aged woman became severely depressed after her husband died in an accident. It proved helpful to establish that she had had several mild, depressive episodes earlier in her life, when she had left home to go to college and after the break-up of an early affair. It was therefore possible to make the current depressive reaction to the loss of her husband somewhat ego-alien by showing her that she had had depressive reactions to other less catastrophic events and presumably had a tendency to react with depression to certain upsets. It was not too difficult to get her to see the common denominator of a loss in all three instances: the separation from the parental home when going to college; the loss of the boy friend—that is, the loss of his affection; and in the current and major instance, the loss of her husband by accidental death.

The patient was thus able to relate a few other minor depressive episodes, including one at the age of ten when she first went to camp. Examination of this episode established that she had been angry at being sent to camp; it then became possible for her to discuss also how angry she had been at the boyfriend who had left her. It now became permissible to ask whether there could have been some anger at her family when she went off to college, and at her husband before his death. Her first response was that she had not wanted him to go on the trip that resulted in the fatal accident. Then, slowly, she was able to discuss other instances when she had been angry at him; in fact, she was angry now for being left with financial concerns and the problems of raising their children alone. She did not find it difficult to see how guilty she must feel over this particular sort of resentment.

She was then offered some intellectual understanding of the dynamics of depression that enabled her to understand that she was not unique. Various cultural forms of mourning were discussed. The orthodox Jewish practice of tearing one's clothes were interpreted as an expression of anger originally directed toward the deceased, the lost object, then deflected upon one's own clothes. The feeling of loss, of being deserted, was related back to the understandable resentment of being sent to camp, and linked with the general phenomenon of the resentment which children feel when parents go away for as little as one evening, or for a vacation without the child, or at any other separation which is felt as reflecting lack of the parents' love or interest. After this intellectual discussion, the patient spoke rather spontaneously of the shame she had felt at camp that she was homesick and depressed. This information led quite naturally to the discussion of a feeling of lack of self-esteem engendered by one's reaction to loss and deprivation: We are ashamed that we need the other person, that we are not able to fend for ourselves. She readily perceived that a decrease of self-esteem was present in her contemporary situation, especially in the feelings that she was not really capable enough to take care of the family and of the special problems created by her husband's death; she saw too that she resented the feelings of passivity and dependence which she was vaguely aware of in herself. It was then clear that she directed critical, denigrating thoughts and sentiments toward herself, and that these also played a role in her depression.

After clarifying these dynamic features, emphasis was put on her ability in the past to handle difficult situations, and upon the fact that indeed she was doing as well as was possible in the current situation, that she had a right to be quite satisfied with her functioning during this admittedly difficult period.

During the ten days following this session, the patient was given instructions to take one dexamyl tablet* each morning—a time she found particularly difficult. During these ten days she was seen for several additional sessions.

The working through of the dynamic features during these sessions, abetted by the gain in self-confidence produced by the drug effect, was sufficient to overcome the reactive depression in this patient.

*This patient was seen well over ten years ago. There might now be more reluctance to use dexamyl (a combination of a barbituate and amphetamine), because of the acute awareness of the possibility of addiction to certain drugs. However, in closely supervised psychotherapy these drugs may still play a selective role (see Chapter 5).

7
Panic—Endogenous and Exogenous

CLINICAL FEATURES

The patient in panic reports a sense of impending disaster, often emphasizing a fear of sudden death—for example, as a result of a heart attack. Another frequently reported feeling is that of becoming insane or of committing an aggressive, destructive act, or generally of losing control and orientation. The patient also may exhibit any or several of the whole range of phobic reactions.

These patients exhibit physiological distress. Their heart beats rapidly, they tremble, they experience nausea, sweating, motor hyperactivity, and their respiration is often deep and rapid and sometimes is accompanied by a feeling of choking or of suffocating. They may experience diarrhea or a compelling need to urinate. The patient may feel faint or dizzy; he may suffer from paresthesias, he perspires, his face is flushed, and his pupils are dilated.

Most striking are the acute feeling of helplessness and the beseeching appeals for assistance.

DYNAMIC CONSIDERATIONS

Freud[73] identified "primary anxiety" arising from the helplessness of the human infant that creates a total feeling of painful tension, evoked by both internal and external stimuli which are experienced passively by the infant. This state is consciously painful and is felt to be unmasterable by the child. The child may fear that his own instinctual demands are painful and dangerous (endogenous panic) or that the environment provides overwhelming, unmasterable stimulation (exogenous panic). Thus primary anxiety is not created by the ego, but is a state of total excitation experienced passively and felt to be unmasterable by the individual; he feels helpless and impotent in dealing with it.

Traumatic anxiety is experienced dynamically in the same fashion as primary anxiety: The individual feels unable to master the stimuli, and experiences a flooding of excitation in the same passive fashion with which primary anxiety is felt.

With development, the ability of the ego to anticipate imaginatively and to plan actions comes into existence. The ego is thus able to judge what experience may become traumatic. This judgment is experienced by the ego as anxiety, which is used as a signal, cautioning one to avoid the situation or to institute defensive measures against the danger of trauma: Neither the situation nor the anxiety is passively experienced and consequently do not flood the self with excitation. For a wide variety of reasons, panic occurs when these defenses fail.

Conceptually, panic should be viewed as both symptom and signal: As a symptom it indicates that the person is experiencing an excess of tension; as a signal it indicates that the person fears an experience which he feels unable to master or control and which may lead to disintegration of the self.

Careful diagnostic appraisal is therefore imperative in the treatment of panic. The therapist must explore in detail the circumstances of the precipitating event in order to identify the stimuli to which the patient was subjected. With equal care he must explore those circumstances in which the panic reoccurs, and particularly, he must identify both the form and the content of the panic reaction.

THERAPEUTIC PROCEDURES IN ENDOGENOUS PANIC

1. Cathartic expression of the affects and ideation associated with the panic should be encouraged. The procedure establishes the therapist as an interested and helpful person, permits him to appraise the dynamic content and form of the fear, and, at the same time, provides discharge of sufficient tension so that the patient will be receptive to further therapeutic interventions.
2. Reassurance and support is then in order. The therapist may reassure the patient that he is in no danger of becoming mentally ill, while identifying the patient's existing strengths and encouraging their utilization. These may be the patient's ability to avoid overstimulating situations, as well as his readiness to call for help. The ability to call for help counteracts the feeling that the panic *must* be helplessly and passively experienced. With this reassurance, the therapist should stress his availability to the patient at any time of the day or night.

3. Increasing the patient's competence is also in order. The identification of strengths contributes to this intervention. His ability to function and plan in other aspects of his life should be pointed out, thus indicating to him that he is not as totally helpless as he feels during the episodes of panic. It may be particularly useful to indicate that panic does not mean that he is a coward, that, in fact, all brave men are frightened during acts of bravery and that this is the typically normal and healthy reaction.

4. Interpretation of the drives which are exciting the patient, along with their genetic antecedents, is a central therapeutic procedure. One patient may need to see that in a specific set of circumstances he was tempted to submit passively, thus creating his manifest fear of falling. Another patient may need to be shown that his fear of being unable to reach help or to have help reach him invokes the same feeling he had as a child when his father playfully set him on a high tree stump from which he feared to jump down. The patient who is obsessively preoccupied both with fantasies and dreams of waves will need to have this related to her fear of passivity during intercourse and her equal fear of orgasm. The male patient who awakes from a dream of his mouth being full of "gooey stuff" will need to have this related to his fear of homosexual submission.

5. The therapist must be alert to the operation of denial and repression and actively interfere with these when they are excessive, pointing out to the patient that his panics always arise when a stimulus or excitation is denied or repressed.

6. Repressing one drive while encouraging another may be indicated with some patients. Those patients who experience their panics with total passivity and helplessness will need to be encouraged into the expression of more active, aggressive behavior. Those who defensively respond to the inherent feelings of passivity with overly aggressive behavior will require modification of this reaction, since it is in turn generating fears of retaliation.

SPECIAL FEATURES OF EXOGENOUS PANIC

Clinical Features

Exogenous panic is touched off by some external circumstance. It may be a catastrophic event, such as the assassination of President Kennedy, or the heightened tension and anxiety of the Cuban missile crisis. A traumatic event such as the ramming and sinking of the *Andrea Doria*[70] may be the precipitant in a passenger. Another example may be an automobile accident. The event may be the death of a loved person, or the serious illness of such a person. The panic may follow a sexual assault such as rape or a homosexual overture. It may follow a physical assault in which the patient has been beaten or mugged. It may follow the experience of having one's home burglarized or it may be the sequelae of witnessing an act of violence or an accident.

Dynamic Considerations

Kris[106] emphasizes the feeling of helplessness as a disorganizing element in traumatic situations. He cites Freud's differentiation of objective from imaginary danger. In objective danger, the signal of anxiety initiates protective actions, whereas in imaginary danger the anxiety signal does not lead to protective actions, or it leads to random actions with the defense mechanisms, such as regression, becoming functional. The feeling of helplessness is characteristic of human infancy and may, in later life, be recreated by external conditions and the internal response to these conditions.

Kris cites two examples from World War II in which disorganizing panic was predicted but did not occur. During the bombings of British cities, the exposure to physical danger from the bombs was found to be not in itself disruptive. People suffered panic when as a result of evacuation families were broken and separated. This disruption caused more damage than did the fear of the bombs. The cohesive feature was the preservation of family unity with the feeling that individuals were not helpless.

The survivors of the Dunkirk evacuation did not manifest the regressed, disorganized, traumatic conditions which had been predicted for them. Examination of the situation indicated that the *orderly, planned,* and *informed* retreat through Flanders to Dunkirk was the decisive feature in the preservation of their morale. The central dynamic consideration therefore in exogenous panic is what is individually aroused by the external experience that is associated with a helpless, passive, planless state—that is, what external factor produces the dynamic situation characteristic of the endogenous panic.

In our experience, the assassination of President Kennedy touched off panic reactions in three patients, all of whom were overwhelmed with a sense of impending disaster. With one, there was identification with the assassin; the man feared the outbreak of his own aggressive drives. He had been looking forward after a period of sexual abstinence to spending that night with a woman. With another patient the central idea was: "If a man as powerful as Kennedy can be killed, what will happen to a simple 'shnook' like myself?" The third patient experienced the loss of President Kennedy with a remembrance of the death of her mother during the patient's childhood which had left her feeling unprotected and helpless.

In cases of sexual assault, there is often an arousal of sado-masochistic fantasies. People who come home to their apartments to find that they have been robbed frequently have touched off in them, if they are women, the fear of rape; among men the event may arouse dread of homosexual passivity.

Therapeutic Procedures

These procedures are essentially similar to those delineated above for endogenous panic: cathartic expression; the provision of reassurance and support; and the improvement of self-esteem.

In addition, one must institute reality testing with the patient, insisting with him that the excessive degree of anxiety present is not appropriate to the external event or situation, and that this disparity requires the patient and therapist to search together for the actual source of the excessive fear.

The features of the exogenous circumstances and the form and content of the panic must be linked in interpretation to the patient's specific dynamics and genetic antecedents. Thus the patient who identified with President Kennedy's assassin was reminded of the event in his childhood when he was four years old and his father struck his mother during a quarrel.

The prescription of specific behavior for specific situations is helpful with patients suffering from recurrence of exogenous panic. The passive patient may be instructed to engage in gross muscular activity when he feels the panic coming on, or he may be told that at the first signal of anxiety, when he is still able to think planfully, he should actively recall the genetic antecedent which has been linked to the exogenous circumstance by the therapist.

ILLUSTRATIVE CASE HISTORIES

Emergency Treatment of Panic

A 25 year old man telephoned for an emergency consultation. In New York to visit a hospitalized friend, he had suffered, the night before, an overwhelming panic on the subway while returning to his hotel. He had managed to tolerate the panic only by calling for the help of another friend with whom he had a few drinks. Gradually, his panic had subsided and he had been able to sleep. This morning the panic had returned as he was entering the subway. The therapist cancelled the session of a patient he could reach by telephone and saw the man in panic.

The subway panic was vague: The patient could only think that he felt trapped, alone, helpless, his heart beat as if it would rupture his chest, sweat poured from all over his body. The ideation became a little clearer: He feared that the train would stop and that he would be caught underground. He felt compelled to stand between cars so that he could get out into the tunnel and find an exit if indeed the train stalled. He knew that trains sometimes stopped between stations in response to signal lights, but he was sure he would die if this happened. This had never happened on earlier visits to New York.

Had the panic suddenly erupted, or had there been a preceding feeling of uneasiness? Of anxiety? In response, he reported three stages of mounting anxiety. The first was a feeling of queasiness while visiting his friend in the hospital the evening before. The second came after he turned away from a bar because it was full of "fairies," and his heart, inexplicably, began to pound. The third, full-blown panic, came as the subway train left the platform and plunged into the tunnel, the dirty walls of which seemed to close in and threaten to crush or smother him.

Why was his friend in the hospital? He had undergone some kind of rectal surgery, and was lying on his stomach. The night was hot and his friend had been nude except for a section of sheet covering his buttocks. The queasiness had begun when he saw his friend; he couldn't look at his body, at his buttocks particularly. He kept expecting that blood would soak through the sheet covering him. The feeling intensified when later he thumbed through a magazine and saw photographs of the burned body of a Vietnamese monk. He had cut short his visit and walked the streets for awhile. He became conscious of being "horny" and decided to enter a bar, perhaps to pick up a woman. He felt guilty as he did so; he loved his wife, they had a child, he had never done this before. When he saw that the bar was frequented by homosexuals he became disgusted and felt like throwing up. He turned away, deciding to go back to his hotel. Several men from the bar passed him, and in the street lights he noticed their tight-fitting trousers revealing the lines of their buttocks. As he turned in the opposite direction to walk around the block his heart began to pound. Then came the subway and his panic.

His work and education history were both good. His marriage was "wonderful"; he and his wife made love every night, even during her menstrual periods. Their preferred position put him on bottom: He could last longer that way, and his wife could be more active which they both liked. His health had always been excellent except for his two years in the army when he had been troubled by a queasy stomach. The Army doctors thought that he might have an incipient ulcer.

His parents had divorced when he was five because his father had been continually unfaithful. He visited his father and stepmother regularly. His stepmother was a "tramp," much younger than his father. On his way to New York this time he had stopped off to see them. While his father was sleeping, she had taken him to the basement on some pretext and they had intercourse standing in an empty coal bin. He had felt terrible and cut his visit short. His mother, too, had remarried and lived in New York. For some reason he felt like not seeing her this time, but she knew he was in town so he would put off seeing her until just before he left.

Before the divorce, his father has been a streetcar motorman. He recalled his pleasure in sometimes waiting on the corner for his father's car and riding to the terminal with him. One time so many people got on the car that he had been unable to board. His father had driven off with a loud clanging of the bell, laughing derisively at the boy who remained paralyzed with fear for a half-hour before a neighbor came to his rescue. His father was cruel in his punishments: He had whipped the boy across the buttocks with the buckle of his belt for infractions. His father had enjoyed hunting and kept several rifles and a pistol at home which the boy had been forbidden to touch, an interdiction he had sometimes ignored with resultant beatings. His mother was by contrast very gentle and loving. In his culture the boy child was adored and he recalled his mother and her sisters admiring his penis. He seemed to recall that they fondled it and kissed it. As a teenager he had felt secure only with a switch blade in his pocket, and would have felt safer if he had had a gun. He had tried to fashion a zip gun from a car-radio antenna but had failed.

The therapist decided to focus on the patient's fear of his father's punishment for the sexual episode with his father's wife, and, unless necessary and advisable, not to touch upon the homosexual temptation. He began by pointing out that the patient had suffered anxiety before—the childhood panic when left by his father on the curb, the adolescent anxiety mitigated only by a knife or gun—and he interpreted the Army stomach as the symptom of anxiety. The patient accepted this and recalled his worry that if sent to Vietnam he would be captured and tortured. He was reminded of the burned monk and shuddered in response. He was then reminded that he had been able to survive these experiences of anxiety, to outgrow them, to marry, and to become a husband and father (the therapist sought here to reinforce his heterosexual feelings).

Then the therapist told him that his panic appeared to be the result of a concern with crime and punishment, that he expected his father to discover that his son had cuckolded him. The patient readily agreed that this was a concern; he feared that his stepmother in a moment of anger would tell his father. And how would the father punish him? With his belt buckle across the buttocks?

The patient nodded with seeming comprehension but then looked puzzled. "But why did it start in the hospital?" he asked. The therapist reminded him that his friend had injured buttocks, that he had expected them to bleed. The patient picked up the association and continued it with a question about why the buttocks of the homosexuals had troubled him. The therapist turned the question back to him for the answer and waited. Slowly, and with great difficulty, the patient threaded his way through his thoughts: Homosexuals had intercourse that way, he had always imagined that it would hurt a great deal, he and his wife sometimes fingered each other's rectum during intercourse, but his wife refused to have anal intercourse because the penis hurt too much.

The therapist then departed from his predetermined program: He interpreted the patient's fear of, but not the wish for, a homosexual attack upon himself by his father. He must have had the fantasy that his father in fury would not only beat his behind but penetrate it as the surgeon had his friend's rectum. Again the patient nodded and picked up the thread with a question: Why had the photograph of the burned monk upset him? "Fury and fire," replied the therapist with the intent of maintaining the emotional level of the working through the patient was doing. "My father's fury," the patient added.

"What about the subway?" he then asked. The therapist asked him to think about the dark, dirty tunnel and what it brought to mind. The patient began to sweat, looked over his shoulder at the door behind him, then rather aimlessly about the room. The therapist pressed him for his thoughts. The patient remained silent for awhile, then hung his head with obvious shame. "The coal bin," he muttered, almost inaudibly.

With the session about to end, the therapist decided to introduce the role of wishes in producing symptoms. "You know, most of us would probably be tempted to go back for a repeat performance. But the more you may wish to do that the more likely you are to be afraid; afraid that your father will attack you." The patient acknowledged this by revealing that his stepmother had performed fellatio upon him. His wife refused to do this, and it was for this pleasure that he was tempted to repeat this episode. He was reminded of the adoration given his penis by the women in his family.

The patient planned to remain in the city three more days. He was asked to telephone the therapist each day at an appointed time, and was assured that he would be seen again if necessary. He was also given the name of a therapist in his home city. It was not necessary to see him again. He was able to ride the subway with some queasiness, but without panic. Had it proved necessary to see the patient again, the therapist planned to go into the patient's wish for his father's love, his rivalry with his father, and the act of sexual submission as accomplishing both the attainment of this love and a placation of his father's fury.

Brief Therapy of Panic

A young woman in her twenties complained of free-floating types of panic accompanied by palpitations, a tight feeling in the chest and throat, and a feeling of impending doom. She was unable to relate these feelings to anything specific. Feelings of unreality, especially a generally foggy feeling, secondarily contributed to the panic.

Care was taken to establish the onset of the panic in order to obtain clues to understanding its dynamic background. It turned out that her husband had worked in his family's business and had then decided to take another job. On this new job, it was necessary for him to accept a much smaller salary for the time being than he had previously received. This seemed a reasonable thing for him to do; the new job gave him increased freedom, and the potentialities for the longer run were much better than in the family business. The net effect of the current situation was, however, that the patient and her family had to live on a much less comfortable basis than she had been accustomed to. This engendered both resentment on her part and the fear of loss of support. Meanwhile, the husband was enjoying himself considerably in his new business activity, in meeting with many people for business lunches and occasionally for the evening. Thus the patient now had reason for feeling that while she was suffering a constricted, house-bound period marked by a compelling need to economize, her husband was enjoying himself in expansive socializing. However, this resentment was denied by her as were the implications of these simple facts. It was necessary to show her the reality situation in slow, easy steps, and at first give her some intellectual awareness of how the denial, and in part the repression, of her anger had caused her upset.

In the first session, she was given reassurance by letting her know that states such as hers were by no means infrequent, and that they usually responded well and quickly to treatment. The mechanism of denial was explained to her, and it was then possible to explain her fogginess as a slight form of depersonalization, the attempt to blot out disturbing features in a contemporary life situation and the resulting anger and resentment. She was able to understand that she was "foggy" because she kept herself in a fog about the factors affecting her life.

Following this session, a conjoint interview with the husband was held. This meeting established that the situation did not demand as much parsimony in living as had appeared. Since the husband was reasonably assured of a rather early improvement in his financial situation, there was no reason for trying to save and put money aside under the current circumstances. To the contrary, it seemed even reasonable that he take a small loan to provide for some of the current needs, such as part-time domestic help and some things for the children. It was necessary also in the conjoint interview situation to remind the patient that the presently lowered income was not really a threat of deprivation, but could be seen as an investment in the future; that her husband, by taking a job which at the moment brought less income, was likely to receive much greater remuneration in the future.

The interventions of reassurance that her panic could be understood, interpretation of her denial of real circumstances as well as of her sentiments, and the conjoint interview with her husband to alleviate some of the conditions resulting from the economic change led to a rather prompt dissolution of the panic.

8
Depersonalization

CLINICAL FEATURES

The individual in a state of depersonalization feels himself to be changed in contrast with his former state of being. He feels himself to be an observer, in effect, a spectator of himself. He senses a loss or loosening of his own personality and of his ego. His sense of identity becomes partially indistinct or totally confused. The patient feels that he no longer has a self to which he can refer directive forces and behavior. He may feel that parts of his body or of his mind are now alien and strange and do not belong to him. In extreme states he will feel that he no longer has a body or that he is not alive. These feelings may extend to the environment, which will seem equally alien and strange to the patient and which will appear to have lost its features of reality. He may believe that there is no world existing.

A phenomenon associated with depersonalization to be kept in mind is that very often the patient will not be able to describe symptoms that the therapist will easily recognize as depersonalization, or will not describe the symptom most clearly associated with depersonalization—that is, a feeling of unrealness. Thus, what appears to be a phobia, for example, may turn out actually to be primarily a state of depersonalization induced by special circumstances.

DYNAMIC CONSIDERATIONS

Depersonalization and feelings of unreality along with feelings of loss of identity receive considerable stress in modern psychopathology. The currently flourishing existentialism revolves almost entirely around variations of these feelings. Bellak[27] has published a review of the theory of depersonalization. Schilder[145] ascribed depersonalization to a withdrawal of libido, Nunberg[132] related it specifically to a loss of love or love object, Bergler and Eidelberg[46] considered it a defense against anal exhibitionism, and Oberndorf[133] saw it as a means of containing anxiety. Reich,[140] Fenichel,[67] and Hartmann[81] stressed the defensive function of depersonalization and feelings of unreality. These concepts were broadened by Blank[51] who suggested that depersonalization is a defense against rage, anxiety, and deprivation. He added, however, that depersonalization takes over as a defense only when hypomania fails. Stamm[163] extended the concept to include hypnagogic states, twilight experience, and even the wish to sleep, and in accordance with Lewin[111] he felt that depersonalization might be expected to occur in individuals with marked oral trends and passive strivings. Jacobson[92] broadened the concept of depersonalization still further. Taking Federn's contribution[63] into account she indicates that depersonalization occurs in normal people as well as in neurotics and psychotics and lists a number of factors which precipitate this experience. She formulates depersonalization as a process in which an intact part of the ego observes an unacceptable part. She distinguishes depersonalization from depression by noting that in depression the conflict is between the superego and the self, whereas in depersonalization the conflict is between the various identifications of different parts of the ego. Although Jacobson identifies depersonalization as occurring in normal individuals and indicates that it may be accompanied by changes in perception of the environment, she views it primarily as a clinical phenomenon. Both Jacobson and Spiegel[159] however, adopt a perceptual frame of reference in considering depersonalization.

In his review, Bellak states that it is imperative to conceive of depersonalization as a more or less extreme variation of the changes in self-perception and feelings of unreality as similar variants of perception of the world that occur constantly in normal life. These changes may often be on a preconscious level, the degree of consciousness depending upon circumstances and individual variations of introspectiveness. He believes that changes in self-perception are probably always associated with changes in perception of the environment. By viewing depersonalization and feeling of unreality as a special aspect of the general problem of perception we can broaden our understanding of the phenomenon, to see its dynamic and genetic relationship to other variants of perception, and to see it as part of a general theory of personality rather than as a form of psychopathology per se.

Everyday life forces a multitude of varying roles on every individual, with concomitant changes of one's self in relation to the environment and coinciding with changes in self-awareness, self-concept, and self-feeling. These changing roles involve those of peer and subordinate and superior, public figure and parent, buyer and seller, and many others; in fact, in subtle ways our role changes in relationship to every person with whom we deal, and every setting in which we move about. In addition, there are of course the more dramatic changes of role from health to illness, civilian to soldier, free man to prisoner, young man to old man.

Even mild feelings of self-consciousness with their altered self-perception may be accompanied by a perceptual distortion of the individual's perception of the world around him, and reactions or observations. In these instances, depersonalization, feelings of unreality, and projection are inextricably linked as a general perceptual distortion of the self and the environment. Bellak's concept of depersonalization as a variation in self-awareness and as a normal phenomenon of the functioning self serves several purposes:

1. It obviates the tendency to identify depersonalization *only* with specific psychiatric disorders even though it may be related to varying degrees of pathology. Thus a patient's history of feelings of depersonalization is in itself of no specific diagnostic value. The severity of depersonalized states probably relates to the extent of the disturbance caused by oral problems and to the extent of the disturbance of ego boundaries. These in turn may be more or less related to the severity of the neurosis or psychosis.

2. It obviates the tendency to define depersonalization too narrowly as a specific psychic process or even simply as a defense. Thus each self-perception, in a different role and to a slight extent, may involve a small degree of depersonalization.

3. Finally, the concept enables us to see that any number of pathways may lead to depersonalization and feelings of unreality. The state may be produced by a wide variety of drugs or even brought about by simple physiological processes. The rigidity of the neck muscles in an extremely anxious person may produce sufficient dizziness and disorientation to account for feelings of estrangement. Hyperventilation may produce a feeling of light-headedness and dizziness, even paresthesias, which arouses changes in proprioception. These changes may result in alterations in self-perception and give rise to feelings of depersonalization. Depersonalization may also be associated with the dizziness produced when the eyes do not focus properly. The resultant blurring or alteration of depth perception may create a sense of unrealness.

Bellak concludes that any change in the customary frame of perceptual reference of any of the senses of proprioception and of time may induce enough disorientation as to cause the individual to experience changes in self-perception including depersonalization. This will be particularly true if the ego boundaries and self-identity are not strongly established.

THERAPEUTIC PROCEDURES

We are primarily concerned with complaints of depersonalization which are accompanied by anxiety or panic engendered by the feeling of depersonalization—syntonic depersonalization is not a concern here. Treatment will depend upon the outstanding dynamic features.

Giving the patient some intellectual awareness of the process is generally useful, and assuring him that this is not a unique, individual phenomenon, but something that the therapist well understands, that has been met with in many other instances and that can be observed under certain normal circumstances—after waking from a deep sleep or anesthesia, from overbreathing, muscular tension, and perceptual distortions. The effect of the various physiological phenomena may be demonstrated to the patient.

One can demonstrate to the patient that overbreathing will induce an alkalosis, a change of the pH of the blood, which in turn can produce a wide range of phenomena, from tingling in various parts of the body (paresthesia, technically) to spasticity of a variety of muscles, such as the intercostal muscles (accounting for some tension in the chest which in turn may produce anxiety), to headaches and tension in the strong muscles of the neck (the nuchal muscles). The nuchal muscles play a definite role in orientation in space. Their inappropriate rigidity may lead to dizziness, which in turn may lead to disturbance of the self-boundaries and of orientation in space and thus precipitate feelings of depersonalization.

If overbreathing plays a frequent role in the induction of depersonalization, the patient may be taught a specific breathing technique: breathing out through a straw or some other small opening with some resistance to exhalation (after free inhalation) while permitting free exhalation in the last moments of exhalation. This will stimulate the Hering-Breuer reflex in the lungs and lead again to an automatically controlled, regular type of breathing which will interfere with the onset of alkalosis and associated depersonalization. The acute states of depersonalization induced by overbreathing and alkalosis can be reversed by the well-known technique of breathing into a paper bag or simply holding one's breath, thereby accumulating more carbon dioxide in the blood stream and reversing the alkalosis and with it the vague feelings associated with depersonalization.

Where depersonalization is primarily induced by an anxiety-arousing experience, one can often alleviate the immediate symptoms by drugs such as meprobamate (Miltown, Equanil), and diazepoxide (Librium, etc.).

Where depersonalization is primarily precipitated by a flooding of aggressive impulses coupled with a denial of impulses and emotions, reversal of the denial by interpretation will be most effective. Relatively precise formulation of the psychodynamic constellation is required in the interpretation. Sometimes the loss of self-boundaries is related primarily to a lack of clear definition of identity in childhood and the need of closeness to some loved person in order to be assured of that wavering identity. Such problems frequently manifest themselves clinically as phobias—for instance, agoraphobia or a fear of traveling. Under such circumstances, the patient reveals a panic which has, primarily, features of depersonalization. Development along these lines usually follows a path in which the patient does not mind traveling certain distances, or is not upset when being on a boat provided that the boat travels closely to the shore—or he does not have any of these symptoms as long as someone close to the patient is with him. In other words, a need of a symbiotic relationship on a deeply oral basis is often related to the feelings of depersonalization.

Problems of orality manifest themselves especially often in feelings of partial depersonalization, such as a feeling of deadness of the perioral area—a feeling as if the mouth were unreal. Relating the onset of feelings of depersonalization in such cases to feelings of oral deprivation, of loss or removal from the symbiotic figure, will be useful.

The déjà vu phenomenon, in which the individual feels that a scene he has never witnessed before has a sense of familiarity, seems to occupy a place somewhere between depersonalization and projection. The experience has an overall quality of strangeness; it seems uncanny, may arouse anxiety, and often makes one feel odd to the point of depersonalization. In this case, external perception may be affected by past fantasies or by congruity with earlier experiences. Interpretation of the connection between contemporary and genetic dynamics is in order. The déjà vu phenomenon may lend itself to an illustration of how nearly everybody may have similar feelings of unreality under certain circumstances—when, for example, modern rapid transportation in a short period of time enables a person to move from one culture or environment to a strange and alien one.

The feeling of having lost one's legs or of "the legs leaving one" as a form of depersonalization, usually accompanied by very unpleasant feelings, occurs almost exclusively in females and often relates to a form of a conversion symptom associated with acutely aroused sexual fears. Interpretation of the dynamics of the situation is likely to be immediately successful.

ILLUSTRATIVE CASE HISTORIES

Emergency Therapy in Depersonalization

A cardiologist, Dr. X, referred a woman patient, Thelma, suffering from anxiety of panic proportions for consultation. The central idea of her panic was that she would die of a heart attack. Thelma is not the patient to be discussed in this case, but her fear of heart failure and the role of the physician who referred her are central to the case to be presented.

Soon after, the same physician also referred his nurse, Susan, for consultation. She too was extremely anxious but her anxiety seemed to center around her identity: Who am I? What am I? What am I doing? Where am I going? It developed that what she was doing was having an affair with the physician, who would not leave his wife and children to marry her. He was, incidentally, 20 years older than she. In her history there was ample evidence of family rivalries among four beautiful sisters for a seductive father who apparently relished his harem. The girls all lived at home, none were married, and two others, like Susan, were having affairs with older married men. Susan agreed to consider a referral to another therapist, and left, having seemingly been led to see that her anxiety and identity crisis were linked to her affair with the physician. She expressed determination to end the affair, get another job. She did not call back.

Two months later, Thelma told the therapist that she had met Susan that morning, that Susan had told her that she had seen the therapist for consultation. The two women, one very young, the other middle-aged, talked about what a "doll" the therapist was.

That very afternoon Susan telephoned the therapist. She was in a panic and feared that she was going crazy. It had. begun with a strange and eerie feeling that she was not herself, which had increased in intensity to where she had to know who she was or she would go out of her mind. Could the therapist himself take her into treatment right then and there? He must! He must! They would talk about that in a moment, the therapist answered, but first some information. She was still working for the physician; the affair continued; he still refused to leave his wife and pleaded with her to take another job and give him up. In fact, he had gotten her a job with a colleague, Dr. Y, who, within a short period after her arrival died of a coronary, which led her to return to the first employer.

When had she first felt the strange feeling that day? What had she been doing? It had been a slow morning with only one patient in the office. She had taken an EKG reading and there in that room it all began.

What had she been thinking about? Nothing? Had she not wondered what the EKG would show? Was she not worried that the patient might die just as Doctor Y had died? That he might die right there on the very examining table where she and Doctor X made love? With these suggestions made, she broke into tears, and when she could speak it was apparent that the sharp edge of panic was dulled and the frantic quality was gone.

"What else happened this morning?"

"Nothing," she replied.

"Well," said the therapist, "my grapevine tells me that you met Thelma. Didn't you do an EKG on her several times? You know she feared she would have a heart attack?"

Susan laughed this time. Yes, she had thought about Thelma in the EKG room. What a silly woman she was, worrying about her heart when it was perfectly all right, and complaining and being neurotic when she had a wonderful husband and a lovely daughter.

"Serve her right if she had a heart attack, huh?"

With this remark from the therapist, Susan laughed.

"And something more," continued the therapist, "any woman in your situation would be bound to have some nice juicy fantasies that Doctor X's wife would suddenly die, that Doctor X would marry you, that you would be a wonderful mother to his children, and that you and he would also have children together."

"Yes," acknowledged Susan, "and when I get desperate about him I think it would be nice if he died or went away and left me alone."

"The thing to remember," the therapist concluded, "is that you are a nurse because you like to help people. How terrible, you feel, if you have thoughts about their dying. You say, 'It can't be me who thinks that way, it must be someone else.' You try to pull away from yourself. And now, you really should get into treatment; let me give you someone's name."

"Can't you take me, Doctor? I feel you know me so well."

"You mean, if Thelma goes away or dies couldn't I take you?"

Susan laughed again, and accepted the referral. Her therapist reports that not once in her successful treatment was there evidence of further depersonalization.

The dynamics seem very clear: the Oedipal situation repeated in young adult life, accompanied by very strong death wishes that she attempts to deny by depersonalization, with the whole complex repeated again in the transference. The interventions in this case may be identified as mediate catharis and intellectualization. The transference manifestation was used to illuminate the contemporary conflict but not the genetic one.

Brief Therapy of Depersonalization

A woman sought psychotherapy for what appeared to be a travel phobia. Interviewing soon revealed that as soon as she was on her way in any kind of conveyance she would have a feeling as if she were in cotton, behind a thick glass wall cut off from all other people, on the outside looking in, and as if she were going somewhere against her will or at least without her participation. She lacked feelings of belongingness and suffered a mild feeling of confusion, without these symptoms taking on psychotic proportions. It was possible to establish that her separation from an accustomed environment played a major role. The strangeness of the new environment and the feeling of being separated from "home" induced a lack of a perceptual frame of reference. It turned out, for instance, that boat travel would not induce this state provided, it was aboard a coast liner. The idea, however, of going out to sea in a boat was most alarming. The degree of apparent phobia, in effect, was related directly to the distance from home; the longer the distance, the greater the panic, and in due course the greater the feelings of depersonalization.

She had suffered similar feelings of panic during childhood when her mother was farther away than the next room. It was possible to establish that, even then, what appeared simply to be panic were actually feelings of depersonalization, of not being quite sure where mother might be, of feeling curiously shrunken in size when in bed. She had often had perspective dreams in which things were perceived as if through the wrong end of a telescope, creating a feeling of distance and smallness. Obviously, these feelings of depersonalization which expressed themselves primarily as anxiety were related to a strong dependent relationship to the mother. Feelings of a loss of perceptual organization and reference emerged as soon as she was separated from her mother. Later, the same feelings occurred when she was separated from mother substitutes—the accustomed home, terra firma, or the shore line. The common denominators operating in various experiences were pointed out to the patient and she was told that her travel anxiety was secondary to a form of depersonalization. Her separation anxiety had to be worked through in order to affect her feelings of depersonalization. The feeling of helplessness, of practically not even existing when out of touch with an accustomed feature of the environment, also had to be worked through.

The patient was instructed to undertake a series of traveling excursions. She was seen by the therapist upon returning from each trip. At these sessions dynamics were again worked through and she was given instructions for the next trip. At first, it was possible for the patient to travel with somebody well known to her and thus avoid the feelings of depersonalization. Then she was able to travel alone by having some clearly defined tasks to perform while traveling, a schedule of work or a reading syllabus. She was encouraged to increase her awareness of geography on the trip, and she was reminded of the ease of communication by telephone with the home base. All of these interventions were helpful in at least decreasing her symptoms. Her anxiety also had manifested itself in marked overbreathing which led to tension and pain in the chest. Making the patient aware of the overbreathing interfered with the alkalosis produced by it, which had in turn been responsible for spasms of the intercostal muscles. These spasms in turn had aroused fears of a heart attack, another part of an interlocking series of symptoms.

9

Incipient and Acute Psychotic States

CLINICAL FEATURES

In the incipient psychotic states, a variety of clinical manifestations are observed. Some patients report a state of general confusion in which they feel their perceptions are not as accurate, their judgments not as sound, and their reasoning not as clear as they were in the past. Patients report memory losses or impairment: They forget appointments, they are late for work or fail to show up, they arrive at a destination without being sure about why they have come there. An intrapsychic awareness of the loss of reality testing is another manifestation. In some patients there is an impairment of the body boundaries, resulting in symptoms which range from depersonalization to delusion states. In almost all incipient psychotic conditions, anxiety is of panic proportions. The patient may be responding with panic to exogenous situations which symbolize an internal conflict; with others the panic is vague and undefined, but most generally is associated with a perception of the serious faltering of ego functions with the implication perceived by the patient that he is becoming psychotic.

In the acute psychotic states, the patient manifests acting-out behavior of the overt psychotic symptoms of delusions, hallucinations, and suicidal and homicidal impulses. In addition, there are manifestations of the perversions, with wildly exhibitionistic behavior, overt homosexual expressions, flagrant transvestism.

The patient who suffers an occasional acute psychotic episode or seems about to enter such an episode must be distinguished diagnostically from the active or chronic psychotic. The transient or incipient psychotic reveals an oscillating level of ego strength: He has not succumbed to a permanent adaptation in psychosis. He is always striving for a more stable adjustment, perhaps neurotic in character, but better integrated and related than the psychotic. Although frequently he may have paranoid feelings and ideation, they have not evolved into a fixed system. His reality testing will falter on occasion, but he will not totally succumb; yet it will remain a constant problem to the patient who consciously or intrapsychically perceives defects in this function. He shifts from one defense to another in his frantic efforts to attain homeostasis.

A complication in the diagnosis of acute and incipient psychosis is described by Small.[157] This complication is encountered in states resembling an acute episode but which are in fact the manifestation of an epileptic condition, often of subclinical nature that cannot be verified by standard neurological procedures, including the EEG and brain scan. Many diagnoses have been verified, however, by extending the EEG to include phobic stimulation, hyperventilation, sleep recordings, needle electrodes and nasopharyngeal leads, or by efforts at a therapeutic diagnosis.

Any of the symptoms described that are associated with acute psychotic states may be present. The clinician must give credence to his social–clinical response to the patient; if despite hallucinations and body delusions, for example, the patient appears not to be psychotic, the clinician should explore further and keep judgment in abeyance while the diagnostic process continues. Frank acknowledgement of and alienation from such symptoms are often a clue to a nonpsychotic state, for example. Monroe[128] has called attention to the repeatedly observed, unfavorable response of some diagnosed psychotics to the phenothiazine drugs—they paradoxically become worse because the phenothiazines potentiate seizure disorders.

Small has described and illustrated with case material a list of symptoms that may be associated with seizure disorders: blurred and double vision, phosphenes, micropsia and macropsia, tension in response to eye movements (following moving lights or reading), ringing and humming high-pitched sounds, parasthesias, episodic disorganization of sound and smell in which an ordinarily pleasant stimulus suddenly becomes unpleasant then pleasant again, automatic behavior, bouts of clumsiness, and altered states of consciousness, among others.

While any of these symptoms may be associated with an epileptic state, they may also be observed in other conditions. The clinician must be cautious, and above all keep in mind that it is possible for an epileptic to be psychotic, and vice versa.

Epileptic-equivalent conditions appear to be occurring with greater frequency in recent decades. Jonas[96] hypothesizes that the introduction of tranquilizing drugs is responsible for this phenomenon; prior to their development and widespread use, the barbituates were prescribed for their tranquilizing effect. Barbiturates are anticonvulsant, so that their use tended to mask seizure phenomena. The newer drugs neither mask nor potentiate the symptoms.

DYNAMIC CONSIDERATIONS

Almost always in psychotic states, we are able to observe that there has been an intensification of the instinctual drives. These have overwhelmed the ego and threatened the personality with a loss of control of the impulses, producing concurrently the impairment in the sense of reality, and in reality perception and testing.

Also usually observable is an increase of the basic conflictual pattern of the individual, which may be heterosexual, homosexual, sado-masochistic, or exhibitionistic–voyeuristic in nature.

Sometimes an already existing depressive dynamic is intensified by situations which stimulate a sense of object loss, a lowering of self-esteem, a disappointment, or an internalization of aggression.

A fourth observable dynamic is the primacy of denial, with resulting manic or hypomanic conditions.

Usually a punitively severe and poorly integrated superego accompanies faulty ego functioning. Assessment of ego function is essential to the understanding of the patient's particular process, to the formulation of a therapeutic procedure, and to the enlistment of therapeutic allies—those intact or nearly intact ego functions.

THERAPEUTIC PROCEDURES

1. An important step is the regulation of the life of the patient. This may require strengthening of the physiological defenses. Careful inquiry into the eating and sleeping patterns of the patient during the crisis must be made, and precautions taken that the patient does not suffer mounting fatigue, producing as it does a lowering of defenses. Prescribing soporifics and carefully regulating their use may be necessary. Firm interdictions against or prescriptions of certain patterns of behavior may be in order: The acting-out heterosexual patient or homosexual patient may be cautioned against such sexual behavior; the overly inactive or passive patient may, by the same token, have to be counseled into a program of activity and exercise.

2. Active but cautious interpretation of the conflict with which the patient is coping is a major therapeutic effort. As described in the section on the choice of interventions (Chapter 4), this involves the double operation of pacifying the patient's superego while at the same time increasing his ego strength by making the drive more syntonic and supporting impulse control.

3. Drug treatment is often of great importance in the therapy of incipient and acute states. A basic rule might well be that whenever any primary process is observable, the use of the more potent tranquilizers such as

Thorazine is indicated. The milder drugs, involving less danger of complications, may be used in less critical situations. The dynamic intention in the use of tranquilizing drugs is to obtain a reduction in the impact of the instinctual drive. With those patients who have suffered an intensification of the depressive dynamics, the utilization of the energizing drugs is indicated. Careful attention to emerging symptoms is required since a balancing of both energizer and tranquilizer may be necessary—for example, with the agitated–depressed patient.

4. A period of brief hospitalization may be desirable to provide safeguards during active interpretation of the conflict. The protection provided by the hospital will enable the therapist to interpret more vigorously and deeply than he might otherwise feel safe in doing. Hospitalization will also protect those patients who do not have family and friends available to guard them against suicidal or homicidal acting out, or during the administration of soporific drugs.

5. The support and reassurance provided by the therapist's availability is a primary therapeutic device in these conditions. A valuable technique is to have some patients report by telephone at appointed times in the period between therapeutic sessions. Many patients are only able to fall asleep because they experience the offered availability by telephone as an immediate presence by the therapist.

ILLUSTRATIVE CASE HISTORIES

Emergency Treatment of an Incipient Psychotic State

A.B., 27, was referred by the counseling service of the university where he was a day student. His symptoms were indicative of an incipient psychotic state: massive anxiety, forgetfulness, inability to sleep, anorexia, compulsive masturbation, picking and eating of whiteheads from his face, ritualistic nose-blowing (neither more nor less than three times for a single nose-clearing episode), an obsessional fear that he would stab his mother with a kitchen knife, attacks of dizziness accompanied by panic on the subway that made him regularly late for work, a tremendous fear of hearing anyone snoring, and, to end this list short of completion, a reliance upon talismans (grapes, which warded off what was to him the horrendous danger of flatus; and aspirins, which acted as "fire extinguishers" in his head).

Despite these limiting and disruptive symptoms, he was an honor student, and an officer in several student organizations, and worked adequately, though with difficulty, at a full-time night job he had held for ten years, receiving regular promotions. Though shy, he was not withdrawn. He was attractive to and sexually successful with women. These relations, however, were fraught with anxiety: As the hour for a date approached, he became increasingly upset, feared that he would be flatulent, and managed to appear only with the aid of his talismans. Upon completion of intercourse his anxiety abated, he became hungry, and could eat without fear of choking.

His history recorded very early disturbances: the death of a sibling, extensive masturbation from the age of five with precocious ejaculation at eight, an early obsessional concern with the genitals and underwear of women, an inability to look at his own genitals, and an increasing absorption with transvestism.

He had made five attempts in the past six years to be helped by psychotherapy. Each effort had ended in similar fashion: The therapist discontinued the treatment feeling that he was intransigent. He seemed to be incapable of insight, to be unable to associate, to be confused by and resistant to interpretation, and to insist upon concrete suggestions from the therapist. He was understandably skeptical about the worth of the present consultation, but he feared that he was "going crazy" and would have to be hospitalized unless he could be helped.

This fear had crystallized during the preceding month. In that interval he had begun an affair with a married woman with whose husband he was friendly. While the husband worked at night, the lovers assignated in the husband's car; then they met the husband at his place of work and the trio enjoyed a midnight snack.

The therapist viewed his task in two dimensions: to help the patient through the present crisis, and to move him into a long-term, supportive relationship. Accordingly he did the following:

1. Intellectually, he delineated A.B.'s problems as stemming from some unknown fears of sexual behavior in general, and the current crisis as specifically associated with his affair with the married woman.
2. He forbade continuation of the affair. It was, he agreed, especially exciting to have relations with a married woman, but it was also especially guilt producing. He was to explain the discontinuation to the woman on this basis, and he was to continue to see the couple. (The therapist reasoned that this would enable him to substitute a sexless, guiltless aura for the more damaging one.)
3. He made himself available to the patient by phone for emergency consultation 24 hours a day, seven days a week.
4. He prescribed an amphetamine to counteract depression and fatigue.

The patient followed instructions to the letter, in the manner one might have expected from his compulsive traits. His panic decreased quickly; several exacerbations were handled during the next two weeks by telephone calls he made to the therapist from subway platforms. He achieved a degree of insight when he discovered that he experienced no appreciable subway anxiety if he masturbated before leaving for work.

This patient continued in treatment for ten years. He was graduated from college with high honors, and promoted to chief of his department at work. Anorexia, subway fears, and fear of insanity have remained under control. The transvestism remains as an impulse which has not been acted out. Periodic episodes of depression have occurred, almost always and predictively associated with anniversaries of object loss. His heterosexual successes have continued; sharp anxiety was experienced when several women on occasions made efforts to convince him of the rightness of marriage. He is probably episodically a lifelong patient, but one functioning and employed.

Brief Therapy of an Incipient Psychotic State

In incipient psychotic states, awareness of changes of perception, intrapsychic awareness of a potential loss of control over impulses, and awareness of decreased acuity of reality testing, all tend to produce anxiety, if not panic, altered-ego states, and a feeling of helplessness. With one young woman, it was most helpful at first to convey to her that these subjective phenomena, which were to her strange and alarming, were not unknown to the therapist. The intellectual aspects of their origin were discussed in some detail, giving examples from other patients and other symptoms in order to assure the patient that, in principle, she could be understood. This procedure gives the patient some feeling of control and considerable reassurance.

In the case of this young woman, a triangular situation had arisen in her office in which she was involved. She acutely felt that one of her male co-workers disliked her. This was quickly understood as a simple form of projection, in which she was jealous of this man's relationship to another woman in the same office. Information she supplied permitted her to be told that she herself had a marked interest in the man, and while she could not admit this to herself, she was actually quite jealous of the man's seeming involvement with the other woman. She expressed all of this by ascribing to him a feeling of dislike for herself. She became dimly aware that some of the evidence upon which she based her strong sentiments of being disliked by him were not entirely sound. This awareness of some distortion of reality itself engendered a good deal of anxiety.

The psychotherapeutic task then was to acquaint her on the one hand with the mechanism of projection in intellectual form, and on the other hand, to make her aware of her true sentiments for the man and the woman at her place of work. Once this was dicussed, a similar situation involving an aunt and an uncle with whom she had spent about a year of her childhood was brought in by the patient, and in turn was related to the contemporary situation. Frightening experiences of a near breakthrough of primary-process material and disturbing hypnagogic phenomena on going to bed were interfered with by the prescription of a nonbarbiturate sleeping pill. (Barbiturates, like alcohol, tend in the beginning few minutes of their effectiveness to further decrease the strength of the secondary process and paradoxically can lead to greater panic by facilitating an emergence of primary-process material before the desired soporific action takes over.)

When this approach plus Librium (10 mg., three times a day) did not prove sufficient to suppress the primary anxiety and the secondary tendency to project, and disruption of the work situation threatened, the patient was put on the combination of Thorazine (25 mg., three times a day) and Imipramine (twice a day). The Thorazine provided tranquilization whereas the Imipramine interfered with the tendency to depression in this patient.

The therapist considered it essential to help her maintain herself at work, since a disruption of her job activity was likely to lead to a secondary regression and considerable trauma. This point should be kept in mind generally with incipient psychotic states: They must be controlled as quickly as possible lest the disruptive experience serve as a major trauma, facilitate future dissociation, induce painful loss of self-esteem, and instill a terrifying fear of loss of control. The use of drugs under such circumstances is especially indicated in an effort to ameliorate the situation as quickly as possible and often before psychotherapy can become effective.

10
Acting Out

CLINICAL MANIFESTATIONS

The concept of acting out involves phenomena of difficult complexity and relates to different clinical syndromes as Bellak has discussed elsewhere.[25] The term acting out is sometimes used to describe brief episodes of a circumscribed and episodic nature; for example, an obese person may be said to be acting out his sense of frustration and his need for gratification by overeating. While the dynamics may be much more complex than this, the essential implication is that such a person, feeling deprived, disappointed, and unloved, translates these feelings, usually unconsciously, into the act of feeding himself. Thus the act of eating would symbolically represent the statement: "Nobody loves me and nobody feeds me, so I feed myself." Alcoholism may provide the same unverbalized expression. In such cases the term acting out is used when behavior seems to make a simple unconscious statement. Frequently the acting-out behavior is ego-syntonic to the individual. At least it is so during the moment of action or behavior. However, many patients who act out express a degree of ego-alienation from the behavior.

The term acting out is frequently used in describing the behavior of psychotic individuals. An assaultive attack, for example, may be considered in relationship to the acting out of delusional and hallucinatory distortions; the behavior is consistent with and caused by the distortions and has little or nothing to do with reality. Our concern very often in the treatment of psychotics is the question: Is this patient likely to act out? We are concerned with the probability that this patient will act upon his unrealistic impulses and perceptions. Fortunately, only a small percentage of psychotic individuals act out their distorted perception. It nonetheless remains an urgent task to understand why certain individuals are able to sustain paranoid feelings without ever doing harm whereas others are pressed into dreadfully destructive acts by similar impulses.

Acting out is found also as a classic characteristic of the hysterical personality. One notes about such individuals tremendous mood variations from love to hate, depression to elation, with corresponding actions of marked polarity in short intervals of time.

In fugue states, one observes also a split-off part of the personality being permitted to act out ordinarily unacceptable impulses.

The psychopath or sociopath, unlike the neurotic, tends to translate his conflicts and drives into direct behavior rather than into the symptoms of the autoplastic neurotic. Narcotic addiction, in itself a form of acting out, leads to further acting out under the influence of the drug.

Acting-out behavior may also be manifested by apparently normal people who suffer from character disorders, through their tendency to react to certain situations in a stereotyped manner. Some behave inappropriately as an unconscious invitation for aggression against themselves. Others persistently respond in a self-destructive way by being attracted to those whose principal aim is to exploit them physically. Some men and women act out childhood conflicts and frustrations in a life of empty promiscuity. Their behavior is perceived as pathological to everyone but themselves; their behavior does not change with realistic experience since it concurs with their unconscious perceptions. They fail to see a causal relationship between their behavior and its manifest results and do not profit from learning. For these individuals their acting-out behavior becomes the characteristic pattern of their life. The acting out is less episodic than would be found in a "repetition–compulsion" with which it is often confused. The acting-out behavior is integrated as a style of life.

DYNAMIC CONSIDERATIONS

Freud first mentioned acting out in *The Psychopathology of Everyday Life*,[72] in which he describes various kinds of symptomatic and faulty actions within the range of normal behavior. In his *Fragment of an Analysis of a Case of Hysteria*,[76] he relates Dora's premature termination of her analysis to an acting out of certain childhood recollections and fantasies. In a paper on technique,[75] he associates acting out in relationship to transference and resistance.

Fenichel[65] describes the acting-out person as one in whom "an unconscious misunderstanding of the present in the sense of the past" is extraordinarily strong; the patients repeatedly perform acts or undergo experiences—identical or very similar ones—that represent unconscious attempts to rid themselves of old instinctual conflicts in order to find a belated gratification of repressed impulses (instinctual demands as well as guilt feelings), or at least to find relief from some inner tension. Fenichel describes these patients as having an intolerance for tension, as being unable to perform the step from acting to thinking. They immediately yield reasonable judgment to all impulses. He believes that their aim is the avoidance of displeasure rather than the attainment of pleasure, and that oral fixations and early traumata play a significant role in their behavior. He emphasizes that the quality of action is in itself especially conspicuous as compared to other neurotic activity; it is a fairly organized activity and not merely a single movement, gesture, or mimicked expression. He characterizes acting out as ego-syntonic and as being an alloplastic rather than an autoplastic defense: People who act out tend to change their environment rather than themselves.

Greenacre[78] says that in acting out ". . . there may be special problems in accepting and understanding current reality." These problems she identifies as: specific problems in the immediate realistic situation; persistence of memories of earlier disturbing experiences; an inadequate sense of reality. In acting out, Greenacre sees a compulsion to reproduce the totality of an experience or episode rather than to manifest a symbolic or token portion of it. She sees habitual, neurotic acting out as the selective distortion of reality. In contrast, she sees psychotic acting out as characterized by a complete taking over of the current situation by early unconscious memories that severely and adversely affect reality perception and bar conscious memories and attitudes.

Both Greenacre and Fenichel consider part of the genesis of habitual acting out to be an oral fixation, a great narcissistic need, an intolerance of frustration, a constitutionally heightened motility, and the presence of severe early tramata which cause repetitive abreactive acting out similar to that found in the traumatic neuroses. Greenacre, however, places special emphasis on visual sensitization, which produces a tendency for dramatization and an unconscious belief in the magic of action. She feels that the important role of acting out is due to disturbances of the development of speech in the second year. When this is the case, motor action is used to take over some of the communication function.

Bellak[25] believes that multiple, diverse identification coupled with a lack of synthesis of ego-nuclei also plays a role. He has observed some patients to intermittently act out highly diverse roles which seem patterned on identification with one or the other parent.

Low frustration tolerance is also considered a dynamic aspect of acting out and is frequently related to a developmental interference: inconsistent rearing, overindulgence, insufficient discipline, general overcharging with sexual and aggressive impulses. Blos[52] views acting out in the adolescent to be in the service of ego synthesis as a phase-specific mechanism. He maintains that adolescence involves a progressive decathexis of primary love objects, involving increased narcissism and autoeroticism, to eventual finding of the heterosexual object. He believes that these changes are "accompanied by a profound sense of loss and isolation, by a severe ego impoverishment which accounts for the adolescent's frantic turn to the outside world, to sensory stimulation, and to activity." Thus action for the normal adolescent is resisting the surrender to primal passivity, "action assumes the quality of a magic gesture: it averts evil, it denies passive wishes, and it affirms a delusional control over reality." Blos finds acting out common among normal adolescents because "the adolescent process can be accomplished only through synthesizing the past with the present and the anticipated future . . . [through] constantly striving to bring the past into harmony with the terminal stage of childhood, with adolescence."

In the more diffuse type of acting out, a much broader genetic basis must be considered. These individuals manifest not merely the visual sensitization described by Greenacre but a proneness to general overstimulation and sensitization for all stimuli. They manifest a much lower threshold for both input and output. While we believe that infants need a certain amount of sensory input for normal development, apparently the infant through overstimulation may get a permanent overload; such a person may then have a lifelong, excessive stimulus hunger, matched only by his inability for containment and the continuous need for discharge.

The defensive aspects of acting out have been related as a cathartic and abreactive experience in which the patient "blows off steam" and reduces tension. Acting out may sometimes, even when violent or harmful to the individual, ward off the more anxiety-laden feeling of depersonalization. Jacobson[91] says that the resistance against remembering effected by acting out constitutes a form of denial, and is regularly linked with a bent for this defense. She sees acting out as action that keeps certain forms of behavior ego-syntonic with the help of denial and repression.

Complex forms of acting out, as in the character neuroses, suggest the operation of repression. These complex forms may be highly overdetermined, and may operate on an unconscious rather than preconscious level—as in denial. One pattern of behavior may be designed defensively to counteract another sequence of behavior pattern: A series of masochistically and passively seductive acts may be followed consistently by active sadistic reactions, and vice versa.

The acting-out individual shows a multitude of ego weaknesses: a lack of fusion of ego-nuclei, a deficiency in the synthetic function, poor impulse control, low frustration tolerance, poor reality testing, an inability to attain and maintain object constancy, and little ability for sublimation and neutralization. He also shows incapacities in the secondary-process functioning and in the ability for detour behavior.

THERAPEUTIC PROCEDURES

Greenacre considers the three basic long-range therapeutic techniques with acting-out patients to be prohibition, interpretation, and strengthening of the ego. These techniques are essentially the same, with modifications, for the short-term treatment of acting out. The diverse and complex nature of acting-out behavior suggests that the therapeutic management of this phenomenon will obviously vary a great deal from patient to patient.[25]

1. Direct prohibition of certain relationships or certain behavior may be indicated. Greenacre, however, has pointed out limitations in the use of such prohibitions, both from the standpoint of immediate effectiveness and because of their potentially detrimental effect on the relationship between therapist and patient.

2. Removing the patient from the situation which precipitates or triggers acting out is a possible procedure in some cases. This may involve changing the geographical milieu, insisting that the patient move out of the parental home, altering the arrangement by which a son works for his father-in-law, and the like. It is infinitely more useful to make such changes immediately, if necessary in consultation with the others involved.

3. Cathartic interpretation which deals directly with the drive expressed in the acting out may sometimes be useful, provided the necessary precautions are kept in mind. The patient must be made aware that the interpretation is not a license for the behavior interpreted.

4. Attempts to make the behavior ego-alien is perhaps the most useful instrument. One points out the repetitive and harmful nature of the behavior pattern and above all indicates to the patient that he is a victim of his own unconscious distortions. By stressing the passive role the patient plays in relationship to his own impulses, one can remove much of the feeling of omnipotence and magic which is inherent in acting out.

5. The early intellectual outlining of the meaning of the patient's behavior may be useful in increasing self-scrutiny and self-criticism. This will require, of course, that the therapist arrive at a dynamic comprehension of the patient's behavior very early in the treatment.

6. Closely linked with the above intervention is the technique of prediction: The therapist tells the patient that he is very likely to act out because of current circumstances or approaching ones. The patient may be told that the purpose of the prediction is the hope of proving it false.

7. The achievement of any kind of delay becomes an important ally in the therapy of the acting-out patient, since immediate action is such a large factor in his behavior. The patient who wants to get married today, who

wants to terminate treatment, who wants to initiate divorce proceedings instantly, may sometimes be deterred by agreement to wait a day, a week, a month. The benefits of such an agreement may be two-fold: The urgency of the moment may be bypassed, and one gains time to interpret usefully.

8.   A strengthening of the superego may be immediately helpful. One appeals persistently to the patient's conscience and points out to him the full implications of his behavior and the detrimental effect it has on others. The therapist attempts to ally himself with the part of the patient's personality that wishes to control the impulses.

9.   Increasing the synthetic ability of the patient by reviewing the feelings and expressions manifested in preceding sessions is a useful device. Acting-out patients, particularly the hysterical ones, have a tendency to forget completely the mood of the day before or the most urgent problem of the last week. These patients must be reminded of the state of affairs of yesterday and the week before, and shown the relationship of today's need for action to events just past. To achieve this effect, one can insist that such a patient begin the therapeutic session by his recalling the main dynamic gist of the previous session, and then intentionally and actively relating current to previous material.

10. The use of appropriate drugs may be indicated to avoid repetitions of acting out. Drugs that will decrease the predisposing anxieties and tensions may provide the breathing spell necessary for therapeutic success and at the same time hinder further strengthening of pathological patterns. Some drugs, especially of the phenothiazine group, may interfere with acting out by decreasing the affective drive directly and thus increasing the synthetic functions indirectly. Ostow[134] believes that the energizers have the ability to increase the synthetic capacity of the ego.

11. In extreme cases, enlisting the help of others may be necessary to curb harmful acting out. Conjoint consultation with a mate, a parent, or a sibling, even a friend, may be required.

12. Reassurance supplied through the availability of the therapist to be reached by telephone is an important technique when the danger of acting out is acute. Stressing the slogan, "Don't act—telephone," is important. The telephone conversation may provide the necessary catharsis, thus reducing the impact of both drive and tension. It may also provide opportunity for strengthening of the superego by pointing out the consequences of the contemplated action.

13. Therapeutic dissolution of *inhibitions* is an intervention sometimes recommended by Deutsch.[60] Very often the acting-out patient is found to be inhibited in "success" efforts: unable to take an exam, not looking for a better job, not moving out of the parents' home, not pursuing a desired course of training or education, etc. Presumably such efforts help dissipate some of the energy-finding outlet in the undesirable act-

ing out; certainly the achievement of success increases the patient's investment in alienating himself from the acting out.

One cannot be too sanguine about the satisfactory treatment of severe cases of acting out. There are many instances in which the behavior remains refractory. A large percentage of these patients do not enter treatment even if they have sought consultation, or they break off very soon. The person who is constantly excited, who has had a sensory overload in early childhood and now lives on a high level of tension with a great need for stimulation and immediate discharge, remains largely unreachable by psychotherapy. Totally new—possibly physiological—forms of therapy must be searched for.

Much of the difficulty in treating acting out stems from the fact that genetic roots of the behavior lie in preverbal experiences. Little wonder then, that acting out shares its therapeutic problems with other pathological syndromes of nonverbal nature and preverbal origin and is often even an exchangeable symptom. Acting out is closely related to hypochrondriasis, psychosomatic conditions, and hysterical phenomena. In all of these, we observe a variety of body language expressions, rather than verbal communication appropriate to the secondary process.

The difficulties of treating relatively minor forms of acting out in otherwise well-integrated personalities make one pessimistic of the success of treating more severe and especially asocial forms of acting out. To expect that addiction and major asocial and antisocial forms of acting out will respond to our current therapeutic armamentarium seems merely wishful, except with a relatively small percentage in whom the severity of the acting out is not primarily related to the degree of psychopathology, but rather to social and other situational factors. Sociopathic or psychotic acting out of major violence will not yield readily to psychotherapy alone, nor can psychotherapy take the place of other forms of humane management which offer society more immediate protection—certainly not until the effectiveness of our diagnostic and therapeutic attempts has increased generally, or until psychotherapy has been proved extensively in each individual case of a social offender.

ILLUSTRATIVE CASE HISTORIES

Brief Therapy of Aggressive Acting Out

A woman in her early thirties sought help for the complaint that her relationship with her husband and her children was dangerously impaired by her inability to control an explosive temper. She shouted and committed other forms of aggression both against the children and the husband, especially around dinner time. This family shared many common denominators with a culturally widespread situation: The husband comes home from work tired and expecting to be taken care of; the wife, having carried the burdens of the household and the children all day, is in no mood to cater to him; the children, at this time of day, particularly if they are young, are at the low ebb of ego strength, and are fussy and demanding. While the many pressures upon the patient were quite real, even typical for mothers of small children, it became the therapist's task to see why these pressures resulted in more difficulties than for most women.

Exploration of her associations and of one dream quickly revealed some of the basic dynamic features. In the dream, she felt that something like zombies hovered around her, crowded her, and walked over her. Asked to associate or talk particularly about the feeling in the dream, she quickly related it to the feeling she had at the most difficult times of the evening: It was as if everybody was crowding in on her, on top of her, tugging at her, making demands on her. Her interpretation of these demands involved the feeling of passivity, of being imposed upon, and, ultimately, of being sexually attacked. At the same time, being tugged at was related to being bitten. This feeling of being devoured was a primitive conception of the demands being made on her. The genetics of these two main trends were then worked through. On the one hand, it led to some primal scene memories; the notion that her mother was being imposed upon by the demands of her father meant literally that her father was on top of her mother, who was in danger of being harmed as well as smothered. Association to the zombies led to childhood fears, fairy tales, and nightmares. The feeling of being tugged at reminded her of an early dream of being in the water, about to be attacked by sharks who tugged at and then bit her. At one point the sharks turned into crocodiles who threatened to devour her completely.

A simple interpretation was now possible: The dinner hour was experienced as a combination of dangers, of being attacked, of being smothered, and being imposed upon; at the same time, the desire of everybody to be fed and their many demands were related to primitive childhood notions of being bitten and devoured. A supportive association was offered when she recalled an excessive fear of her nipple being bitten when she breast-fed one of the children. From other interview material, it became clear that she suffered in a variety of situations in which the common denominator appeared to be "too much impact": noises, social situations with too many people in them, fear of sitting in the middle of the row in threatres, discomfort at crowded parties, and some claustrophobia-like feelings in elevators. These too were worked through in relation to her sexual and oral distortions, and in turn related to the impact of the dinner situation.

The therapist decided not to bring in other genetic material that suggested that some of the fear of being imposed upon and squashed related back to problems with her mother. Instead, the shouting at and hitting of the children was interpreted as a defense; in order not to feel passive, endangered, imposed upon, overcome, and attacked, she took the active, aggressive role and struck out first.

A totally different tack was taken with an essentially intellectual discussion of the pleasures of being able to act out—the feeling of relief after "blowing up." The patient acknowledged that while her conscience troubled her, some time after having acted out angrily, there was a feeling of relief. This discussion led to a study in detail of her daily life. She indeed led an overburdened life with no chance to care for herself, no opportunity for release in a pleasurable time. As a supportive measure for decreasing the need for acting out, she was urged to take an hour for herself just prior to the difficult dinner time, preferably to remove herself from the house and engage in some pleasant and relaxing activity (a walk, shopping without great pressure for something that is not urgently needed, going to the library, or visiting a friend).

In almost all instances of this nature, it seems paramount that the woman actually leave the house for a period to escape the demands of the children, the telephone, or her own superego. Considerable ingenuity may be needed "to assure" the mother some time to herself, particularly if the socioeconomic status does not permit the hiring of somebody who can fill in for her. Sometimes, it is wise to have the mother take a part-time job which enables her to pay for child-care services. The work alone drains off some of the aggression. Where feasible, bowling or other athletics may be suggested as a release of aggression.

Drugs that provide relief from tension or overcome fatigue or depression may be useful in halting the vicious cycle of similar situations. Breaks in the cycle often permit both children and husband to react differently, so that they in turn generate less tension. Moreover, recesses from acting out makes the patient more readily appreciative of the gains inherent in giving up the acting out. Finally, the time thus won may permit the necessary working through of dynamics and the making of burden-relieving arrangements.

Brief Therapy of Sexual Acting Out

A married man, nearly 30, engaged in promiscuous activity which had the earmarks of acting out. His behavior, at least *after* the event, was very much against his better judgment and desire, especially since he seemed to arrange matters so that, sooner or later, his escapades became known to his wife. Though a very intelligent and capable man, he felt markedly inferior to his attractive, bright wife who was not without managerial tendencies. Some occasions of his acting out were provoked by domestic events, others by situations at work, when he had reason to feel his self-esteem lowered. At such times, he experienced an irresistible urge to engage in some heterosexual activity. This served the rather simple function of elevating his feelings of self-esteem again: If the acting out was related to problems with his wife, it also was a way of taking revenge on her and engaging in retribution. This latter feature made it necessary for him to conduct these affairs so that they would, however inadvertently, come to her knowledge. At the same time, the ensuing unpleasantness satisfied his superego.

As these dynamics were worked through they were also related back to masturbation fantasies in his adolescence which possessed sado-masochistic features. The fantasies might start out with a rescue scene in which he manifestly was the noble knight, but latently he was the passive one who was being rescued. Sometimes, to his alarm, fantasies would develop in which the rescued damsel was now entirely in his power for unspecified acts of sexually tinged sadism. The "rescue fantasy" was easily related to the problems of his self-esteem, whereas the more obviously sadistic-sexual fantasies lent themselves to interpretation with the relationship to his wife. Successfully predicting two or three instances of temptation to act out led to control of the impulse at first; working through a number of situations led apparently to a cessation—to judge by a revisit six months after the brief intervention.

11
Severe Somatic Conditions

CLINICAL FEATURES

The psychological effect of an illness is a function of the patient's previously existing personality, and in most situations correlation is positive between degree of disturbance in the premorbid personality and degree of pathological response to the disability.

Schematically, Bellak[16] presents five types of response to illness or disability:

1. A "normal" reaction of some anxiety and depression, which soon, however, decreases to a concern approximately commensurate with the actual degree of illness or impairment.
2. An avoidance reaction exhibited in a denial of the illness, expressed in an unperturbed demeanor, and often accompanied by overactivity and false gaiety. This attitude frequently turns into a depression with anxiety, and disobedience of medical instructions.
3. A reactive depression which may be prolonged and involve hypochondriasis.
4. A channeling of all previously existing anxiety into the new focus of concern. Sometimes these patients, usually rather disturbed persons, give up earlier, more diffuse manifestations of disturbance and thus appear to be more tractable.
5. Psychological invalidism, as when a patient who is physically able to function both socially and occupationally develops fears, symptoms, or attitudes which are incapacitating.

Such manifestations are observable in some patients who have suffered only minor ailments, whereas the full range is observed more frequently among patients who have suffered a severe organic illness or disability, including cancer, cardiac disease, tuberculosis or amputation.

DYNAMIC CONSIDERATIONS

The psychodynamics involved in some somatic problems have been reviewed by Bellak and Haselkorn.[18] They found that for most people the initial trauma resulting from the diagnosis or experience of a major illness is followed by a process that might be called "organization." Gradually the meaning to the patient of his illness undergoes certain changes. His initial diffuse anxiety is replaced by a more personalized concept; the nature of the pathology and how the illness looks and feels to him takes on special meaning on unconscious, preconscious, and conscious levels. He becomes familiar with his symptoms; in general his relationship to his illness is characterized by phases that resemble the changes that take place in an ambivalent relationship to people and places over a period of time. He learns to live with his illness and achieve some degree of acceptance. Thus with time and increasing emotional distance from the original episode, a relatively successful adaptation in psychic economy takes place. Observable in most patients is the operation of intact ego functions striving for and achieving psychic homeostasis.

For other patients, however, the trauma of illness and the resulting disability bring with them a pathological organization of distorted ideational content that is not readily relinquished. Emotion is withdrawn from object relations, and the self becomes the center of all concern. This withdrawal represents the patient's regression to an earlier level of development, when as a child he invested most of his feelings in his own body. If his previous object relationships were impoverished, the illness intensifies his narcissistic fixation.

This process of increased narcissism includes changes in self-image, body image, and organ image.

A painful organ or one known to be diseased attracts attention. If the illness is chronic and of major importance, the ill portion is treated in a nearly anthropomorphized fashion as a separate being. Special provisions are made for it, care is provided, and an attitude is established which closely corresponds to that of a mother toward her child. Solicitous overconcern may in varying degrees be demanded from the outside world as well as tendered by the person toward himself. In the healthy person, a large emotional investment is made in a variety of figures which change as he develops. In the neurotic, an excessive investment in himself has been maintained. A physically ill person makes an increased investment in himself as a defensive measure against further harm. In the neurotic, this reinvestment will be greater, as will be the reluctance to give it up when the crisis is past. This reinvestment is an increase of secondary narcissism.

The clinical importance of the body image was originally described by Paul Schilder.[145] "The image of the human body means the picture of our body which we form in our mind . . . the way in which the body appears to ourself." The child needs to learn to differentiate its own body from the rest of the world. More pertinent is that everyone develops some idiosyncratic concepts of their own body, frequently an overidealized and/or a greatly underrated one. Illness distorts this body image. An affected organ may loom so prominently as to affect the concept profoundly. One is reminded of an old humorous map of the United States as drawn by a New Yorker, with New York City covering two-thirds or more of the entire North American continent. The clinical manifestations of this increased narcissism and the disturbance of the body image are obvious and familiar: hypochondriacal concern, depression, many body complaints that cannot be correlated with physical findings, persistent self-observation, and anxiety. Increased oral needs and passivity also result.

Misconceptions about anatomy, or ignorance of it, invite conscious misinterpretation of body injury. On the unconscious level, irrational elaboration of these distortions takes place. Organic disease often has symbolic connotations for the patient which determine the particular meaning the illness will have for him. Naturally, the greater his original fear of passivity, the more severe will be the threat to his ego. Psychoanalysis has demonstrated the wide divergence that can exist between objective reality and the patient's self-image and body image. The content of the patient's fantasies in free association illuminates the significance of behavior that would otherwise be utterly unintelligible. A powerful and virile male who unhesitatingly engages in physical combat may unconsciously conceive of himself as a fragile little girl in constant danger of being attacked. His aggression may then be a defensive reaction to his fear of being hurt. Everyone is familiar with the person who is said to "carry himself with an air." It becomes apparent that such a person is acting out a fantasy predicated on an inflated self-image that may be vastly different from what is consistent with reality.

Irrational attitudes toward illness become further comprehensible when organ imagery is understood. One female patient, when informed that she had a stomach ulcer, perceived it as an "oozing, pus-like hole" and was extremely revolted by it. Her association was to a relative's leg ulcer which she had observed. Needless to say, there were anal and vaginal implications. A frequent interpretation of illness is that it is something dirty. On the other hand, the bacterial invasion of an organ, such as the lung, is frequently perceived by the patient as a form of oral impregnation.

The diseased organ may become anthropomorphized. The patient will see it as separate from himself but in a definite relationship as, for example, perceiving the sick organ to be similar to a controlling agent, "My stomach doesn't permit me. . . ." On the other hand, the patient's relationship to the diseased organ may be that of a mother to a sick child in which the patient plays mother to the sick organ.

The specific personal meaning of an illness is often incorrectly, though even consciously, derived from some other ill person the patient knows. Identification with a parent or relative who may have had a similar or seemingly similar disease can cause the patient much anxiety, especially if the patient had hostile wishes toward this person. He now sees his illness as retaliation and punishment for this hostility, a response to the guilt feelings engendered. If a patient has been excessively competitive in the past, chronic disease may permit him to justify his escape into passive dependency; he can now accept attention whereas previously this was psychically intolerable. One must not overlook the psychic distress and anguish that misinformation and misconception concerning the nature of the disease can cause the patient.

A phenomenon of all psychopathology and a common ally to organic illness is *secondary gain*. Gaining attention, avoiding responsibility, controlling and tyrannizing the family, and similar means of capitalizing on and exploiting illness are all too familiar and can be seen most dramatically in "insurance neurosis," or "pension syndrome," where illness has brought some advantage to the patient and may operate unconsciously to retard his recovery. Thus an investigation of the patient's anxieties must include an examination of the superficial meaning that the illness holds for him, as well as the factors that derive from earlier notions that have been deeply repressed and find contemporary representation in psychic overlay.

Specific Problems of Cardiac Illness

Heart disease has certain unique sequelae: It is experienced as a *severe threat to life,* associated as it is with sudden death. Misconception about the diagnosis itself—for example, confusion of rheumatic heart disease with coronary disease—can result in inappropriate fear. More frequently, however, intrapsychic factors that have their dynamic roots in repressed fear of powerlessness, abandonment, and castration and which are now reawakened, account for the incapacitating fear of death.

Whereas the amputee, for example, does not often think of work as impairing his health, the cardiac patient frequently focuses on work as a hazard. His overwhelming fear that any exertion may shorten his life poses a special problem in his psychotherapy and especially in his rehabilitation. On the other hand, a cardiac patient with a defensive need to deny his illness may be self-destructive—for example, the patient who needs to push a piano around.

By the very nature of the organ involved, cardiac illness poses another unique problem. The heart is the symbol of basic human emotions—love, affection, and hatred—and therefore holds the position of primacy among all body organs. The cardiovascular system is a special participant in affect syndromes; arrhythmia, tachycardia, and dyspnea are somatic equivalents of anxiety and need not be referable to heart disease. Psychosomatic studies have shown that the cardiovascular system can respond to stress situations with increased heart rate, rise in systolic pressure, and increase in cardiac output. Physiological changes and disturbances in autonomic rhythm can in turn create apprehension and set in motion a psychosomatic circuit that challenges the most perceptive diagnostic skills. With anxiety manifestations that stimulate cardiac symptoms, and chronic tension states that effect internal physiological responses, the diagnostic problem created understandably adds nourishment to the hypochondriacal concerns of the cardiac patient.

Another factor that contributes to the disproportionate disability of some cardiac patients is what has come to be known as the *iatrogenic factor*. Physicians are likely to contribute more to the invalidism of the cardiac patient than to that of any other type of patient. This is probably related to the fact that as a group physicians are more likely than the general population to develop heart disease, and tend on the whole to be extremely apprehensive about having a coronary episode. They are apt to project onto their patients their own anxieties according to their own psychological needs and to advise their patients to be unduly restrictive.

Bellak and Haselkorn[18] were unable from their study material to establish any specific emotional constellations that were significantly correlated with the development of coronary disease. They found, however, that patients with a premorbid history of overcompensatory, competitive, aggressive behavior (used as a denial against excessive underlying passivity) appeared more emotionally threatened by coronary disease. For these patients, outlets for discharge of anxiety in excessive activity were denied by the cardiac disease. The resulting psychic conflict contributed further to the somatopsychological problem. Currently, a theory is prevalent that indeed, the aggressive person (Type A) is more prone to develop coronary artery disease than the more lighthearted person (Type B).

Specific Problems in Tuberculosis

Bellak[13] had the opportunity to study intimately and directly 46 tuberculosis patients, and through casework and treatment conferences was familiar with the histories of about two hundred fifty others. He reports that the first response to being informed of the diagnosis of tuberculosis was frequently an attempt at denial, the patient maintaining that it could not be so. Only in a very few patients was this denial pathologically prolonged. In the majority it was followed by a more or less pronounced depression. A catastrophic reaction was frequently based on some very primitive concept of tuberculosis, or occurred because it was seen in terms of the experience of another family member or acquaintance. The most profoundly disturbing effects seemed to exist in those cases with a familial history where the diagnosis led to identification with a previously affected family member. This was, of course, most traumatic in the case of men identifying with a previously ill mother. Acceptance of the illness also brought about a profound disturbance of the body image. In the case of men with a great libidinal investment in their masculine prowess, this was particularly upsetting. (This observation also holds true for several other chronic diseases, as most observations reported here hold true for the totally incapaciting or chronic diseases.)

A more specific response to the diagnosis of tuberculosis in some patients was the tendency to nausea and vomiting. This was particularly marked in one young man who started this symptom the day of the diagnosis and maintained it for years. In another young man, the idea of vomiting was associated from early childhood with being ill and the idea became reactivated when informed that he had tuberculosis. In a third young man, the nausea was associated with anorexia and he had to be hospitalized because of the danger of starvation.

In a young woman seen in private practice, the fear of tuberculosis manifested itself as a fear of pregnancy. Her father had died ot tuberculosis in her childhood, and an older sister died of the same illness during the patient's adolescence. The patient identified tuberculosis germs with sperm in an infantile fantasy of oral impregnantion. All her symptoms were related to this fantasy—the fear of having holes made in her and bleeding to death. In men, too, neurotic disturbances relate to oral-passive wishes and defenses against them.

Again, there was no evidence to indicate that a particular personality type appears more frequently among tuberculosis patients than in the general population. Their response to the illness could be clearly seen in relation to their pre-existing personalities; they varied in basic dynamics as much as any other group. Any similarity appeared to be a secondary change in response to the threatening disease and the chronic invalidism necessarily imposed for some years.

Two major responses to illness among the tubercular were noted which are most likely applicable to all or to the vast majority of patients who suffer a severe illness or disability: *increased secondary narcissism with changes in the body image;* and *increased oral needs and passivity.*

Rest is extremely important in the care of the tubercular, and all of his needs should be met. A premium is put on his paying attention to his illness, on his being passive, accepting all but spoon feeding; he is generally forced to accept, for the time being, the image of being a baby. (However, the current trend is to decrease passivity by permitting the patient as much self-direction as possible.)

That a good percentage of patients have a hard time giving up this attitude immediately upon being discharged from the sanatorium is thus not surprising. They have seen other patients return with relapses and they doubt with justification the doctor's criteria of heatlh. Those relatively healthy psychologically, are the ones who always had strong defenses against passivity and oral wishes: They will pass through this stage more or less easily. The more neurotic patients, who to begin with had a more infantile attitude or strong oral wishes, will hold on to the regressed position.

The problems of secondary gain of illness are most manifest among the neurotic tuberculosis patient; since he is an invalid, the patient is unconsciously set to enjoy all the advantages of being under constant care.

Organ Transplants, Hemodialysis, Open-Heart Surgery

These dramatic and heroic procedures—transplanting hearts and kidneys from donors to seriously ill patients, rigging patients to artificial kidney machines, opening the heart to repair or replace valves and create bypasses—induce severe psychological and emotional problems for the patients, the patients' families, and for the donor, if alive.

ORGAN TRANSPLANTS

The patient's illness, and its severity and locus in an emotionally significant organ, are likely to affect the patient's body image, and to increase narcissism, dependency, and social isolation. When renal or cardiac disease has existed since childhood or adolescence, stunted growth and retarded sexual and social development result, and are compounded by a confusion of identity, social aversiveness, protracted and increased dependency, depersonalization, and intense anxiety, especially the fear of death.

The literature on the psychological effects of kidney transplants on child and adolescent recipients has been reviewed by Zarensky.[174] Most of her observations are pertinent for adults and for recipients of donor hearts as well.

Among the crucial issues are:

1. Fantasies concerning the intermingling of the body images of recipient and donor—especially where the life of the patient is dependent upon the death of another—are severely disturbing and may provoke a psychosis if the premorbid ego functions are weak or tentative. Often, in renal transplants, the donor is a relative (success of the procedure is increased where there is a blood relationship between donor and recip-

ient). This relationship may either decrease or increase the severity of the reactions to body image, depending on the nature of the pretransplant relationship.

2. The recipient must deal with the likelihood of rejection of the transplanted organ, as well as the disturbing effects of the suppressive drugs which intensify the fear of death.
3. The recipient must struggle also with the need to accept emotionally (internalize) the donor organ. The process usually begins with feelings of strangeness and separation, of alienation from the organ. Gradually incorporation develops until full acceptance is achieved. Without completion of these latter steps the patient's discomfort may be extreme.
4. Family relationship problems are frequent. Dependency is likely to be encouraged, paralleled by excessive restrictions imposed on the patient by family members. These responses of family members will intensify the patient's fantasies of helplessness in the face of attack and mutilation, generated by the nature of the surgery. If the donor is a relative, the relationship between donor and recipient may intensify to a pathological level what previously were relatively dormant interactions.

HEMODIALYSIS

Where kidney function is inadequate to sustain life and an organ for transplant is not yet available, the patient is attached at regular intervals to a hemodialyzer. The machine removes toxic substances from the blood and excess water from the body. The process takes several hours, and must be repeated frequently.

These patients may exhibit any or all of the emotional difficulties and distortions to which any seriously ill person is vulnerable. Additionally, there are the patient's feelings of relationship to his lifesaver, the machine itself. The machine may become anthropomorphized, deified, or endowed with magical powers. It may be fantasized as a sexual partner whose connecting needles penetrate the patient's body, or as a sucking vampire that drains the blood from the patient and may not return it. Structuring reality is important in helping patients with such reactions endure the long period of passivity inherent in the treatment.

OPEN-HEART AND BY-PASS SURGERY

These procedures probably are the most frequently performed of all the recently developed heroic surgical procedures. Success rates are high, and the accompanying beneficial changes are dramatic. During 1975, 952 cardiovascular operations were performed at New York University Hospital in New York City (New York Times, March 17, 1976).

Essentially, the psychological difficulties encountered by the open-heart and by-pass surgery patient are similar to those of patients undergoing other types of surgery. All major surgery involves feelings of passivity and helplessness under the effects of anesthesia, the threat of the scalpel invading the body, the fears of attack and mutilation, the particular significance the individual patient ascribes to the area of the body and the organ being operated on, and the transference phenomena the patient frequently associates with the surgeon.

Open-heart surgery stimulates other specific reactions in addition to these. Because of the heart's function in sustaining life, the images of it stopping, of it being lifted out of the chest, of being attached to an artificial heart, all intensify the question of life and death for the patient. Many patients fear brain damage because of the long period of anesthesia that open-heart surgery requires. The chest-long incision, and the image of the ribs being sawed, dramatically affects the body image. Indeed, delirious episodes after open heart surgery are not rare.

SUMMARY OF DYNAMIC CONSIDERATIONS

The foregoing review of dynamic features observable in cardiac, tuberculosis, and surgical patients discloses a number of features applicable to victims of all severe illness and disability, including amputees and cancer patients. These are: (1) secondary narcissistic injury; (2) depression; (3) denial; (4) changes in the body image and self-image; (5) increased passivity and dependency, accompanied by an increase in oral demands and anger stemming from the disappointments and frustration; and (6) secondary gains.

THERAPEUTIC PROCEDURES

Psychotherapy is aimed at the isolation of the irrational aspects of the responses to an admittedly difficult reality situation, and to the peculiarly strong transference problems in the patient who is reduced almost to helplessness by his illness. Psychosomatic problems need simple, convincing explanation first, and then further interpretation. Depression and extensive denial of illness need prompt attention.

1. The therapist must assume a realistic attitude toward the seriousness of the patient's illness or disability; he must not minimize the realistic fears or the realistic extent of damage, nor the disabling effect of the illness. In large measure, the therapist's interventions will be directed toward clarification of misconceptions and distortions in the patient's body image and self-image, and in alienating the patient from the idea of

succumbing to the death process. With these considerations in mind, the therapist has available a number of therapeutic procedures.

2. The structure of the patient's unconscious, preconscious, or even conscious notion of his injury or illness should be established through the history, often with the aid of projective techniques such as the Draw-A-Person test and Thematic Apperception Test. With these misconceptions identified, the therapist may initiate a period of intellectual education. For instance, a discussion of the anatomy of a coronary and anastomotic repair (with a comparison to the healing of a fractured arm bone) may vastly improve the patient's body image.

3. The specific meaning of the illness to the patient must also be identified and insight achieved therapeutically. Thus a male patient's identification of his illness with the illness of his mother may lead to false conscious expectations and pathogenic female identification. A tuberculosis patient may need to be shown that his conception of the bleeding hole in his lung actually reveals childhood conceptions of female genitalia and castration. Among cancer patients, the oral aggressive features of the patient's personality may find exaggeration in the disease so that he perceives the cancer as an eating, boring, destroying phenomenon. With others in whom the sado-masochistic features are predominant, the cancer may be perceived as a brutal, sadistic, attacking introject. In a similar fashion, the specific meaning of death to the patient must be identified and dealt with.

    At least two therapeutic approaches are available for interfering with or preventing the patient's tendency to succumb to the death process: improving object relations, and increasing denial in certain areas without, at the same time, denying the seriousness of the illness. Both procedures are intended to utilize, even exploit, certain narcissistic attitudes in the service of making continued existence tolerable, acceptable, and even desirable.

4. Improvement of object relations may be sought by removing or mitigating conflictual elements between patient and spouse; emphasizing the positive features in relationships; helping the patient reestablish or strengthen ties between himself and parents, siblings, children, or other relatives; and by presenting the biological immortality inherent in survivors. These steps are indicated particularly when there is danger that the patient will commit suicide.

5. Serviceable denial may be achieved by helping the patient identify with prominent individuals who have survived a serious episode of the same disease or disability from which the patient suffers. Examples are Presidents Eisenhower and Johnson for the cardiac patient, General Curtis LeMay and Arthur Godfrey for the cancer patient, and Franklin D. Roosevelt for the orthopedically impaired.

ILLUSTRATIVE CASE HISTORIES

Depression and Passivity in an Orthopedically Disabled Man of Forty

Ten years after World War II, a disabled veteran of 40 was referred to a psychologist for psychotherapy. Both legs were severely crippled during the war, and he could walk only with great effort and the aid of braces and crutches. Repeated rehabilitation efforts by the Veterans Administration appeared to have failed: He was severely depressed, bitter, and hostile. He was seen for six sessions in brief psychotherapy.

A college graudate, he was intellectually perceptive, widely read. Prior to his disability he had been active, friendly, and sociable. Now he was withdrawn, and spent most of his time in passive, glowering rumination about his misfortune. As she had during his childhood illnesses, his now aged mother hovered over and served him.

During the first interview he expressed discontent that the therapist was not a "medical doctor." Much of the session he cried in bitter disappointment over the frustration of his young manhood wishes and ambitions. The therapist actively linked the two expressions and told the patient that he seemed to keep hoping that "the doctors" would give him back a pair of sound, healthy legs. This indeed was the criterion by which he had measured the outcome of his various rehabilitation programs, and by which he was about to evaluate his experience with psychotherapy. His intelligence and perceptiveness now entered into the service of insight and working through. A series of antecedent experiences were brought to light in which the theme was similar: a damaged bike he destroyed when he had difficulty repairing it; his persistent refusal for two years to learn to read when his first efforts encountered the usual, but to him unexpected difficulties. He came to see that his disturbance was due only in part to his disability, and in equal part, if not greater measure, to the failure of his omnipotence.

One experience followed another in his comprehension, self-assessment, and finally planning. Subsequent to his brief therapy he obtained a specially equipped car that increased his mobility and conserved his strength; he entered and completed a graduate program in vocational rehabilitation; and found employment as a counselor in that field.

Brief Therapy of Dangerous Defenses in the Victim of a Coronary Attack

An occasional patient will find the threat and enforced passivity of serious illness so intolerable that he will prefer to deny his illness by engaging in self-harming overexertion. The following may serve as a fairly representative case:

Mr. J., 45 at the time of his coronary attack, had led an energetic and ambitious physical life. As a young man, he had worked in many strenuous jobs, and for a while prided himself on being the fastest driver on a bus line. Later he had worked as a truck driver, delivering heavy material on a crowded schedule, making an excellent salary, and exulting in his stamina.

He now suffered from a depression reactive to a recent coronary attack and felt that life was not at all worthwhile as a "cripple"; he was obviously distressed by a loss of self-esteem and a loss of masculinity as a defense. He related that he had shared a bed with his father until he was 16, and had frequently awakened to see his father move to his mother's bed for a clearly overheard sexual interlude, and then return after that to the patient's bed. These experiences had engendered a good deal of homosexual anxiety in the patient, which of course he could not acknowledge. He had a conflictual relationship toward an older sister, and felt neglected by the mother who was a chronic invalid, having been said to have heart trouble since the patient's boyhood. To him, his coronary attack meant being a cripple, being a woman like his mother. The homosexual fears (manifested earlier in nightmares) became accentuated; they were largely related to the feminine identification aroused by sleeping with his father. He had defended against these fears by adopting an overbearing attitude toward his wife and by ventures that tended to convince him of his masculinity and power. The therapist was quickly able to see that the heart attack meant castration. Indeed, the patient's physical imagery of the coronary embolism was clearly of a phallic object having been inserted into a hollow tube—not so unrealistic and yet symbolically overinvested. Although he complained daily about his inability to provide for his family, in his responses to the T.A.T. he chose primarily female identification figures and projected feelings of being crippled and incapacitated.

The coronary occlusion was severely traumatic to Mr. J. He expressed suicidal ideas and made one half-hearted attempt by swallowing pills he had received from his doctor. During the rehabilitation period, he was often depressed, felt worthless, and attempted self-reassurance by physical feats. He assisted strangers in moving a piano, showed someone else how to lift a heavy burden, and cracked a door when it failed to open. He obtained great but temporary satisfaction from these deeds. He also insisted on spending money unnecessarily at times, as though to prove to himself that he still could.

Notions of invalidism because of the coronary were central in this patient's problem, and these notions were usefully explored. They were modeled on his observation of severe decompensation with swelling of limbs and immobility in his mother. This was explained to him as due to something similar to a leaky pump and quite different from his affliction. The coronary condition was not made light of but discussed with the help of a simple diagram illustrating the fact that the blood supply was shut off from part of the muscle, impairing its power. It was explained that as part of the repair, new blood vessels were growing, substituting for the occluded vessel. Instead of seeing regular work as dangerous, it was explained that moderate activity would encourage the growth of new blood vessels, while excessive work could be dangerous.

The concept of excessive masculine defense was explored with him. One day he felt somebody had pushed him intentionally in the subway, and he was very upset about having to restrain himself from retribution. That night he dreamed of a seal being shot by a big powerful man. It was not clear whether he primarily identified with the seal, or wishfully with the big man, but it was easily related to the day's event. An attempt was made to devalue the idea of physical combat among civilized men of mature age.

At the same time an effort was made to establish an informal man-to-man type relationship. He had considerable knowledge of photography, and it was easy for the therapist genuinely to show interest in learning from the patient. This gave the patient's self-esteem an obvious boost. The therapist even joined the patient in some slightly chauvinistic male viewpoints about women to help him feel less threatened by his wife's emerging role as contributor to the family's sustenance. The various defensive maneuvers of dangerous nature (e.g., the lifting of a heavy box) however, were vigorously interpreted as infantile, compensatory, and dangerous. An attempt was made to change the value system of "toughness" to one of "reasonableness."

As his physical condition improved with his rehabilitation work, his emotional growth seemed to keep pace, particularly as he had reason to feel less incapacitated and less acutely threatened.

12
Brief Psychotherapy in Sex Therapies

The past decade has witnessed a rapid proliferation of therapeutic services designed to ameliorate or cure sexual problems in a short time. For the most part these treatments are based on behavioral psychological procedures. The emphasis is usually upon what might be termed the mechanics of sexual behavior. Instructions are given for positions and procedures of giving and taking pleasure, along with instructions for inducing relaxation and the delay of orgasm. Little or no attention is given to the possible psychodynamics of the sexual dysfunction being treated—psychodynamics having little, if any, role in the behavioral approach. The presumption is probably that the sexually dysfunctional person who seeks sex therapy is motivated to change by the discomfort the sexual problem creates, and that such motivation is sufficient for the success of the process.

A notable exception is Kaplan's approach described by Sollod and Kaplan[158] in which the therapist moves through a therapeutic strategy that utilizes psychodynamic and interpersonal techniques along with the behavioral. The rationale is that the sexual response has an autonomic component that is easily affected by anxiety and which may either have a superficial etiology or may arise from deeply rooted conflicts or character traits. The borrowing from psychodynamic approaches involves the awareness of transference manifestations that facilitate or block the progress of sex therapy, the defensive structure of the personality, and resistance manifestations to the sexual exercises of the behavioral treatment. Kaplan emphasizes the behavioral intervention in preference to the dynamic and interpersonal, but shifts to the latter two whenever the behavioral approach fails.

Our practice has provided us the opportunity to participate in a number of sexual-therapy cases, both before the sex therapy was initiated and after the patients had encountered difficulty and failed to progress to their desired goal. Our experience with these cases indicated that some sessions of brief therapy oriented to uncovering the psychodynamic elements in the sexual dysfunction facilitated the success of the behavioral sex therapy. Brief therapy enlarged insight and increased cooperation by minimizing or even eliminating emotional blocks.

The therapist offering short-term approaches need not insist upon his services as a prelude to the sex treatment. Brief therapy may serve as an introductory exploration and preparation, or it may become part of the process only after the patient has failed to respond to the behavioral methods. The failure, should it occur, often intensifies and reinforces the motivation for a psychodynamic change: it increases the patient's willingness to form a therapeutic alliance, to give a meaningful history, and hence to become more open to developing insight. Our observation is that the failure to develop insight tends to sharpen the conflict and bring more dynamic material into a preconscious level of awareness. Concentration upon the mechanical aspects of sex in many instances brings conflicts involving disgust, aggression, fear of insanity, loss of control of bladder or bowels, and other impulses closer to the surface where they are more available for psychotherapeutic work. In other instances these same mechanics may arouse aversion and resistance.

Several prognostic cautions should be kept in mind. Brief therapy in sex treatments usually depends on the participation of both partners for a successful outcome. But as always there are exceptions to the rule. Sometimes one member of a couple is clearly identifiable as the dysfunctional partner in emotional conflict, so that work with one partner alone is justified. Usually, however, the procedure moves along best when neither partner bears the entire onus for the difficulties the couple has been experiencing; and when an emotional involvement exists between partners, an established pattern of sexual relationship that can best be analyzed through their mutual cooperation and the opportunity for ongoing sexual activity.

Prognosis also may depend on the duration of the dysfunction. The more recently emergent problem in a person or couple who have functioned reasonably well before is, on the surface, more likely to be an acute reaction to a currently provoking event. A man's impotence or premature ejaculation or a woman's frigidity may be a response to a partner's insult or infidelity, to grief induced by the loss of a loved person, or to exposure to a guilt-provoking situation. Normally functioning persons have become disrupted on visits to the home of parents, where unconscious interdictions inhibit sexual arousal, activity, or pleasure.

The clinician must always be cautious in judging recency of etiology. What may seem to be a recently emergent problem may have been mobilizing slowly over a period of years, during which the manifestations were largely unconscious or barely discernable as symptoms. Recalled dreams may give clues to earlier efforts to recognize and state the problem. On inquiry brief, inexplicable, or displaced periods of mood disturbance in retrospect may have been eruptions of the anxiety or depression presaging the sexual difficulty or conflict.

As is the case in most conflicts, long-established dysfunctions usually are more stubborn, more incorporated into character structure, and more resistant to change. Major exceptions occur when a long-enduring dysfunction results from a conflict between partners that has been kept alive but not engaged.

PROCEDURES

Since this is so often couple therapy, the major variant in the brief psychotherapy of sex problems is the ordering of the sessions governing when the couple is to be seen together or individually.

Usually both partners are seen together for the first session when, as is customary, a history of the problem and the couple's relationship is taken, and the therapist begins to formulate hypotheses concerning dynamics and contributing causes. It is advisable that the therapist not structure this meeting, so that the couple may be allowed to present and discuss the problem in their own way. Which of the partners will begin, for example, is left to the dynamics of their relationship; the resolution often identifies forces of dominance and passivity. The encouragement of the exchange of fantasies is a valuable technique. The therapist identifies the less inhibited of the partners, elicits fantasies related to the problem or to sex in general, and then asks the more reticent partner to participate. It is to be expected that the more innocuous fantasies will be offered first and that others might be seriously modified or not recalled at all. Yet the approach is often successful and unusually illuminating both for the couple and for the therapist's comprehension of the dynamics. Most important, the technique has the potential for bringing the partners to a more candid and intimate level of communication, one that may be initiated in the first session and continued by each partner in individual sessions and when they reassemble jointly for later work.

In the second and third sessions, each partner is seen individually. Their personal histories are pursued in greater depth, enabling formulations concerning their particular contribution to the joint problem. Often, material of a critical diagnostic nature emerges for the first time, or heretofore unexpressed complaints that are central to the problem are voiced. Sometimes the basic complaint emerges as a very simple matter; the husband doesn't wash his hands before lovemaking or the wife's breath is malodorous. Interpretations may be made in these individual sessions, along with suggestions, if they are indicated.

The fourth and fifth sessions bring the partners together again. In the fourth session their reactions to, and thoughts and feelings about, the preceding joint and individual sessions are discussed. Interpretations and clarifications are offered. The interplay of their indiviudal conflicts is delineated by the therapist, along with the effects upon their sexual relationship. This session is significant for both prognosis and the therapist's planning for future recommendations. What becomes clearest in this session is the degree to which both partners can exchange their feelings and thoughts that were stimulated by the individual meetings. Moreover, the therapist can sense whether there is an alliance in which the individuals are striving to preserve their relationship, or whether, as is often the case, one or both partners are resolved to break it up. The nature of their interchange also will permit the therapist to determine if one or both partner's problems are so entrenched that long-term therapy is indicated because sex therapy will probably fail.

The fifth session is similar to the fourth in working through the preceding material. Also, of course, there is a summing up with recommendations for the future. The couple is invited to return after sex therapy or during it if further critical material emerges. A follow-up meeting is arranged.

ILLUSTRATIVE CASE HISTORIES

Brief Therapy in a Case of Impotence and Frigidity

Jill and Dan were referred by Jill's gynecologist. Jill complained of a low-key sexual relationship. Jill was nonorgasmic although she got pleasure from sex, and Dan experienced great difficulty in achieving erection. They were nearly 40, handsome, well dressed, athletic, financially comfortable, and socially active. They had one child.

Their marriage had started badly. Dan had been very much attracted to Jill and very much in love with her, but she had not cared as much for him. She became pregnant by another man (she gave much emphasis to the fact that conception took place during foreplay, not intercourse) and decided to induce Dan to marry her by getting him to believe that he had made her pregnant. He found her behavior so unreasonable that he pursued her reasoning, uncovered the true story, then married her and saw her through an abortion—"the knight in shining armor."

Through the 15 years of their marriage Dan was obsessed with the thought that she had attempted to deceive him and that she really had not loved him. He had come to believe that she did love him now, but this conviction was not stable and was subject to periods of uncertainty. Priding himself on gentleness and understanding, he withheld rage and recrimination to the point that he did not know he was experiencing them. He was also vindictive, brooding on this "injustice," and waiting for an opportunity to retaliate. Jill appeared to carry a burden of shame more than guilt; she had done something dirty and was caught, and then lied. They had joined each other in a conspiracy of denial: "Except for sex ours is a fine, open, communicative marriage." But they had never talked this matter out.

Although this history seemed to provide a rather dramatic etiology for their difficulties, the individual sessions indicated that it would be seriously erroneous to rely upon it as the major, let alone the sole cause of their sexual problems. Their individual histories indicated the probability that they would have had sexual problems in any case.

Jill was narcissistic and frigid. Appearance was everything for her and she had not begun to take pride in herself until her teens when she had her nose bobbed and her teeth capped, and she reduced her weight by heroic dieting. Sex between her parents was often embarrassingly audible. She listened, but denied any feelings of excitement or revulsion. She also denied being affected by perceiving her mother in a submissive, devalued role. Puritanical and inhibited, she had never masturbated, refused to have lights on during sex, and was unwilling to initiate sex or be assertive during it. However, she needed to know that she was desirable, and knew it only through Dan's wish for her. The less he had to do with her, the more she needed his sexual attention, not for genital gratification but for assurance. And the guiltier she felt about deceiving him, the more she needed these demonstrations from him. She, in her inhibition, could not respond to him, and by withholding his attentions, he had the perfect weapon to punish her.

Dan had developed surface self-control to a fine art. He prided himself, "I can manage anything." He had had to manage the early established evidence that his mother overvalued his older brother and depreciated him, that he was never of primary priority in her values, and that nothing new was ever purchased for him but came down second-hand from his brother. He was very ill as a child and in one particular illness felt he was neglected to the point of being in danger of dying. He denied his rage at feeling deprived and indeed became intensely aversive to its experience. He sought acceptance in achievement and in being sensitive, tender, and agreeable. Ironically, his personality developed in a way that later enabled Jill to easily deceive him.

The restraint of rage led to restraint of sexuality. He always had been low-keyed and never had a more intense sexual relationship than with Jill. He had had a few brief and tangential relations, more to prove he was functional than from feelings of sexual deprivation, just as Jill now considered the possibility of having an affair to reestablish her desirability. A recent myocardial infarction contributed to his current need to restrain intensity of affect.

The prognosis did not appear favorable. Fixed character traits in each partner suggested a rigidity that would not respond to either brief psychotherapy or sex treatment. When it became evident that neither would accept a more intensive approach to psychotherapy, the briefer method was attempted.

Two additional individual sessions were used to interpret their individual dynamics in relation to their past, and the mode of their interaction. An effort was made not to bring about a significant change in these dynamics, but rather to obtain agreement for more openness in communication between them. They agreed to meet together again with the therapist to talk through the experience of deceit and their ongoing feelings about it and their subsequent relationship.

Two joint sessions followed. In these they talked through their roles and reactions for the first time. Dan mildly expressed his anger. Jill asked his forgiveness, admitting that her behavior had been deceitful, and that she had been and was holding back. Dan also acknowledged his fear of death if he became too excited. They agreed to try to communicate better with each other, to concentrate on giving each other more time, more caring, and more pleasure rather than focusing only on orgasm for Jill. They were referred for sex therapy with the goal of fostering their agreement to give each other more pleasure, and to mobilize this agreement into a course of action.

Three times during the next year they returned for joint sessions to facilitate their talking through periods in which they were slipping back into the former mold of silent hostility. The relationship had improved somewhat, though it was still low-keyed. Dissatisfactions were less intense. Eighteen months later the referring gynecologist reported that they appeared to be reasonably content with each other. Jill no longer manifested sexual dissatisfaction. They were planning to have a second child

From many points of view this was a compromise situation. One may reason that a more satisfactory equilibrium and more favorable prognosis would have been probable, had this couple been convinced to accept more intensive individual therapy. However, their character structures and manifest resistance to the recommendation of a longer therapy warranted this compromise.

Brief Therapy with a Couple with Negative Body Images

A couple in their mid-thirties, married for ten years, with two children, complained that they were constantly out of phase with each other. The husband, Alan, wanted more physical expression; it upset him that his wife, Sandra, resisted. He stated that his wife had been disturbed by his sexual reticence early in their marriage. He conjectured that she had borne this resentment and now was "paying him back." When she wanted him, he withdrew; when he wanted her, she withdrew. There were many positive aspects of their relationship. Most important, they expressed a great deal of genuine caring for each other.

Each spouse was burdened by intensely negative feelings about selfhood and body image. From these feelings emerged strong doubts that they were loved or lovable. The self-esteem of each was badly damaged, and they were constantly out of phase with each other in their efforts to communciate. Sex therapy had begun but was not progressing; their scheduled and structured sexual couplings appeared to intensify their conflict rather than ameliorate it.

Individual sessions brought out pertinent histories indicating that each was laboring under strongly negative feelings, most significantly about body image. As a young girl Sandra had been flattered by her father's seductiveness, but later experienced a painful rejection by him when she developed from a beautiful pre-Oedipal child into an overweight and acned Oedipal-and-latency child and then to an adolescent. She became confused and doubtful about her desirability, and feared that her body was being used while her real self was being devalued. She wanted to talk, to share ideas, feelings, values: "Sex is no great deal." So she held back. Beneath this dynamic was the feeling that she was not worthy of pleasure. Resentment mounted in a defensive way, and to restore and preserve her self-esteem she denied her husband the opportunity to give or derive pleasure.

Alan had been reared by a domineering mother who neglected her children for her own career. He felt deprived and became furious, but he restrained and denied his anger. Early in college this defense backfired and he developed ulcerative colitis, underwent two surgeries, and now had a permanent ileostomy. Certainly this situation posed a real damage to his body as well as to his body image. Nonetheless he experienced two sexual affairs after the surgery. Despite the two affairs (one with Sandra before she became his wife), he continued to doubt that he was sexually acceptable. While he had difficulty communicating verbally, he obtained relief for his tension by physical activity, and regularly played tennis to exhaustion.

Each felt that something vital to their continued lives was missing from their relationship; they did not want to continue what appeared to be senseless routines of work and child care. They both were affect hungry.

In subsequent joint sessions, they were induced to tell each other how they felt about their past lives and how their thinking affected their body images. Moreover, they were encouraged to tell each other their fantasies about their bodies and the body of their partner. Sandra feared that Alan would emit feces through the ileostomy, and cover her body with it. The therapist related this fantasy to her acne and suggested that acne and feces were equated in her mind. Alan had a related fantasy, that his ejaculation would take place through the ileostomy rather than his penis.

Working through the negative feelings about body image manifestly decreased the tension between this essentially caring couple. Their subsequent sex therapy was successful, and promoted a freer, more frequent exchange, both sexually and in other areas of communication.

13
The Elderly Patient

This chapter discusses principles and procedures for dealing psychotherapeutically with the aged and their short-term major problems that are likely to respond to psychotherapy. Although considerable material has been written about emergency and brief therapy for the average adult, and a fair amount about children,[9, 10, 104, 156] little deals specifically with the subject of the aged.

BASIC PRINCIPLES AND PROCEDURES

The general principles for emergency psychotherapy for the aged are the same as for younger populations. However, the therapist also must have knowledge and experience with the geriatric population in general, and with the special ills and problems of the aged in particular.

Emergency psychotherapy may be chosen for several reasons. Some elderly people will be impatient with intensive therapy, though they may clearly require some assistance in times of crisis. The therapist can use an emergency approach to alleviate the crisis, thus helping the person to continue functioning, while preventively forestalling more serious maladaptations. Many elderly patients have limited insurance coverage, and centers which cater to a heavily aged population may be short staffed.

The major principles employed in brief therapy are particularly appro-

Some of the material in this chapter has been taken from Bellak, L., and Karasu, B. in *Geriatric Psychiatry*. New York: Grune & Stratton, 1976. By permission of the publisher.

priate in treating elderly patients; because they often feel they have little time left in life, the brevity and directness of approach are welcomed by elderly patients who seek quick relief from emotional discomfort. Those with little family or few friends respond favorably to establishing and maintaining a positive transference, and to the emphasis on support and interpretation, coupled with medical and environmental intervention.

Brief psychotherapy can be utilized over the telephone if the patient is immobilized. The sessions themselves may have to be appropriately brief, with 15 minutes suitable for those patients with reduced attention span. However, if the patient's attention span is not diminished and there is no physical exhaustion, the usual psychotherapeutic session of 45 or 50 minutes can be employed readily.

It is essential for the therapist to keep in mind that emergency therapy demands precision of thought and economy of intervention. Our ability to help the elderly patient will come from *understanding nearly everything and doing only the little that makes a difference*. Thus it is as necessary to begin by obtaining a complete history from the elderly patient as from the younger adult. In fact, it is even more necessary; for the aged patient, history giving itself provides gratification, especially if the person has been suffering from a lack of meaningful communication or attention. If the patient cannot give an adequate history, relatives should be consulted if they are available and caring.

Understanding the precipitating event in its proper relation to the current situation and general history is also necessary. For example, any significant loss, especially of a loved one, always has dynamic effects. The therapist should expect marked individual reactions, ranging from severe depression (including suicidal thoughts), to appropriate grieving followed by continued growth. If the patient's particular reaction to loss is understood, the therapist can deal more effectively with the effects of a current loss. The patterns of the patient's current life in areas such as social functioning, physical illness, and the family network are secondary major aspects which should be incorporated into the overall comprehension of the loss.

Identification of problem areas may be facilitated through the use of projective techniques. The Senior Apperception Technique (SAT)[34] was designed specifically to identify some of the more frequent situations leading to psychiatric problems in the aged. The test consists of 16 pictures of people in various situations common to the elderly. Only the pictures relevant to the patient need be used. The patient is asked to tell a story about what is happening in the picture as each individual card is presented. Information about the patient's anxieties, conflicts, and problems is gained from the content of the stories and the manner in which they are told.

The following three stories, told by a 72-year-old woman, serve as a brief example.

The story to Picture 3 is somewhat unusual. The popular theme in response to this picture is usually one of competition for the affection of the

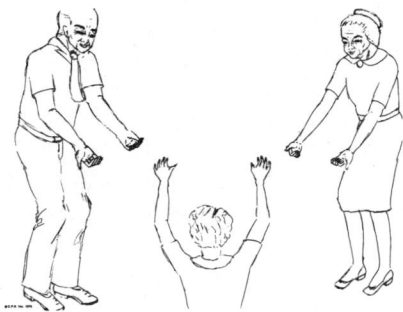

Picture 3

The grandparents are stretching their arms out to catch their little grandson before he falls. His hands are up in the air as he is about to tumble. Grandmother catches him in time and embraces him

Picture 8

This woman has a neighbor in for a little snack. She slips a little and the bowl slips out of her hand. She is annoyed because this neighbor is a gossip and might tell others that the woman is losing her grip, but she gets a mop and cleans up the mess.

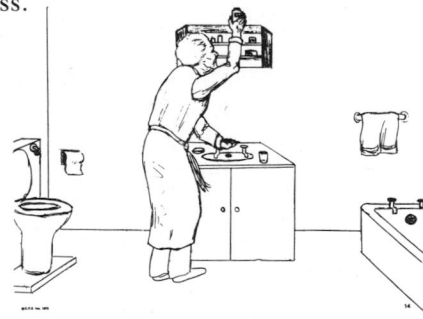

Picture 14

This man is just going to bed. He is taking some medicine for his digestion. He supports himself with his other hand on the washbasin. He hates taking medicine, but when you get older, nothing works the way it used to.

small central figure. In this case the story may communicate a positive asset available to this elderly person, a sense of love and communication with family. On the other hand, the story to Picture 8 revolves around loss of motor control, and in Picture 14, the detail of the man supporting himself with one hand is noted and the remark made that "nothing works the way it used to." Thus it may be that the story to Picture 3 is a projection of this woman's concern with loss of control onto the grandson, or identification with his helpless infantile state. She expresses the wish to be helped in this lightly defensive disguise. In the story to Picture 8, which involves a figure who is manifestly closer to her, she is afraid of loss of control to the other woman and gathers her strength for dealing with the mess effectively.

The stories illuminate some aspects of this woman's problems. She requested a consultation because she worried about dreaming too much—more than ever in her life, sometimes in color. She felt her dreams were whole reveries of her past and wondered whether this was normal. She appeared to suffer from a mild agitated depression.

Her complaint showed a concern about her sanity, a fear of losing control of her mind. A brief history revealed that her mother had become psychotic in middle age, which upset the patient a great deal. The mother had had to be hospitalized.

In the course of the interview, this elderly woman complained about the insufficient interest she felt her two daughters were taking in her, and she worried about her own future. The stories to the SAT made it clear that she was also concerned about some loss of motor control and the general functioning of her body. In the stories, she made slight use of projection. This made it more understandable that she was projecting some of her feelings toward her own mother onto her daughters in wondering if they were going to put her in an old age home as soon as she could not manage well enough in her small apartment. It appeared likely that she dreaded her loss of control as a psychosis, similar to her mother's, and that she also had some conflict about her dependency wishes.

She was reassured about the normalcy of dreaming with a discussion of the findings of recent sleep research. She was told that the occasional dreams in color might be due to a drug she had been taking for arthritic pains. It was not difficult to make her aware that she was afraid of "going crazy" as her mother did. Some reality testing and a discussion of her situation, her feelings about herself, the ambivalent feelings toward her mother, and her expectations from her daughters, brought a considerable relief in four half-hour sessions.

After formulating an understanding of the contemporary disorder and the precipitating event, the selection of the psychological areas of intervention, the methods of intervention to be employed, and the sequence of areas and methods are guided by the principles set forth in earlier chapters.

Intrapsychic awareness of cognitive defects may be a specific factor in the crises of the aged. Depression is a frequently encountered reaction signalling loss of loved ones, or self-esteem lowered by infirmity, physical changes, sexual changes, and anger inwardly deflected.

Attention to possible physical ailments or physiological problems causing emotional crises are other specific concerns for brief therapy. The drug factor deserves specific consideration because it plays such a large role with the elderly. Various crises of the aged—confusion, panic, sleeplessness—may be due to excessive drug intake or to a mixture of drugs ingested more frequently than by robust younger adults.

Attempts at adaptive constructions in the aged may take the form of delusions, hallucinations, and other disturbances. Frequently these symptoms are easily reversible. The method, not unlike what Rosen[141] described as the "direct analysis" of psychotics, is direct interpretation of the content of the delusion, hallucination, or other symptomatology.

Again, we emphasize the advisability of brief sessions and extensive work with the family, occasionally even to the exclusion of the patient. In every instance the therapist should try to establish a warm relationship; even prescribing and dispensing drugs should assume the nature of serious personal transactions, with careful explanations and written instructions.

Teamwork is important to all phases of geriatric psychiatry. Especially in brief and emergency psychotherapy, it is often necessary to direct both the patient and family to helping agencies which provide family guidance, housing, medical care, social opportunities, and job-finding services.

SOME SPECIFIC PROBLEMS OF THE ELDERLY

Occasionally geriatric patients will experience some disturbances of a relatively minor nature that nevertheless make life miserable for them, their families, and their associates. Most of these problems occur in nongeriatric patients as well, but are not likely to bring them into brief therapy. However, inherent in these problems are certain unique geriatric aspects, foremost of which is their ability to produce panic in the patient or relatives.

Absentmindedness and forgetfulness are the most frequent complaints. Etiology and meaning are varied and still under question. Some research findings maintain that forgetfulness correlates with depression rather than cortical changes. Registration, storage, and retrieval are three components of memory; in any given case all three aspects may be involved, or any combination thereof, with or without organic changes. Clinically speaking, we have found that preoccupation is likely to be the most frequent cause of absentmindedness, aside from depression and organic deterioration.

Absentmindedness and forgetfulness come to the clinician's attention when they involve some danger to the patient: The elderly person forgets to lock doors or turn off heaters, leaves keys in locks, etc. Unless a mental status examination reveals organic changes, discussion and reassurance may be the only therapy needed. Since absentmindedness may in fact be caused by increasing self-preoccupation, social contact and constructive activities are somewhat successful remedies. Mild anxiety-reducing drugs also may be indicated if the patient exhibits prolonged agitation.

Accumulations of mementoes and objectively useless objects is also a relatively frequent symptom in some aged people. Unless trash accumulation constitutes a danger or a major nuisance, there is no reason to be concerned clinically. It is important to remember that these accumulated objects are the patient's attempts to maintain an identity and relationship with the past. They often serve a gratifying need if they remind the patient of a happier time—a time with greater dignity and health.

Sometimes accumulations of objects are a response to a feeling of loss: the loss of a variety of faculties and abilities, of love objects, and unconsciously, the loss of life.

If anal-retentive tendencies played a major role in the personality in earlier life, accumulation of useless objects may be a reversion to earlier defenses against the feeling of loss or of getting lost or losing control.

Bizarre accusations, like persecutory ideas, may be a way of expressing a need for more attention and contact: They may be an exaggerated version of something that is really happening—a way of describing hostility that the patient feels on the part of someone taking care of him or her—or they may be delusional. In the aged, they are a defense mechanism and are often quite transparent. Decreased blood supply and poor nutrition may be responsible. Social isolation usually plays a large part.

These accusations, including statements that the patient is being plotted against, poisoned, raped, or otherwise physically abused may be particularly trying for family members. They may center on certain individuals or may shift from family member to family member, nurse to nurse.

Bodily preoccupation.   Generally speaking, there is more preoccupation with the body in the aged because the body tends to function less smoothly than in the healthy adult. Furthermore, its deterioration or alteration is a visible sign of the individual's changing identity.

People with a great deal of *body narcissism* in their earlier life are likely to experience an increase in narcissism with aging. Women for whom beauty was of prime importance, and men for whom machismo played a major role, are likely to be especially affected by the aging process per se. Whatever the earlier level of narcissism may have been, the body changes accompanying aging are likely to be upsetting to one's self-image: the decrease in strength, the limiting of physical effectiveness, the decrease in sexual response, the changes in skin, etc.

Concern about elimination and *anxiety over incontinence* are frequent problems. In some cases, a lifelong concern about elimination may become more noticeable to others when the older person becomes dependent. Alternatively, the aged individual may use concern about elimination as a means of gaining attention, or may overinvest in elimination as a focus of other concerns.

Bowel problems may respond to a change in diet. Adhering to a schedule of toileting, refraining from liquids prior to bedtime, and wearing pads or special undergarments may help an elderly person with a frequent need to go to the bathroom, who may feel in danger of embarrassing himself in public. These preventive measures also reassure him that he has not lost all self-control.

Illness tends to lead to distortions and excessive preoccupation with the body image and the organ image. As in younger patients, a split identification may occur, and one part of the self may treat the rest as if one were a nurturing parent and the other an ailing child. Sometimes an organ or organ system is anthropomorphized in a similar way.

Emphasis on the body part may be initiated by others, a nurse or relatives, who become excessively preoccupied by the patient's physical symptoms until their interaction with the patient is distorted. In such instances family counseling is important.

Often irrational ideas and faddish notions concerning bodily function, health, and remedies for ailments can best be dealt with by information and education. If the patient becomes conscious of playing the role of the indulgent parent with himself and can understand that disadvantages result from such excessive preoccupation—namely, worry, absentmindedness, and unnecessary invalidism—an ameliorization may occur.

Confusion frequently brings the aged person, or more often the patient's children, to seek help. Lack of orientation to time, place, and person is a very alarming symptom that can lead to many everyday complications, such as not finding the way home, and not recognizing, or misidentifying, close relatives. In the absence of very definite organic changes, such confusion is usually due to the lack of daily contacts and will respond to variations of what has been called *reality therapy*—a repeated discussion of the facts of everyday life.

Delusions and **hallucinations** are attempts to deal with fears, anxieties, hopelessness, and helplessness, which may or may not be successful. Sometimes they are useful to the patient but troubling to those interacting with him, and sometimes they are disturbing to the patient as well.

Delusions are false beliefs maintained in the face of good evidence to the contrary. Hallucinations are things seen or heard by someone but by no one else. They may occur separately or in combination. A person may form a delusion to compensate for an unpleasant reality, such as the elderly individual who insists she is young, wealthy, and sexually desirable, or the person who hallucinates a love object who is not physically present, not unlike the imaginary friends of childhood.

Other delusions and hallucinations are painful to the individual, like a nightmare that continues into the waking hours. Some delusions are caused by guilt. For example, an old man suddenly believed he had syphilis of the brain. He was fearful and distraught and cried in shame. As it turned out, he had had a sexual dream and was overwhelmed with guilt. Early adolescent fears emerged. He knew he was not functioning mentally as well as he used to, and had been troubled by this. Now all these factors merged and he suffered a painful delusion.

Sometimes repressed sexual desires are projected onto someone else if they are considered objectionable by the conscience. A person may then accuse others of making sexual advances toward him and may even go so far as to develop elaborate defenses against the imagined behavior.

Loss of control over events in the elderly person's life, memory, or physical functions plays a role in the formation of delusions that things are being taken away from him.

Sometimes delusions come and go spontaneously in old age. Increasing contacts and activities may help. In some cases, hallucinations may be due to visual or auditory impairment. Delusions may result from malnutrition or reduced blood supply to the brain. In some cases, small doses of phenothiazines may be effective, with caution taken against excessive doses and undesirable side effects.

Death, and its imminence.   Our society increasingly has come to recognize that death is a preoccupation of many elderly persons, and that many are made more comfortable by being allowed to discuss its imminence and their feelings about it. The preoccupation may encompass primitive fears about death, the separation from loved ones, or a review of one's past life and its worth. Relatives often are uncomfortable with an open discussion of the topic and attempt to silence or falsely reassure the elderly person. The preoccupation is intensified by illness, surgery, and increased incapacity. It is assuaged in those who have a firm belief in a good life in a hereafter, a belief that should not be challenged. It is especially important that elderly persons be tested for the degree of death denial being exercised, and that care be taken for it not to be penetrated too rapidly, if at all.

Emotional lability may perturb elderly patients. Some older people have a tendency to extreme or inappropriate moods, especially to cry very readily. They may fear that this indicates a general childishness or senility and may require support in various forms.

Insomnia, with various attending complications, is a frequent complaint of older people. It is often due to their sleeping too much in the daytime out of boredom, depression, or in response to some medication which has a hypnotic side effect. Some drugs, including drinking too much coffee or tea, may keep people awake. Loneliness and a variety of fears prevent some people from falling asleep. In that case, it is often found useful to keep a light on or a radio or television going. Rather than having a disturbing effect, this provides some feeling of contact. If the older person's room is far from the rest of the family, moving closer to others may provide the necessary comfort.

Of course, some older people may not require much sleep, and simply be worried about this, or their family may dislike their moving around at night when everyone else is sleeping. In that case, reassurance that sleep requirements vary and devising activities for the person at night may be all that is needed.

Sometimes older people insist that neighbors are intentionally keeping them awake at night and respond by banging on the walls or ceilings. It may be that neighbors are playing music very loudly, or the bass vibrations may be particularly disturbing. Sometimes neighbors, impatient with the old person, *may* be making unwarranted noise. Or it may be that the older person is expressing a desire to have someone take an interest in him, a need to have someone close by at night, or a feeling of lack of control over the environment, by projecting onto the neighbors. In such cases, appropriate intervention can affect a change.

Loquaciousness and *clinging behavior* in the elderly are particularly annoying to those around them. Sometimes an endlessly embroidered story is a desperate attempt to maintain contact with others. The old person may cause embarrassment or pain by telling old secrets. In some cases, this is because the aged person does not want to take the secret to the grave; in other instances, it may be an expression of spite or revenge. Sometimes the stories may be fabricated as an attention-getting device.

Physical clinging may be the only way the older person knows to obtain affection and physical contact. Reassurance and physical contact in the form of handholding, back rubs, hair brushing, relaxing baths, and the like will probably limit loquaciousness and clinging behavior.

Manic states are less frequent in the aged than depression and almost exclusively occur in individuals who have had earlier manic episodes. Manic behavior in the elderly may cause anger or embarrassment to their families because it is often considered inappropriate, particularly if it involves excessive sexual acting out, grandiose plans, or extreme anger.

Nagging and *repeated questions* are often a form of reality testing on the part of the older person who feels his hold on reality is slipping. This symptom may also be the patient's way of maintaining some object relationship and thus signal that there is not enough of it. Reassurance, confirmation of reality, and increased interaction may minimize this behavior.

Persecutory ideas are often the result of the patient's diminished hold on reality. Less able to engage in reality testing and to fend for himself, the individual is more concerned about being deceived or having things taken. Less able to trust himself, the patient becomes more suspicious of others. Some persecutory ideas are a simple desire to have others take an interest; occasionally they present a more complex phenomenon of projection.

In urban neighborhoods where the elderly are the routine prey of muggers, if an older person expresses a fear of injury or molestation, protection in the form of companionship or a move to another neighborhood is necessary.

Reality denial may be the elderly person's means of holding on to autonomy, such as when the aged individual insists on being able to live alone when this is clearly impossible.

Emotional and physical *regression* may occur because the older person has a need to be dependent and cared for. Sometimes the regression is exaggerated because the older person thinks this role is expected. Sometimes those caring for the elderly individual reinforce this behavior. It is important for the older person to retain as much independence as possible and to satisfy dependency needs without reverting unnecessarily to childlike behavior.

Uncustomary *selfishness* sometimes occurs in the elderly. The need for gratification may be so great that the older person is unaware of how his behavior affects others. It may be that the old person starts putting himself first when he feels time is running short. Or, sensing resentment on the part of those who care for him, the aged person becomes miserly. Hostility or anger at being old, and jealously of the young, may be expressed through selfishness.

On the other hand, adult children accusing their parents of selfishness may be expressing an unrealistic desire that their parents continue to respond to them with the selfless generosity appropriate for very young children. This may represent the wish that their parents are not becoming old.

Sexual acting out.　The idea that someone is making advances to the patient is often a very simple expression of the *wish* to be found interesting and attractive, as a denial of manifest physical and sexual changes. Or it may be a way of expressing the patient's own feelings of sexuality, which may be repressed out of a belief that older people no longer have such feelings, or that such feelings are bad. With complaints of infidelity, there is probably a pre-existing personality pattern of jealousy. As at any other age, feelings of inadequacy or latent homosexual needs may be projected.

Sexual behavior may include reaching for breasts or genitals, and in such a case, is frequently primarily an attempt to establish some general physical contact. This behavior, often disturbing to the people around the aged person, can probably be modified by providing attention and some acceptable bodily contact.

In both sexes, in the case of considerable confusion and other regression, exhibitionism in the aged expresses the need to be found attractive and desirable, just as it does in children. Sometimes, males accused of exhibitionism have actually been urinating in the absence of public toilet facilities. Older people are especially appreciative of the beauty of young skin, and an innocent reaching out to touch a child's cheek may be misinterpreted as a more sinister act. In such cases, contact with children or pets, or even sensuous fabrics or luscious fruit, may provide gratification.

It should be kept in mind that sometimes when older people claim they are being followed or molested, they are telling the truth. News reports of old women who have been raped and murdered are not uncommon. Sometimes patients are physically mistreated in old age homes. Thus, one must always take such claims seriously and provide for the older person's safety.

Stealing in the aged, as with children, may represent the need for love, or a feeling of impoverishment. It may indicate a need for greater excitement in daily life. Of course, it may also be a realistic response to an inadequate income.

14
Some Critical Life Situations and Extrinsic Traumata

All contemporary events are influenced by unique past experiences in terms of each individual's constellation of congenital, physiological, cognitive, structural, and experiental factors. This unique whole results from the interaction of the biological Anlage with the experiental factors.

In discussing some critical life situations and extrinsic traumata, we can only outline some of the specific aspects but must otherwise firmly adhere to the general principles of brief psychotherapy discussed throughout this volume.

Whatever the contemporary problem may be, it has to be brought into relationship not only with the entire contemporary situation and whatever precipitating factors may have contributed to it: Above all, it must be related to the *entire life history of the person involved,* the entire persona. The contemporary event has to be understood in terms of its apperceptive distortion by all previous life events.

To the extent to which insight plays a role, continuity has to be established between the common denominators in the current problem and those of earlier life situations. As in all instances, the most useful proposition to keep in mind is the attempt to understand by finding a continuity between childhood and adulthood, between waking and dreaming thought, and between normal and adaptive behavior and pathology.

If insight is not a primary tool, then all the other methods of interventions, whatever they may be, must still be based on the understanding gained by bridging the discontinuities. This holds true for support in case of an accident, education in case of illness, or a decision not to interfere with denial in some cases of dire circumstance. Whether we deal with mugging, malignancy, rape, joblessness or an accident, we must help with our vast armamentarium in terms of what we can understand about this particular person, aided by what we know generally about one or the other kinds of problems.

We emphasize again that whatever crisis brings the patient to therapy, it is important to try to understand the impact of the contemporary crisis in terms of the patient's life situation. One accident victim may respond by primarily feeling a threat to his ability to control, while another will have fears of mutilation or problems of narcissism. The word "primarily" deserves special attention: Each crisis usually involves five or six basic factors whose rank order of importance will vary from person to person so that an overriding factor in one person but will be of minimal importance in another.

The therapist should be knowledgeable about the factors generally relevant for each crisis; without general propositions we have no science. In this sense, the psychotherapist uses the knowledge and rules of his profession much as the surgeon uses guidelines for the optimal sequence of surgical interventions: anatomical areas and structures to be dealt with, physiological considerations concerning stress, and complicating factors.

Jacobson and his colleagues[94] at the Benjamin Rush Institute identified the generic and the individual approaches to crisis as guides to the application of interventions. The *generic* concept holds that each type of crisis provokes its own unique pattern of response. The *individual* concept embraces the importance of the bio-psycho-social events in the individual's life. At the same time that a general frame of reference is utilized, the therapist must be flexible by adapting to and conceptually incorporating the individual responses of each patient that derive from his personal bio-psycho-social past.

The subject of a divorce action is likely to have feelings of rejection and problems of separation. For one husband, his wife's bringing suit—rather than both partners agreeing that lawyers negotiate conditions—meant to him that she did not trust him to be fair and reasonable. His personal concern with feelings of trustworthiness and honesty provoked a severe crisis, so that it was necessary to understand why this contemporary event produced such intense concern about his trustworthiness. What life history factors caused him to perceive the situation in this particular way? The usual feelings of rejection and separation were secondary to this question.

Although many crisis-producing events will cut dynamically across these lines, most critical life situations may be grouped under three headings: those that involve violence and arouse fears for one's life, health, and sense of self; the loss of self esteem; and the loss of love or of loved ones.

A serious accident, mugging, or rape; a serious illness or death-threatening incident; or the disorganizing effect of hallucinogenic drugs may all arouse fears about one's sense of self, frequently accompanied by feelings of depersonalization and fears of regressive disorganization. Those crises provoking loss of self-esteem and the experience of rejection or separation include job loss, divorce, an unhappy love affair, financial reverses, and aging, among others.

Medical and surgical problems often cut across these lines and involve fears of death, incapacity, and disfiguration. Certain situations such as abortion and decisions about heroic methods of life support systems are likely to stimulate conflicts involving conscience, aggression, and identification.

Hospitalization often produces a crisis in self-esteem which has been vividly described by both physicians and patients.[137a] Suddenly one is a unit to be moved, turned, injected, exposed, and at times treated callously enough to elicit intense anxiety, anger, or depression. Severe physical conditions such as malignancies, cardiac conditions, or neurological afflictions often evoke unique distortions and anxieties.

The following sections explore several specific crisis situations. Our purpose is not to encompass all or even most crises, rather to illustrate the principles of general and individual responses and to offer some generalizations which link all crises conceptually.

DIVORCE

Divorce is an increasingly prevalent fact of life in our mobile and fast-paced society, and many couples or individuals will seek brief psychotherapy to help discuss marital problems, which may lead to resolution or reinforce the decision to divorce.

Divorce may be divided into three types:

1. Long and drawn out, where there is much fluctuation and indecision, but divorce appears to be eventually inevitable. The couple might have attempted to live apart at least once, and usually one partner wants divorce more than the other.
2. Developmental crisis, where the nexus of the relationship has changed, or each partner's self-image has changed. This often occurs in mid-life, when children leave home, and when the wife or husband experience a change in role or a psychological or physiological "change of life," sometimes accompanied by an operation such as hysterectomy or prostatectomy, which upsets the body image and can affect the relationship;
3. Impulsive gesture, which is most common in younger married couples whose marriage is frequently stormy and divorce often is threatened.

Many mental health professionals try to perform marriage counseling when in fact they should realistically be preparing the couple for divorce. The tenuousness of some marital situations should become apparent within the first few sessions, especially if both partners are present. One or both partners will often try to sidestep the primary issue by attempting to talk about the desire to temper one or the other partner's personality for the sake of the marriage or by making other suggestions or accusations that are not relevant to the situation. It is important that the therapist help the couple face their decision by talking frankly about the issues.

If only one partner wants a divorce, the therapist can help avoid one partner's potential manipulation of the other by inviting both for at least one joint session of brief therapy. By so doing, the therapist also lessens the possibility of his own value judgments influencing the situation. Having the couple or even the entire family present in most cases will clarify the problem that has been shared by the family as a whole. An imminent divorce discussed and shared by the family also can help expedite the process of separation in a less traumatic manner. There should be no age restriction on the children included. Even a very young child can be enlightening regarding his parents' marital problems. Each partner's lawyer should also be present if possible during the family session or sessions so that they have the opportunity to observe the family interaction.

Brief therapy for divorce in a crisis clinic may follow the following temporal sequence.

Sessions 1 and 2.   The therapist deals with any suicidal or homicidal risk. He identifies the events that led to the decision to divorce, and helps the couple find out what went wrong and build a fence around the "trouble." There are civilized and uncivilized ways to go through a divorce, and isolating the trouble helps give the couple perspective about each other and discourages the danger of discomfort or reprisal. It is important to discuss the basic arrangements for the children and for the wife, if she is dependent upon the husband for financial support.

Sessions 2, 3, and 4.   The therapist helps each partner cope with the new situation. Fear of living alone, anxiety about being separated from the children, or sadness, remorse, or rage concerning the new situation or past interactions between partners are common. The therapist helps each partner reconstitute a sense of mastery to alleviate feelings of being overwhelmed.

Session 5, and possibly the few preceding it.   The therapist works on confirming each partner's stabilization, discussing feelings about a sense of loss, if present. The therapist systematically explores all facets when helping each partner deal with new problems and situations, and by so doing attempts to give each partner a broad base for his and her new life situations. The therapist helps each partner decide if he wants to choose future therapy, and acts as a guide to the best situation for each partner's particular needs. These needs might be realized in conventional therapy, or in a more specific group situation such as Alcoholics Anonymous or Parents Without Partners.

Termination of brief psychotherapy should pose no outstanding problems if the therapist has made its goals and time limit clear from the beginning, and if many, if not all, of these goals have been met. Because of the nature of the situation which brought the couple to therapy, termination may make one or both partners susceptible to feelings toward the therapist that he has had toward his partner, such as feelings of abandonment or rejection. The therapist keeps this in mind throughout brief psychotherapy, and helps each partner deal with these feelings that are often most pronounced concurrent with the termination of psychotherapy.

JOB SEPARATION

For many people, job separation is an unwanted and unexpected event that can occur at any time in one's career, and often more than once. It is especially a burden for those who are unprepared for it. Symptomalogically, the reaction to job loss can be a form of bereavement much like the loss of a loved one. However, one's reaction is to the loss of part, often a major part, of one's identity; the job is often closely linked to self-image and to ties to the community.

Therapists recently have been treating more and more victims of job separation as a result of a new wave of unemployment. These victims include the younger person who is unable to find work after completing his education; the individual who has been laid off but has many working years ahead of him; the older person who has been retired early or has chosen to retire early; and the middle-aged person who has been laid off or whose career has been limited by the inaccessibility of promotions, again due in large part to the recessive job market.

The meaning of work is threefold—economic, psychological, and social. Studies of the 45 to 70-year-old age group to determine whether work or leisure is more satisfying revealed that only one in six found leisure more satisfying; this group was also the least happy. Research, both of those presently working and of those who have retired, showed that most would continue to work even if they could be financially comfortable without the need to work.

Although therapists have less exposure to blue-collar than white-collar workers, it seems generally that blue-collar workers look forward to retirement as relief from a boring and unfulfilling job situation. White-collar workers, who usually have more stimulating jobs and who tend to view their career goals in terms of upward mobility, usually invest more of their identity in their work and therefore are more threatened by job separation. However, white-collar workers are often not as financially threatened by retirement and are more likely to maintain a reasonably satisfactory standard of living, because they have more financial resources to fall back on and have planned better in this area.

Those who plan, anticipate, and arrange for retirement are much better prepared for it and do best during it than those individuals who simply drift toward retirement. With the older, retired patient, it is important that the therapist explore the patient's concept of adaptation as necessary for the cessation of his job. The therapist will have to work through these problems with the older patient who has not made adaptation a concept of retirement by not having planned or having planned poorly for retirement. The therapist can use role models of those who have retired successfully, especially from the patient's own peer or economic group.

The most vigorous and healthy people continue to work in some capacity, with the concept of work given in its broadest definition. Durkheim[61a] states that those who maintain at least peripheral ties with institutions are least apt to be suicide risks. We can emphasize one aspect of this thesis: People manage better with some form of structure to their lives that includes interaction with and recognition by the community.

The patient should be helped to structure and manage his new time schedule. The degree of structure that each person needs to establish and maintain will vary; the therapist should discuss these needs with the patient and help him to establish a schedule and activities which are best suited to his needs. Most people are conditioned over the years to equate work with monetary reward. The therapist can help the retired patient shift the emphasis from monetary reward; in retirement, work can more fully be equated with pleasure. The therapist may want to suggest sources for activity, such as foster grandparents and numerous other volunteer activities. If the patient wishes to and is physically able to work for a salary, he should be encouraged to do so. However, the therapist should be alert to the retired patient's feeling of loss of identity as a possible reason for seeking paid work. If this is the patient's major reason for seeking paid work, the therapist should help the patient establish a newer, or another aspect of his identity through diverse and pleasurable activities.

A Cornell University study of retirement found that single women cope with retirement better than married women. This could be due to the fact that married women usually have worked full time within the home for a number of years and only sought work outside the home later in life. Therefore, having spent many years doing household work, they might be more hesitant to return to it after having experienced a broader work environment outside the home. Many woman also feel that the experience of working outside the home enables them to contribute more to the intellectual fulfillment of their marriages, to have more in common with their husbands, and to feel more a part of the mainstream of life. On the other hand, single women (that is, women who have worked full time during their working years, which also applies to married women who have done the same) find it easier to retire. These women are often similar to blue-collar men, in that both groups realize the limitations often imposed upon their work experience, and seek fulfillment elsewhere.

There is a dual problem for women and the retirement situation that has forced therapists to change their notion that retirement is solely the man's burden. Working women not only have to deal with their own retirement but their husbands' as well, and both working and nonworking women are affected by changes in their life styles when the husband retires. Both nonworking and working women usually have an expanded life style outside the home which is somewhat related to the community, whereas the man's primary social activities are usually more closely related to and dependent upon his work situation. Therefore, the retired husband can often be a burden to himself and to his wife because much of his social identity has been lost along with his job. The couple that shares household and community activities fares better in retirement than the couple that does not. Because retirement is a period of change and adjustment that affects both partners, the therapist is often called upon to help both spouses, no matter which is facing retirement.

Job loss for those in mid-career can be especially devastating. This group is less likely to be considered for similar employment in another company. Group therapy can offer peer support for members of this age group who still have many working years ahead of them. Group discussion helps relieve negative self-esteem and often provides the stimulus to further one's efforts to find employment by the discussion of shared problems and by meeting others who are in various stages of coping with a common dilemma, which includes economic problems, social isolation, and loss of meaningful activities.

Though the younger victim of job loss suffers, he usually has the advantages of fewer economic burdens and of greater flexibility in terms of career choice. The therapist may encourage him to explore an unfulfilled career desire or an avocation that possibly has career potential. A discussion of the difference between future-oriented retirement planning and the sudden loss of a job, and often the career goals that go with this loss, may necessitate a therapeutic session for the purpose of catharsis. Massive ventilation on the part of the patient will help give perspective both to the therapist and the patient concerning the patient's feelings and fears about his job loss.

Unanticipated job loss often causes panic that can be immobilizing to the patient. This will detract from his ability to seek employment and is part of a working-through process that, if carefully guided by the therapist, can be the beginning of the formation of a job-seeking structure. People react to job loss in a variety of ways, and the therapist should be alert to all possibilities. Some attempt to use denial to cope with their job loss, and when that begins to fail, they collapse into panic. With professional help, they will eventually begin to rebuild. Others withdraw and refuse to interact with their family and the community, and will not attempt to seek employment. When Studebaker closed its plant in South Bend, Indiana, a team of former Studebaker employees knocked on doors of laid-off workers and, often with much resistance, urged them to come to a newly opened counseling center so they could be helped to find new jobs. Situations such as this one, where one plant employs most members of a community, can be especially devastating to the economic and social welfare of the community. However, there is the advantage of readily available group support in a shared dilemma. Without the support of interventions—such as in this example, or group therapy, or brief therapy—there is danger of depression and loss of self-esteem becoming chronic, bitterness setting in, and the victim of job loss becoming steadily less employable. In all cases, the key to intervention is helping the person build a structure for finding a new job.

The person who has lost his job often insists on denying his plight and leaving the house every morning with the pretense of going to work. After eight hours he returns home as if he had spent the day at work. The family's declining economic situation forces it to realize what has happened. However, often the major problem of finding new employment cannot be dealt with, and the family copes obliquely by applying for food stamps or some other form of public assistance, and denying itself services and goods that reinforce the loss of self-esteem in the person upon whom the family has depended financially. This can be particularly difficult to someone whose standing in his family and in his community has rested in large part upon the prestige of his job.

The skidding phenomenon is common to those in whom the loss of self-esteem is combined with the inability, or the lack of faith in one's ability, to find similar employment. The individual accepts employment at a lower prestige and salary level; if this situation is allowed to persist, often long after the economic or other circumstances which precipitated the job loss have disappeared, his self-esteem and confidence will erode over the years. Studies have shown that these people do just as poorly psychologically as those without jobs. The therapist should help the patient adjust to his lower job level if all other avenues of seeking employment have brought negative results. This job situation may be of temporary but unknown duration, usually depending on economic factors and trends which take time to reverse. If the patient has accepted a lower job level primarily out of panic, the therapist should help him strengthen his ego functions and lay a good foundation for the search for an appropriate job.

The speed and intensity of the therapist's intervention depends on factors indicated by the patient's age and his reaction to the job loss. Intervention should be swifter with older people; they have less time to seek employment, are usually less flexible to change, and therefore are more adversely affected by job loss. The therapist should be less hesitant to over-direct older people or those in a panic. The victim of job loss should be encouraged to be active, even if activity is at first minimal, and perhaps not even directly related to finding a job. At the crucial point—when unemployment first occurs—even minimal activity is far better than no activity at all.

Inactivity can be painful and regressive. The vice-president of a large manufacturing company retired at age 65. Expecting to live only a few more years, he had planned well only for the first two years following retirement. However, at 78 he was alive and had little to keep himself busy. Furthermore, his physician began treating him for minimal heart disease by restricting his activity and prescribing heart medication. Consequently, he spent much of his time lying down and staring at the ceiling. This chain of events led him to brief therapy, where the therapist's first intervention was to have this still healthy and intelligent man consider his possibilities for meaningful activity. Based on information gained from the preliminary interview, the therapist suggested that he write down his fascinating life history. The patient complained that he couldn't type, and the therapist encouraged him to learn. Shortly thereafter, the patient began writing his autobiography, and was able to discontinue heart medication.

The therapist can help the victim of job loss or unplanned retirement regain lost self-confidence and the will to again participate and take pleasure in his activities. For those who have retired, activities can be explored for which time was previously unavailable. Some have recommended a mental health check-up prior to retirement to determine other adversities in the patient's life and how these were handled, in order to ascertain the patient's resources in the retirement situation. In both retirement and job loss, the therapist should be alert to the continuity of the patient's reaction to crisis throughout his life cycle, and help the patient apply these resources to the present crisis. The therapist's greatest task is to determine the patient's hidden but existing resources.

DEATH, THREAT OF DEATH, BEREAVEMENT

Life-and-death situations such as the threat of death due to physical illness, or bereavement resulting from the loss of a loved one, produce crises in the individual. Some sociologists tend to view this type of assault upon the individual's life as naturally producing disruption and crisis. The therapeutic profession, however, does not regard such assaults as automatically and pathologically disruptive. Working through of normal mourning is adaptive and not to be interfered with or even added to, unless absolutely necessary. Each patient's crisis is viewed and handled individually, due to the unique constellation of experiental factors. Disruptive dismay, anger, or depression may be the components of crisis in some individuals, whereas in others an apparent crisis may be passed through without the necessity of professional aid or intervention. Other individuals may superficially appear to be adapting very well to crisis while actually suffering great interior, emotional upheaval.

In the 1950s physicians routinely avoided creating and therefore having to deal with crisis in the patient by informing a friend or family member, rather than the patient himself, that he was terminally ill. This technique was rarely successful: It simply transferred crisis from the patient to his family or friends, and did not eliminate the chance that the patient would be informed indirectly. Such transfer of crisis can be especially harmful for a spouse who may find it extremely difficult to maintain the pretense that a dying husband or wife is merely seriously ill and will recover. In this instance the transfer of crisis only complicates matters by forcing the healthy spouse to mask his or her true emotions regarding the patient's condition. This masking in turn interferes with, and in some cases circumscribes, a close supportive relationship which may be critical to both individuals at that time.

Today physicians are much more aware of the relationship between medicine, therapy, and the terminally ill patient. Many physicians now realize that there are ways to inform the dying patient of his true condition in a manner that will not cause him to decompensate. The psychological crisis inherent in terminal illness can be aided, and often resolved, with therapeutic techniques. The physician can help the patient choose whatever defensive arrangement appears to work best for him. Following the diagnosis of terminal illness, the physician should also be prepared to stand by the patient and his family as a supportive figure if such a need should arise.

Although the physician should be alert to the emotional needs of the patient and his family, he often feels after diagnosis and establishment of a treatment plan that his professional duties have been completed. It is during this period of crisis that the therapist may be called upon. He should initially determine the primary source of the patient's concern. If death is threatening to the patient, the intervenor should examine with the patient his specific notions, fantasies, and fears about his own death. The patient may fear nonbeing; he may be afraid of dying but not of death itself; or he may be obsessively concerned with the reasons for his becoming ill, among a variety of possibilities.

As the individual's *understanding* of his particular physical complaint is enhanced, so will be his anticiaptory mechanism and his ability to cope with the symptomatic development of his illness. The therapist should be prepared to discuss with the patient not only the hazards of his illness, but also the various medical treatments which may be employed to combat these hazards, and to see that the patient plays as active a role in his treatment program as possible. *Being the passive victim is often the greatest burden!* The therapist may further relieve the patient's psychological pain by informing him of other terminally ill individuals who have successfully adapted to similar psychological conditions.

Under such serious circimstances it is not rare for the patient to consider suicide. A spouse, especially an elderly spouse, may consider suicide if his or her partner has recently died and life has suddenly become intolerable. All that has previously been dreamed concerning this topic should be kept in mind by the therapist.

Professional intervention in the case of an individual with a diagnosed *malignancy* generally follows one or two procedures. The first allows the patient to respond and adjust to his condition in his own way, with the aid of the therapist who strives only to enhance the adaptive response. The second procedure applies to instances in which the patient cannot deal with the monumental crisis of terminal illness and requries massive therapeutic support. In both instances the patient is permitted to take the lead, although he should always be able to feel the supportive presence of the therapist. The therapist should discuss medical advances with the patient without inappropriately raising his hopes for survival. He can help educate the patient about the nature of his illness, and anticipate his questions to help ease his anxiety, or help him discuss treatment priorities. In many of the better hospitals there is excellent liaison between the oncology and psychiatry services.

Heart patients are often frightened and depressed by their brush with death. They should be given a full understanding and prognosis of their condition with as much optimism as possible. Coronary patients, especially young patients who feel less mortally threatened and consequently less vulnerable, should not be smothered with reassurances which might prove more harmful than beneficial. The younger heart patient often is not readily able to assimilate what has happened to him. In this case intervention may involve interpretation of denial without unduly frightening the patient.

The therapist must anticipate the patient's feeling of depression following discharge from the hospital, and be prepared to take a supportive role in the follow-up treatment. The patient who is informed that he may weaken and tire easily following a heart attack will be in a far better position to cope with these symptoms should they develop after his return to his home and family. The therapist should encourage the patient to follow an exercise program prescribed by his physician, or to be sure an exercise program has been prescribed. Many heart patients are reluctant to tax themselves physically, but the therapist can help overcome the patient's fears by pointing out that appropriate activity in fact strengthens the heart.

The *loss of a loved one* is a major event in the life of an individual. In the case of the death of a spouse, close friend, or family member, the therapist must evaluate the degree of disruption the event has caused in the survivor's life. For many, the sudden death of a loved one is followed by so severe a sensation of shock that the crisis may be delayed until the event is given time to sink in. Individuals who suffer unanticipated loss due to accidents or heart attacks may respond to the event with distrust and bitterness toward a world in which sudden death can occur at any time. The husband who was accustomed to having his home life totally orchestrated by his wife may, following her death, be so overwhelmed by problems of coping with immediate realities that he fails to feel immediate grief. Acceptance of death in such a situation is often a gradual process; many people decide instinctively how much reality they can accept at one time.

There are certain handholds which may be employed by the therapist to help the survivor relate to his new relationship with reality following the death of a loved one. Each individual reacts differently to grief and the therapist should help the patient understand his form of grieving to be natural and expected. Though the therapist should be flexible in his concept of grief, the apparent absence of grief can be harmful to the patient in that it may appear later in symptomatic forms. Therefore, the patient should be encouraged to grieve, no matter how short or long the duration of grief. The survivor should also be made to understand that certain symptoms of loss— reliving scenes from his marriage, the inability to sleep soundly, a sense of tiredness and lassitude, or other somatic conditions—may well be the physical and mental manifestations of hidden depression.

The therapist should not harbor any preconceived opinions on how well or badly the survivor will adjust to the loss of a loved one. This is particularly important since some individuals adjust to the reality of death far better and more quickly than others, especially if their relationship was unambivalent. This crisis situation occasionally may stimulate a better adjustment with reality than existed before the confrontation with death. Understanding the survivor as well as the terminally ill patient in terms of his unique needs and expectations is therefore of primary importance in helping him adjust to sudden, and often inexplicable, loss.

THE SURGICAL DECISION

Surgery can be a psychological as well as a physical trauma. In this type of crisis situation, the therapist is often called upon to act as liaison between the patient, his family, the surgeon, and the participating hospital staff. He can serve as displacement for the anxieties of all involved, and can help open paths of communication that otherwise might remain closed. Though the therapist should involve himself with all aspects of this crisis situation, his primary emphasis will be on the patient and the patient's family.

The therapist cannot replace the primary physician in the eyes of the patient. However, a sufficient knowledge of surgical procedures provides a basis for communication. The patient often is reluctant to discuss certain aspects of surgery with his surgeon, including any ambivalence he may have, due to the fact that he is dependent upon the surgeon for his life. The therapist therefore can help enlighten the patient about areas he might otherwise be unwilling to discuss. The therapist can also determine whether the patient anticipates psychological benefits or deficits unrelated to the realistic physiological compensations of the surgery, and provide appropriate counsel to both patient and surgeon.

Surgeons may appear overly optimistic about the proposed surgery, or will not divulge certain unpleasant aspects of the operation for fear of discouraging or frightening the patient and his family. The therapist seeing a preoperative patient in hospital is dealing with a crisis situation even though the patient may not be aware that there is a crisis. The area of patient–therapist confidentiality is modified by agreement under these circumstances to include, inform, and prepare everyone concerned. Thus they become affective participants in the patient's experience with surgery.

The patient's expectations about the surgery and its aftereffects are valuable clues to the therapist. He should develop a strong preoperative relationship with the patient. The patient is medically better prepared to face surgery if he is psychologically prepared beforehand. The therapist's supportive and educational role is strengthened if he leaves his phone number with the patient.

The experience after surgery of waking up in an intensive care unit—disoriented, fatigued, immobilized, surrounded by machines, possibly in pain, and completely dependent on others—is frightening even when the patient has been prepared. It is important that the patient be informed how he will feel upon awakening. The postoperative environment of the intensive care unit should also be discussed in detail. By being able to orient himself in space and time, the patient is less likely to react psychotically; "structures" such as a clock, calendar, and windows lend themselves to proper reorientation. In a similar way, the therapist becomes the supportive link between the preoperative and postoperative experience.

Should the patient's need for continued medical service cause tensions between him and his family or the participating hospital staff, the therapist can serve as a vehicle for the clarification and resolution of anxieties or conflicts.

In situations where posoperative psychoses occur, the therapist should consider possible physical contributing factors of toxic nature. Dislike of the staff toward the patient may affect him and also contribute to a postoperative psychosis.

The patient's family can help the patient adjust and recover in a manner that is not overtaxing to him physically or psychologically. The therapist should caution the patient and his family against overexpectation of the patient's physical abilities after surgery, at the same time discouraging passivity.

The therapist's continued support is important in the postoperative phase, and should include follow-up visits. If any conflict or discomfort persists, the surgeon and the patient's family can be called in to further support and encourage the patient.

VICTIMS OF VIOLENCE

The victim of violence suffers a swift and severe act perpetrated against his person or his possessions, a trauma which can be both physically and psychologically debilitating. The psychological injury often lingers long after the body has healed. The victim is plagued by questions such as: Could I have prevented this act? Did I in some way encourage it? Is it possible to avoid its recurrence? He may be troubled by other anxieties, such as the fear of passivity. We have selected three examples of victims of violence, and the ways in which the therapist can help the patient through his trauma.

Accidents

A significant percentage of all automobile accidents are estimated as being a form of suicide. To a lesser degree, the same may be true for other types of accidents which the patient dismisses as having been caused by fatigue or distraction. The therapist should explore impulse control with the patient to be certain that the accident was not an acting out of some self-harming component.

A discussion of fantasies and dreams related to the accident, as well as the circumstances surrounding the patient before and during the accident, helps to sort out the reality of the situation from any possible denial of it. The therapist can help the patient avoid a reaction akin to a traumatic neurosis with lingering aftereffects. The therapist should interpret any denial and help the patient work through the significance of the accident, both symbolically and realistically. As Lindemann[112] discovered, surviving victims and relatives have a high incidence of psychomatic disorders, as well as strictly psychological and psychiatric disturbances, when the working through of the experience is not accomplished. At times an accident precipitates the reemergence of childhood anxieites, resulting in fears of helplessness and passivity, fear of castration, or fear of poor impulse control. The therapist's job is to find the common denominators between the precipitating event and historical situations in the patient's life in order to help the patient understand and work through his trauma.

Rape

The traditional assumption has been that a rape victim is the victim of a sexual assault. Due in great part to the educational thrust of the women's movement, rape is now seen primarily as a crime of violence that the victim neither encouraged nor participated in willingly.

As for any victim of violence, it is important to explore and work through the conscious and unconscious anxieties and fantasies associated with the event. Each victim's reaction depends on her general mental condition, the circumstances of the rape, and the responses of those from whom she seeks support; in every case, the victim needs immediate and sustained psychological counseling.

Certain situations increase the complexity of the victim's reaction. For example, rape by a friend or relative has to be worked through more extensively than for a woman who was accosted by a stranger.

The major psychological effects suffered by rape victims are: generalized and prolonged fear of physical vulnerability, including being alone; generalized fear and anger, with the natural anger often directed inward as guilt; and depression, especially if the woman is repressing or denying her anger and feelings of helplessness. Guilt in some form is nearly always present, no matter what the circumstances of the rape.

Changes in life style are prominent, involving impaired levels of functioning at work, home, or school. Feelings of isolation may be intensified by family or friends, or denial by society of the assault or its seriousness. Psychological problems or maladaptive behavior that existed prior to the rape increase the likelihood of maladaptive patterns following the rape.

If there were childhood experiences involving seduction, active sex play, or primal scene fears, the rape will bring them to the fore and precipitate a marked response. If the rape is a woman's first sexual experience, she may become confused about the relationship between sexuality, violence, and humiliation.

There is considerable literature on the psychological aspects of rape. In *The Rape Victim*[85a] Elaine Hilberman deals extensively with the sociocultural aspects of rape and the rape victim. Hilberman divides the victim's reactions to rape into four phases:

1. *Anticipatory or threat phase.* This phase involves the fine balance between the victim's need to protect her illusion of invulnerability and her awareness of reality as she attempts to provide some protection against and preparation for the impending rape.
2. *Actual rape or impact phase.* This phase is often accompanied by increased vigilance as a defense mechanism, followed by diminished alertness, numbness, affective and memory disturbances, and a general disorganization and bewilderment.
3. *Recoil phase.* Emotional expression and awareness return. Depending on how the victim feels about her behavior during the rape, there follows either increased or sharply decreased self-esteem and self-confidence. A critical issue for the victim is the support or nonsupport of those around her.

   The therapist ordinarily sees the rape victim at this phase and should be particularly concerned with helping the patient deal with reconstituting. Although it is a period of seemingly outward adjustment, this is pseudo-adjustment and does not represent the final resolution of the traumatic event or the feelings it aroused. Often there is a heavy measure of denial and suppression.

4. *Post-traumatic phase*. The patient has by now maximally reconstituted and is able to recall the event and to repair the damages, including anxiety. The sequelae that have not been worked through can be manifested by anything from claustrophobia to social withdrawal, depression, guilt, anxiety attacks, and anger due to feelings of helplessness and violation of the woman's self. Sleep disturbances are common, as are dreams about violence, either thinly disguised reenactments of the rape or a mastering of the rape with the victim committing the violent act. Appetite disturbances are also frequent, including anorexia, vomiting, and nausea. Medical procedures for the prevention of pregnancy and venereal disease.

There are many problems attendant on rape that the therapist can help the patient work through: intensified conflicts about dependence and independence; rebuilding trusting relationships with men; difficulties in handling anger and aggression; and persistent feelings of vulnerability. Phobic reactions may also persist in the woman, along with a variety of sexual disturbances such as a decline of interest, withdrawal from her partner and a concern about sexual adequacy. The victim may be afraid to tell her family, husband or lover, friends, or coworkers about the event, and concerned about the implications of not telling. She may also be concerned about the possibility of pregnancy or venereal disease; and about deciding whether to report the rape to the police, and to identify and prosecute the rapist if he is found. Many people hesitate to report crimes of violence to the police for fear of retaliation from the attacker. In the case of rape, this fear is further complicated by the possibility of censure from friends or family and unwanted publicity.

Mugging and Burglary

The more the patient's personality contains fears of passivity or helplessness, the more he will be affected by a mugging or burglary. His self-esteem may also be threatened by his inability or unwillingness to act—even when passivity may have been the wisest choice with regard to personal safety. Some patients may not be troubled by fears of passivity, but be disturbed in other ways. Fantasies and dreams are helpful to the therapist in exploring other contributing factors. Women seem to be less affected by fears of passivity, perhaps due to cultural factors whereby a woman's self-image is usually less threatened by passivity.

The bystander to violence is also often affected. He may feel that he should have acted to help prevent the violence, or may suffer from a survivor syndrome similar to that experienced by survivors of concentrations camps, or battlefields.

The therapist's task is to help the patient work through his trauma in terms of his personal dynamics, his history, and the specifics of the overall situation.

UNWANTED PREGNANCY WITH SPECIAL EMPHASIS ON ABORTION

An unwanted pregnancy—and the decisions and repercussions of keeping the child to term or terminating the pregnancy—is crisis producing, depending on the woman's ego strengths and a variety of other important factors. The 1973 Supreme Court decision to legalize abortion was instrumental in decreasing crises caused by the legal and physical risks inherent in illegal abortion. Although enlightened legislation has minimized or eliminated some crises, others remain. The woman who seeks abortion should be referred to a reputable clinic or doctor and educated about the methods of abortion and about what each procedure involves. Many referral agencies whose main task is to determine pregnancy and to refer the woman to an abortion center have proved surprisingly inefficient, if not willfully outside the law. When it is to the agency's interest to refer as many women for abortion as possible in order to receive a percentage from the clinic as its referral fee, women who are not really pregnant occasionally and unsuspectingly undergo "abortion." Many efforts by local agencies have helped curb the proliferation of dishonest referral agencies, and the honest agencies have provided a needed service.

Although most women today have addressed themselves to the question of unwanted pregnancy and have contemplated their choices in the abstract, a surprising number of women are uninformed in crucial areas, from conception to birth or termination of pregnancy. The therapist's first concern with a pregnant woman in crisis who comes to brief therapy is her history in relation to the unwanted pregnancy. The therapist should determine the cultural milieu in which the patient functions, as well as her understanding of the pregnancy in terms of her life situation and the alternatives available to her. The therapist should learn who the supportive persons are in the woman's life that she can call on; how she presently is coping with her pregnancy; and specifically how she felt when she learned she was pregnant. This information enables the therapist to help the patient take the most appropriate course of action. The therapist's role is *not* that of the patient's counselor. He acts as educator and guide, laying out all options, and by so doing enabling the woman to make a decision that weighs all factors and is best for her life circumstances. She is likely to be influenced by existing cultural and religious factors, as well as by her friends and family. These influences often cause conflict and anxiety, but once a decision is made—one in which the woman has participated and is comfortable with—she will benefit greatly in terms of her self-growth.

It is very likely that the therapeutic sequlae to abortion are not always appropriate in their intensity of application. A relatively healthy woman who is strongly motivated to have a legal abortion will usually come through it not with feelings of conflict, but with a strong feeling of relief.

The therapist should look for and explore the following points in the woman in crisis who has an unwanted pregnancy.

The woman may have ambivalent feelings about keeping or not keeping the child, with many factors affecting her decision. She may be under pressure to have or not have an abortion, and these pressures will interfere with her ability to recognize her own feelings and wishes about her pregnancy.

Strong feelings of love or hatred for the father can affect the woman's decision and often obscure her real feelings and perceptions of her own best interests. Less intense feelings toward the father lessen the possibility that that woman will carry the fetus to term as a romantic notion, or terminate the pregnancy for psychologically pathological reasons.

If the woman has a history of psychiatric illness, the therapist should attempt to determine whether the pregnancy is an acting out of some unconscious drive or unfulfilled need. The reason for recurring pregnancies in which all have been terminated may be that the woman considers abortion a viable form of birth control. She should be disabused of this notion.

Hostility or moral censure by any of the medical staff with whom the patient comes into contact can threaten her self-esteem and make therapeutic sequelae more likely. Specialized abortion clinics are less likely to have hostile personnel; they usually provide a setting suited to the needs of the patient.

The decision to terminate a pregnancy is often made regardless of the patient's religious or moral tenets against such action. This dichotomy is not usually a problem if other factors have been properly evaluated and if the patient is otherwise comfortable with her decision.

An abortion in the second or third trimester presents greater physical and emotional difficulties. Late or delayed termination is usually indicative of problems that will not be resolved adequately by termination of the pregnancy. Indeed, the very difficulties and complications inherent in late termination may be perceived by the patient as retribution for her transgression, thus further adding to her psychological burden. Early evlauation and referral are crucial both for proper medical and emotional sequalae.

Even if the decision to terminate has been carefully weighed beforehand, the patient may display some feelings of despondency after the abortion. This emotional response is natural and possibly even physiological. In cases where there is no such emotional response, the therapist should look for feelings and attitudes which were unresolved prior to the decision to terminate the pregnancy. A history of psychopathology, concomitant medical illness, or medical complications resulting from the abortion, usually contribute to an abnormal post-abortion response. Suicide, however, is a rare occurrence.

The woman's decision to bear the child and give it up for adoption is often the result of a conscious acceptance of the pregnancy. Many women who decide to have the child, though they know they will give it up, see pregnancy and childbirth as a positive personal experience and abortion as alien. If the woman is strong enough to go against societal norms in order to have the child, as is usually the case with the unmarried woman, she is often concomitantly realistic about the problems of raising a child alone and can give the child up for adoption without severe crisis. However, she may depend on the therapist to help her redefine or affirm the factors she has considered in reaching her decision.

In contrast, the decision of some women to bear the child and give it up for adoption is not the result of a conscious acceptance of the pregnancy at all, rather a "discovery" too late that they are in the second or third trimester of pregnancy. They are often younger women, living at or near home with strong, even dominant ties to the family, particularly the father. Such women may be reluctant to assert themselves in the face of strong parental opposition to abortion, or they may have the opinion that bearing the child, and even raising it independently, is proper punishment for the "sin" of having sex. These women are not acting out of the belief that pregnancy and childbirth are positive personal experiences and that abortion is conversely alien. They see pregnancy as a time of entrapment and estrangement from their peers, friends, and family. Often, even today, they do not understand how to go about getting an abortion, or family and religious ties are strong enough to prevent their actively seeking that information.

In addition, these women may not be at all realistic about the problems of raising a child alone. When and if they do give the child up for adoption, it is with severe crisis: no grieving, no explanation of the loss, and no definition or affirmation of the factors leading to such a decision. They go on either to having further unwanted pregnancies, or to other types of severe emotional crises, with which they can only cope by extreme passivity and dependency on the very people who originally fostered the problem. Therapy has to deal with the passivity that played a role in *getting* pregnant and *staying* pregnant.

An accidental pregnancy usually precludes any real planning beyond the decision of whether or not to continue the pregnancy. The problems of rearing and maintaining a child are often obscured by the anticipated emotional benefits of being a mother. The woman must be made to realize and begin planning for major changes in her life situation if she decides to bear and keep the child. Possibly more important than the realities of the woman's age and economic status are the reasons and attitudes behind the decision to continue the pregnancy. The therapist should help the woman explore her expectations in continuing *this* pregnancy versus her motivations to bear and raise a child or children.

Because sterilization is most safely accomplished after abortion or delivery, such a step may be considered by the patient during initial evaluation. For the stable women who wants no more children, sterilization can be a logical decision and need not create any real problem. If the woman is ambivalent, however, the therapist should try to explore the conflcits. Contraception is preferable to sterilization for the younger woman who may still want to bear children. In all cases, the therapist should educate the patient regarding birth control and family planning to help her avoid the misfortune of another unwanted pregnancy in her life.

Men are increasingly choosing sterilization by vasectomy as an alternative to less permanent and unsure birth control methods available to both men and women. This operation is most common with the married man who has had the number of children he and his wife desire, and who wants to ease the burden of birth control for his wife. Sterilization for both men and women is on the rise, although resistance to the vasectomy persists among men who adhere to the more macho cultural influences, and who therefore have less regard for the dangers of unwanted pregnancy and the risks of many birth control methods available to women.

PART III

Appendices

Appendix A
A Multiple Level Study of Brief Psychotherapy in a Trouble Shooting Clinic

THE SETTING OF THE STUDY

The tremendous need for psychotherapy constitutes the impetus for brief psychotherapy and allied techniques. Such measures as the Community Mental Health Act may provide the financial means and administrative settings for offering brief psychotherapy, but the burden of proof that brief psychotherapy can indeed be useful and successful is still on those who practice it.

Therefore, part of the work done at the Trouble Shooting Clinic (TSC) of City Hospital Center at Elmhurst in New York City was a research program concerned with the evaluation of brief psychotherapy offered there.

The Trouble Shooting Clinic was originated by L. Bellak in November 1958* to offer immediate, walk-in care of emotional problems of minor or major degree, from advice to the lovelorn to care of acute psychoses, around the clock. The Clinic treated minor disturbances in order to arrest their

This material is based upon an NIMH sponsored study (5-R11 MH-0915) conducted by L. Bellak, E. J. Meyer, M. Prola, S. Rosenberg, and M. Zuckerman. More detailed reports of this research project have been published elsewhere.[30]

Aside from our indebtedness to these colleagues, we are especially grateful to Dr. David E. Lehine who was very helpful as the Director of the Mental Hygiene Clinic, and to Ruth Cooper, Ph.D., Tim Dineem, M.A., and Renata Saffrin, Ph.D. for their many helpful suggestions.

We are also especially grateful to A. Antonovsky, Ph.D., M. H. Hurwitz, M.D., M. Brzostovski, M.D., M. Malev, M.D., and H. H. Schlossman, M.D., who served as judges and predictors in part of the study.

*Terminated in July, 1964, as part of an administrative change of the entire hospital, resulting in a mass resignation of staff, including four of the authors.

further development, thus serving a preventive as well as a therapeutic function. Furthermore, one of the hypotheses involved was that to assist a patient in dealing with his problems on one occasion might help him to resolve future problems on his own. Some aspects of this clinic have been briefly described before.[21,26] The general viewpoint of Community Psychiatry,[22] both preventive and therapeutic, underly the conception of this innovation.

The community response to the establishment of the Trouble Shooting Clinic was enthusiastic. When demand exceeded those services which could be provided within the meager budgetary provisions of the Department of Hospitals, a grant allowing a gratifying extension of services was obtained from the National Institute of Mental Health. The award made it possible to provide service by a whole team from 9:00 A.M. to 10:00 P.M. seven days a week, rather than by only a single person. At first, only a resident psychiatrist was available at other hours of the night. Later, a psychologist, social worker, and/or a staff psychiatrist were available in the medical–surgical emergency clinic not only for consultation but to see every patient brought in, offering first aid and arranging follow-up treatment where necessary.[28] Thus 24-hour service was provided above and beyond the availability of a psychiatric resident.

All who applied to the out-patient psychiatric service of the hospital for help were seen in the Trouble Shooting Clinic, with the exception of court referrals, drug addicts, and children under 18 years.* These latter were all offered specialized services through the Mental Hygiene Clinic. In this sense, one function of the TSC was as the intake service of the Mental Hygiene Clinic. No appointments were required for the initial contact in the TSC: Patients were interviewed as they arrived; they were not put on waiting lists or referred elsewhere, but were immediately given subsequent appointments in the TSC, usually at weekly intervals. Thus, the clinic offered its treatment to all persons who sought it, and not only to those who were deemed "suitable" for brief psychotherapy. However, when the clinic became well-known in outlying districts as well as in the hospital area, its staff was unable to handle the resulting enormous caseload. Consequently, in April 1963 the clinic had to limit its services to persons with low income who resided in the geographical area assigned to the hospital.

The effort in the initial interview was to describe the service to the patient, clarify the presenting problem, set up working hypotheses about the patient's illness, and make an appropriate treatment plan. Patients were allotted from three to five interviews, with some variation as therapeutically required. An attempt was made within these interviews to bring about some

---

*This administrative decision was reluctantly based on the experience that children would very often be brought when a school complaint was the immediate reason, and that little could be done without having complete records and interviews with the family first.

kind of ameliorative restructuring of the problem. If the problem was successfully resolved, then no further referrals were made. If, on the other hand, short-term psychotherapy had not been adequate in dealing with the problem, the patient was referred for further treatment to the other treatment modalities within the Mental Hygiene Clinic (individual psychotherapy, group psychotherapy, the Day Care Clinic, Medication Clinic) or to other services.

Service to the community was the *raison d'être* of the program, yet both administrative and professional personnel beleived that the usefulness of the treatment offered—specifically, dynamically oriented, psychoanalytically conceptualized, and very brief psychotherapy—should be tested.

ORGANIZATION OF THE RESEARCH PROJECT

The evaluation of brief psychotherapy proceeded on three levels of intensity and extensity:

1. Project I was an epidemiological study of the caseload, utilizing a "Keysort" system for this purpose.
2. In Project II, a sample of 472 patients was followed up by interview and rating scales seeking to evaluate the success of the therapeutic intervention.
3. Project II was the most intensive investigation, using only a small number of patients. The method used rapid, short-range predictions and judgments to test the proposition that it is possible to arrive at a diagnostic appraisal or treatment plan and successful treatment by such a brief method. To illustrate this, recorded and transcribed interviews were submitted to independent raters for prediction of and judgment on a complex set of variables.

EPIDEMIOLOGICAL ASPECTS (PROJECT I)

This part of the research was designed to describe the broad epidemiological characteristics of the population and certain aspects of the treatment process. The approach is a multivariate one in which numerous items of information are analyzed.

Collection of Data

Data were collected from 1,414 patients during a 12-month period from February 1, 1963 to January 31, 1964.

Data were collected by: an admitting clerk before the initiation of treatment; and the patient's therapist at various stages of the treatment process. Clerical workers punched the information on specially designed Royal-McBee Keysort cards.

Review of Significant Data

More women (62.6 percent) than men were seen at the clinic, and 86.8 percent of the patients were white. In the 1960 Census, 94 percent of the population residing in the geographical area of Queens and assigned to the hospital were white. Thus the percentage of nonwhites seeking the clinic's services was higher than the percentage of nonwhites in the community, but as this figure was not adjusted for income level, it may not be meaningful.

About three-fifths of the patients were Catholic, one-fifth Protestant, and one-fifth Jewish. As the official census does not offer percentages for religious groups in order to avoid discriminatory questions, we are unable to draw any conclusions about the relationship between the size of the clinic samples and the size of community groups.

Almost half of the patients were married (first marriage), and a little more than one-fourth were single. The remaining one-fourth either had been married more than once, or were divorced, separated, or widowed.

Fifty-six and six-tenths percent were between ages 20 to 40. More than one-third were over 40: This age group is usually less frequent in most clinic populations.

Occupation, income, and education of the "head of the household" were used to determine socioeconomic status. Twenty-seven and seven-tenths percent of the population were high school graduates (this figure includes 19.8 percent of the total sample who had gone beyond high school), 39.0 percent had not completed high school.

Eighty-two and eight-tenths percent of the heads of the patients' households were in the lower half of the occupation scale:[87] one-third were unemployed or unskilled workers; one-fourth were semiskilled manual workers; one-fifth were clerical or sales workers. The reader will recall that clinic services could be offered only to patients of limited income. The following guide to income eligibility was used:

Number in Family	Maximum Weekly Income Take-Home Pay
1	$ 75.
2	90.
3	100.
4	110.
5	120.

The occupational data by themselves are neither surprising nor significant. What deserves reflection is that the percentage of patients in low occupational categories is more than might be expected from the data on educational attainment. The data do not permit us to say how long patients had been in the economic group reported at the time of treatment. We can speculate that emotional difficulties impaired their abilities or earning capacities. We cannot, however, say whether this disability had been chronic, or relatively recent in origin, although a causal relationship between emotional difficulties and earning capacities must be considered extremely likely.

We note that, following Hollingshead and Redlich, both socioeconomic and educational data refer always to the head of the family; where the patient was a woman, her husband's educational and socioeconomic status was recorded.

If a correlation between educational level and socioeconomic status seems valid at all, we would have to engage in a two-step speculation: that there is a high correlation between disturbances in spouses; and that emotional problems affect earning capacity. Contrary to some reports in the literature,[87] patients with low socioeconomic status seemed well able to profit from psychotherapy.

Almost half of the patients reported no income, or derived their income from pensions, unemployment insurance, etc.; 38.1 percent reported an income of $3,000 to $6,000.

Patients sought treatment for problems of recent origin rather than for chronic complaints: Two-thirds reported a duration of "one year or less" since onset of the presenting problem; one-third reported "no occurrence" of the problem prior to its present onset. Three-fourths of the patients had had no previous psychiatric hospitalization, and two-thirds had had no previous psychotherapy.

The most prevalent complaints* were depression (53.5 percent) and anxiety (50.4 percent). These were followed by marital problems (29.7 percent), somatic problems (26.4 percent), miscellaneous family problems (25.2 percent), and work problems (21.4 percent).

Therapists diagnosed 45.5 percent of the patients as suffering psychoneurotic disorders, 28.5 percent as character disorders, 21.1 percent as psychotic disorders, and 11.6 percent as transient situational personality disorders.

The effective operation of the TSC on an nonappointment "walk-in" basis is illustrated by the fact that 92.2 percent of the patients came initially without an appointment—they "walked in." Yet only 6.5 percent of all

---

*Many patients, of course, presented several complaints.

patients had to wait longer than two hours to be seen, 32.1 percent had to wait a half-hour or less before being seen by a therapist, and 27.5 percent had to wait between half-hour and an hour. Patients were not put on waiting lists or referred elsewhere, but were immediately given further appointments at the TSC, usually at weekly intervals. About 27 percent of the patients had one contact at the clinic; nearly 58 percent were seen three to five times.

Open in the evening and on weekends, the TSC serviced those people who could not meet the 9:00 A.M. to 5:00 P.M. weekday hours of most clinics: 48.2 percent of the patients were seen either in the evenings or on weekends. There is a clear need for evening and weekend psychotherapeutic services.

EVALUATION* BY THERAPISTS' RATINGS AND PATIENTS' SELF-JUDGMENTS (PROJECT II)

In the TSC, the primary responsibility was upon service to the local community. Procedures involving precise preselection of patients or intricate "matching" techniques typical of many psychotherapy research designs were to some extent sacrificed in the attempt to fulfill our basic commitment.

Nevertheless, we sought to move beyond purely descriptive analysis and to explore two areas of significance for the planning and execution of community mental health programs:

1. The development of a self-administered Symptom Check List, both as an aid in patient characterization and assignment to an appropriate therapeutic regimen, and also as an independent method for evaluating outcomes;
2. Identification of factors relating to successful and unsuccessful outcome.

A REVIEW OF OUTCOME BY DISPOSITION

Of the 1,414 patients treated during the 12-month period, about 70 percent received brief psychotherapy; 8.8 percent were referred for hospitalization in the in-patient service of the department; 23.6 percent did not return by their own choice.[7, 110]

Of nearly 1,000 patients who received brief psychotherapy, 35 percent

---

*Evaluation of psychotherapy is a complex task whch has been approached by many others including the senior author.[19, 24, 165] For the most comprehensive published bibliography, see Strupp.[166]

had to be referred for further treatment; after brief therapy, 45 percent were considered not in need of any further treatment; 13.6 percent were maintained on medication after psychotherapy; 7.6 percent were referred for medical, vocational, or other aid; 8.1 percent refused further treatment. Multiple disposition occasionally was involved.

THERAPISTS' JUDGMENT OF CLINICAL CHANGE

Each therapist rated his patients on a five-point scale ranging from "much improved" through "no change" to "much worse." He did this for *all* patients seen by him regardless of the number of times the patient was seen or the nature of termination (premature termination, referral for medication list, referral for individual or group therapy, etc.).

The most relevant for evaluation are those patients who received the full course of five interviews; of these, *85.3 percent were rated as "improved."* No significant differences were found in the percentage of patients rated as improved by social workers, psychiatrists, or psychologists. This suggests that the three disciplines either did equally well in treating patients, or were equally biased about their therapeutic accomplishments.

FACTORS RELATED TO OUTCOME

Three classes of variables were considered in this analysis: patient demography; symptomatology and clinical status; clinic factors. Statistical analysis revealed the following factors to be associated with successful outcome: female, unmarried, between 18 and 30 years old, higher occupational level, problems in the work area, a diagnosis of "neurosis," receiving psychotropic drugs along with psychotherapy, a relative lack of chronicity, and used more of the five psychotherapy sessions offered. Degree of improvement was unrelated to the professional identification of the therapist. The patient's subjective evaluation of improvement was maintained for at least six months (the period of following investigation).

THE SYMPTOM CHECK LIST AS EVALUATION

The Symptom Check List utilizes the patient's own evaluation of his relative comfort as an indication of how much he has benefited by treatment. An index of this kind has inherent limitations and is appropriate only in the context of all other efforts in this study to gauge the merits of brief therapy.

Since the brief psychotherapy offered by the TSC was aimed at the removal or amelioration of symptoms, an instrument was selected which would provide data at this level. Form S of the KAS Behavior Inventories, devised by Katz and Lyerly,[102, 136] was adapted to provide a measure of symptomatic relief. The items on Form S of the KAS Behavior Inventories were classified into subscales which corresponded to the presenting problems described in Project I. Additional items were added, so that the final form of the Symptom Check List (SCL) consists of sixteen subscales: somatic problems, anxiety, depression, hostility and aggression, dependency, obsessive–compulsive problems, psychoses, sexual problems, homosexual problems, marital problems, family conflicts, work problems, travel phobia, alcohol problems, drug problems, other problems. The patient is presented with 97 statements descriptive of problems and symptoms (e.g., "feeling blue," "afraid to take the bus"). He identifies on a four-point scale the extent to which he has felt bothered by the symptoms during the week before.

The SCL was administered to the patient on three occasions: immediately before seeing the therapist for the first time; immediately after the final interview; and six months after completion of treatment. A sample of 300 consecutive cases was used as a standardization population to transform raw scores into standard scores, to permit comparsion of subscales within a patient, and to make other analyses.

Two approaches were studied to determine the most effective method for obtaining the greatest number of returns of the List from patients at the six-month follow up: mailing the List to each patient; requesting each patient to return to the TSC for a personal interview, during which the List was administered.

Fifty patients were selected who had treatment terminated between January 1962 and March 1963. In all these cases, no further referral for therapy was made. These 50 were divided into two groups of 25, matched for:

1. Number of months since termination of treatment.
2. Number of interviews received in the TSC.
3. Diagnosis.
4. Withdrawal from treatment before termination.

Persons in one group were mailed the SCL, a covering letter, and a stamped, addressed return envelope. A reminder was sent to those who did not reply within ten days; after another ten days, the nonrespondent was telephoned. Through these procedures a return of 82 percent was obtained.

Persons in the second group were contacted by telephone and asked to come in to the TSC for an interview; no mention was made of the SCL. Two advanced psychology interns conducted the interviews, administered the SCL, and recorded their evaluation of the patient's present case. They had familiarized themselves with each case before the interview by reading the patient's record and filling out a prepared form. Only nine (36 percent) of the 25 patients in this group were willing to come to the TSC for a follow-up interview.

The mailing procedure was selected with the addition of a questionnaire of three items:

1. Since coming to the Trouble Shooting Clinic, did you apply for further help with your personal problems somewhere else? If so, please describe the kind of help you received.
2. What do you think of the service you received at the Trouble Shooting Clinic?
3. In what way could the Trouble Shooting Clinic be changed to be of greater help to people who have personal problems?

A reminder was sent if the person did not reply after two weeks; he was telephoned after another week if he still failed to respond. These procedures obtained a response from 55.6 percent of the 491 patients followed.

The mean score of the SCL at first administration (immediately before treatment) was 164, at second administration (immediately after last session) 143. The difference is significant at the .001 level. At the third administration (six months later), the mean score was 143. These findings indicate a significant lessening of patient discomfort in response to brief psychotherapy, and that the improvement was maintained for at least six months.

Clinicians' judgments of the patients' improvements correlated at the .05 level of significance with self-evaluations by patients immediately after therapy.

INTENSIVE EVALUATION OF SHORT-TERM PSYCHOANALYTIC PSYCHOTHERAPY (PROJECT III)

Most of the research in psychotherapy has been of long-term treatment. Investigations of brief psychotherapy are few[54, 80, 113, 129, 165] despite research advantages offered by brief psychotherapy: a short time span; the identification of a specific treatment goal which reduces some of the difficulties in evaluating outcome (i.e., the "criterion problem"); and the designation of specific treatment techniques.

Bellak and Smith[19] published the first sytematic, experimental study of psychoanalytic sessions by independent judges and predictors. In a subsequent paper on problems of research in psychoanalysis, Bellak[24] discussed topics relevant to the present consideration: the problems of quantification and of obtaining ratings which are meaningful as well as uncontaminated and statistically treatable; and the use of short-range predictions as a test of hypotheses and as a criterion of validity. This method of repeated short-range prediction and judgment is particularly applicable to the profitable study of brief therapy. (See Figures 1– 4.)

Fig. 1. Dynamic Appraisal

Primary Impulses Aroused

Passivity	0	1	2	3
Activity	0	1	2	3
Homosexuality	0	1	2	3
Heterosexuality	0	1	2	3
Aggress-hostility	0	1	2	3
Sadism	0	1	2	3
Masochism	0	1	2	3

Rating scales

Primary impulses aroused

0	not aroused
1	slight arousal
2	moderate arousal
3	strong arousal

Intensity of manifest second reactions

-3	strong decrease
-2	moderate decrease
-1	slight decrease
0	no change
$+1$	slight increase
$+2$	moderate increase
$+3$	strong increase

Strength of ego functions

-3	strong impairment
-2	moderate impairment
-1	slight impairment
0	no change
$+1$	slight improvement
$+2$	moderate improvement
$+3$	strong improvement

Intensity of Manifest Secondary Reactions

Drives as defenses

passivity	-3	-2	-1	0	$+1$	$+2$	$+3$
activity	-3	-2	-1	0	$+1$	$+2$	$+3$
homosexuality	-3	-2	-1	0	$+1$	$+2$	$+3$
heterosexuality	-3	-2	-1	0	$+1$	$+2$	$+3$
aggress-hostility	-3	-2	-1	0	$+1$	$+2$	$+3$
sadism	-3	-2	-1	0	$+1$	$+2$	$+3$
masochism	-3	-2	-1	0	$+1$	$+2$	$+3$
_____	-3	-2	-1	0	$+1$	$+2$	$+3$
_____	-3	-2	-1	0	$+1$	$+2$	$+3$

Affects and feelings

anxiety, fear	-3	-2	-1	0	$+1$	$+2$	$+3$
elation	-3	-2	-1	0	$+1$	$+2$	$+3$
depression	-3	-2	-1	0	$+1$	$+2$	$+3$
self-esteem	-3	-2	-1	0	$+1$	$+2$	$+3$
guilt, shame	-3	-2	-1	0	$+1$	$+2$	$+3$
anger, rage	-3	-2	-1	0	$+1$	$+2$	$+3$
_____	-3	-2	-1	0	$+1$	$+2$	$+3$
_____	-3	-2	-1	0	$+1$	$+2$	$+3$
_____	-3	-2	-1	0	$+1$	$+2$	$+3$

Ego defenses

repress-denial	-3	-2	-1	0	$+1$	$+2$	$+3$
projection	-3	-2	-1	0	$+1$	$+2$	$+3$
rational-intell.	-3	-2	-1	0	$+1$	$+2$	$+3$
displacement	-3	-2	-1	0	$+1$	$+2$	$+3$
isolation	-3	-2	-1	0	$+1$	$+2$	$+3$
reaction-form.	-3	-2	-1	0	$+1$	$+2$	$+3$
ident. w. agg.	-3	-2	-1	0	$+1$	$+2$	$+3$
_____	-3	-2	-1	0	$+1$	$+2$	$+3$
_____	-3	-2	-1	0	$+1$	$+2$	$+3$

Superego reactions

intensity	-3	-2	-1	0	$+1$	$+2$	$+3$
consistency	-3	-2	-1	0	$+1$	$+2$	$+3$
_____	-3	-2	-1	0	$+1$	$+2$	$+3$
_____	-3	-2	-1	0	$+1$	$+2$	$+3$
_____	-3	-2	-1	0	$+1$	$+2$	$+3$

Strength of ego functions

reality testing	-3	-2	-1	0	$+1$	$+2$	$+3$
object relations	-3	-2	-1	0	$+1$	$+2$	$+3$
thinking	-3	-2	-1	0	$+1$	$+2$	$+3$
impulse control	-3	-2	-1	0	$+1$	$+2$	$+3$
synthesizing	-3	-2	-1	0	$+1$	$+2$	$+3U$
autonomous	-3	-2	-1	0	$+1$	$+2$	$+3U$
_____	-3	-2	-1	0	$+1$	$+2$	$+3$
_____	-3	-2	-1	0	$+1$	$+2$	$+3$
_____	-3	-2	-1	0	$+1$	$+2$	$+3$

Patient_____ Rater_____ Date_____ Int. #_____

Therapist   Judge

(circle one)

Fig. 2. Treatment Plan: Goals of Treatment

Impulses
passivity	−3	−2	−1	0	+1	+2	+3
activity	−3	−2	−1	0	+1	+2	+3
homosexuality	−3	−2	−1	0	+1	+2	+3
heterosexuality	−3	−2	−1	0	+1	+2	+3
aggression-hostility	−3	−2	−1	0	+1	+2	+3
sadism	−3	−2	−1	0	+1	+2	+3
masochism	−3	−2	−1	0	+1	+2	+3
_____	−3	−2	−1	0	+1	+2	+3
_____	−3	−2	−1	0	+1	+2	+3
_____	−3	−2	−1	0	+1	+2	+3

Affects and feeling   *Scales*
anxiety	−3	−2	−1	0	+1	+2	+3		
elation	−3	−2	−1	0	+1	+2	+3	−3	strong decrease
depression	−3	−2	−1	0	+1	+2	+3	−2	moderate decrease
self-esteem	−3	−2	−1	0	+1	+2	+3	−1	slight decrease
guilt, shame	−3	−2	−1	0	+1	+2	+3	0	no change
anger, rage	−3	−2	−1	0	+1	+2	+3	+2	slight increase
_____	−3	−2	−1	0	+1	+2	+3	+1	moderate increase
_____	−3	−2	−1	0	+1	+2	+3	+3	strong increase
_____	−3	−2	−1	0	+1	+2	+3		

Ego defenses
repression-denial	−3	−2	−1	0	+1	+2	+3
projection	−3	−2	−1	0	+1	+2	+3
rational-intellect.	−3	−2	−1	0	+1	+2	+3
displacement	−3	−2	−1	0	+1	+2	+3
isolation	−3	−2	−1	0	+1	+2	+3
reaction formation	−3	−2	−1	0	+1	+2	+3
identif. w. aggress.	−3	−2	−1	0	+1	+2	+3
_____	−3	−2	−1	0	+1	+2	+3
_____	−3	−2	−1	0	+1	+2	+3
_____	−3	−2	−1	0	+1	+2	+3

Superego reactions
intensity	−3	−2	−1	0	+1	+2	+3
consistency	−3	−2	−1	0	+1	+2	+3
_____	−3	−2	−1	0	+1	+2	+3
_____	−3	−2	−1	0	+1	+2	+3
_____	−3	−2	−1	0	+1	+2	+3

Strength of ego functions
reality testing	−3	−2	−1	0	+1	+2	+3
object relations	−3	−2	−1	0	+1	+2	+3
thinking	−3	−2	−1	0	+1	+2	+3
impulse control	−3	−2	−1	0	+1	+2	+3
synthesizing	−3	−2	−1	0	+1	+2	+3
autonomous	−3	−2	−1	0	+1	+2	+3
_____	−3	−2	−1	0	+1	+2	+3
_____	−3	−2	−1	0	+1	+2	+3
_____	−3	−2	−1	0	+1	+2	+3

Patient _____ Rater _____ Date _____ Int. # _____

Therapist   Judge
(circle one)

Fig. 3.   Session Observation: Therapist

Area of Intervention	Rank Cluster	Methods of Intervention	Rank Cluster
Impulses		Catharsis _____	
passivity _____			
activity _____		Mediate catharsis _____	
homosexuality _____			
heterosexuality _____		Understanding—interpreting _____	
aggress-hostility _____			
sadism _____		Sensitization _____	
masochism _____			
_____		Repression and restraint _____	
_____			
Affects and feelings		Making something ego-alien _____	
anxiety, fear _____			
elation _____		Support _____	
depression _____			
self-esteem _____		Intellectualization _____	
guilt, shame _____			
anger, rage _____		Counseling & advising _____	
_____			
_____		Direct environmental manipulation _____	
Ego defenses			
repress-denial _____			
projection _____			
ration-intell. _____			
displacement _____			
isolation _____			
react-form. _____			
ident. w. aggress. _____			
_____			
_____			
Superego reactions			
intensity _____			
consistency _____			
_____			
Ego functions			
reality testing _____			
object relations _____			
thinking _____			
impulse control _____			
synthesizing _____			
autonomous _____			

Patient _____ Rater _____ Date _____ Int.# _____

Therapist   Judge
(circle one)

Fig. 4. Session Observation: Patient

Impulses
- passivity
- activity
- homosexuality
- heterosexuality
- aggression-hostility
- sadism
- masochism

Affects and feelings
- anxiety, fear
- elation
- depression
- self-esteem
- guilt, shame
- anger, rage

Ego defenses
- repression-denial
- projection
- rational-intellect.
- displacement
- isolation
- reaction-formation
- ident. w. aggressor

Superego reactions
- intensity
- consistency

Strength of ego functions
- reality testing
- object relations
- thinking
- impulse control
- synthesizing
- autonomous

Relationship to Therapist
- cooperative
- submissive-dep.
- active re probs.
- hostile
- suspicious
- demanding
- seductive
- aloof
- intellectual
- open to interp.
- anxious

Rating scale

3   strong
2   moderate
1   slight
0   absent
X   no basis for rating

Patient_____ Rater_____ Date_____ Int.#_____

Therapist   Judge
(circle one)

SUMMARY OF RESULTS OF STUDY*

With respect to the overall evaluation of the program, it was found that:

1. The rate of judged improvement among patients treated for five sessions was above the average usually reported in the literature.
2. There was a continuing demand for services during the term of the Clinic.
3. A six-month follow-up study indicated that therapeutic gains were maintained to a significant extent.
4. The data also indicated that self-report inventories, such as the Symptom Check List used in the Clinic, have real utility as devices for screening patients as well as for providing some measure of subjective evaluation of improvement.
5. An intensive process study was made by means of judgments and predictions of a wide variety of clinical variables by six independently rating clinicians. It appears that it was possible—to a statistically, highly significant extent—to agree on the formulation of the psychodynamics, a concise treatment plan, and the actual therapeutic process. Aside from strictly conceptual inferences, predictions were also successfully made against actual extrapolated case material; it appears that, to a given situation, independent observers respond with significantly similar impressions, formulations of interventions, and other clinical judgments.

   The present study strongly supports the contention that very brief, well conceptualized, psychoanalytically oriented psychotherapy has a demonstrable rationale and success, and merits a place in the clinical armamentarium.
6. All the data strongly supported the concept of *brief emergency psychotherapy* as a valuable technique. When applied to patients who were in a state of crisis, and particularly when such patients did not present a history of chronic emotional disturbance, contracts as brief as the three to five sessions offered by the Clinic were strikingly effective. In a significant number of cases, improvement—at least to the extent that it was subjectively appreciated—could be maintained for periods of up to six months. Whether the improvement could be maintained beyond this period cannot be determined from the present data.

---

*Details of the study were reported in the first edition of this volume.

The raw instruments used and the data found also were reported in Bellak, L., Rosenberg, S., et al: Factors related to improvement in brief psychotherapy, and An experimental study of brief psychotherapy. In: Lesse, S., ed. *An Evaluation of the Results of the Psychotherapies*. Springfield, Ill.: Charles C. Thomas, 1968.

Appendix B
Case Histories

A DEPRESSED WOMAN WITH SUICIDAL IMPULSES

Introduction

The patient was a 32 year-old woman of about average intelligence. She had not completed high school, and her vocabulary comprehension was accordingly limited. She was dressed rather carelessly: Her clothes were spotted, and her hair was in need of control.

Her intense anxiety and depression demanded emergency treatment. The decision to treat her within the limits of brief psychotherapy was dictated by her limited financial resources, and the therapist's judgment—formed during the first session—that her ego strength and capacity for insight promised a worthwhile degree of success.

This case illuminates three significant aspects of brief psychotherapy:

1. The appropriateness of the brief therapeutic method is demonstrated with an unsophisticated woman of average intelligence, and limited education and means. Her capacity for cognitive and affective comprehension of the necessary dynamics, and her ability to affect changes in herself, suggest that valuable psychoanalytic principles may indeed be used beneficially with patients other than the well-to-do, the educated, and the sophisticated.

2. Material relevant to the resolution of conflict, though anxiety producing, may be elicited and resolved during brief psychotherapy, provided that there is sufficient ego strength. The emergence of such material advances and accelerates dynamic comprehension; its incorporation as

comprehension and resolution leaves the personality stronger and better able to tolerate impulse and stimulation.

3. In its unfolding, the case provides an excellent example of an occasionally observed exception from one of the basic principles set forth in this book—that the dynamic elements of the precipitating situation and their relationship to preceding developments and events in the patient's life are usually discovered within the first or second session. The dynamics of this patient's depression and anxiety are potentially accessible during the first session, but the actual precipitating event is not discovered until the fifth and last session. The therapist could have investigated a clue in the first session that might have elicited the material more fully during that time. Despite a departure such as this, the authors let stand the principle of early formulation of dynamic causality as an aim of brief therapy. Such early formulation is indeed achievable, and should be sought.

It is unusual that the precipitating factor did not clearly emerge in the first or second session. Nonetheless, the case is used here for demonstration because the patient clearly depicts a "nonideal" case for psychotherapy by virtue of her limited intelligence, vocabulary, and sophistication.

FIRST SESSION

The patient's presenting problems were suicidal thoughts provoked by irritation and anger with her three children, particularly the second, a five-year-old boy whom she described as frequently whining and tearful. While other young mothers in the neighborhood told her that their children too had passed through stages like this, she felt that her control was poorer than theirs must be. (The therapist was alerted to look for anger and rage which the patient must feel to be ego-alien and which she deflected against herself.) By questioning, the therapist learned that her depressive reaction to this irritation began about a month before she came to the clinic, although she had been depressed in recent years.

Her first recalled depression had occurred three years earlier; she was pregnant with her third child, and felt she could not cope with the two older children. Moreover, she feared that her husband would be angry when he learned of her pregnancy. She began to telephone her husband at work as the depression deepened, making him come home from work early to help care for the children. At this time she first began to have thoughts of stabbing herself. She was admitted to a psychiatric hospital, where immediately on admission she "snapped out of it." A second bout of deep depression came during Christmas a year prior to the present consultation.

The therapist's efforts to obtain details of precipitating causes led the patient to reveal the two preceding depressions, and her extreme dependency upon her husband when she became depressed. Her dependency needs raised two questions in the therapist's mind: Did they serve as a form of impulse control? Or did they simply provide some secondary gains? Her acceptance of hospitalization suggested the impulse control mechanism. The therapist also noted that she may have used her quick passage through the crisis when she was hospitalized to bolster her feelings of control and self-esteem. He told her that if she ever got into that condition again she should call him. She should know that while she had a tendency to get depressed, she had shown the ability to snap out of it; talking to someone would help her should the problem arise in the future; and hospitalization most probably would not be necessary.

This encouragement led the patient to describe fears she had had while in the psychiatric hospital, that if she cried and was depressed or moody she would be put in a straitjacket and placed in the "violent ward."

They then explored some historical data. The patient told of an earlier marriage, and of a child by that marriage who was now living with her first husband. She felt much happier with her present husband because he treated her "like a woman should be treated," meaning that he bought her presents, remembered her birthday, and told her that he loved her. Her first marriage broke up because of her husband's infidelity. Her account of her own calmness and lack of agitation, nervousness, and depression in response to her first husband's infidelity were noted by the therapist to himself as containing a suspicious degree of forebearance for her first husband's behavior, and indicative of the repression and denial of anger which she must have exercised. At one point she seemed to recognize the connection between repressed anger and depression, stating, "I didn't get really angry—angry to the point of being depressed or nervous." Following the divorce, she worked, socialized, and met her present husband. These postdivorce experiences indicated good ego functioning in her ability to tolerate the impact of the break-up, and to adapt to a changed social role.

Asked for an autobiography, she described an unhappy home life as a child. When her parents quarrelled, her father would strike her mother. At first she had blamed her father for the distress in the home, but as she grew older she came to see that her mother also contributed to the disharmony; the mother would say things that hurt her father and provoked him into anger. Her parents separated finally when she was 12 years old. She continued to live with her father and his mother.

After her marriage to her present husband, who is nine years her senior, she had become increasingly close to her father. "This past month, when I would get depressed or lonely, instead of wanting to be with my husband, who is very good to me, I would want to be with my father. I don't know why." While visiting her father, she felt relaxed, but as soon as she came home to her husband "my depression would start all over again."

She had intimated quite openly to her husband that she did not expect to live very long. She was aware that this tormented him because his first wife died slowly of a brain tumor. She wondered whether she wanted to hurt him, but didn't know why she would have this wish. She suggested that perhaps it was because of the pain she suffered in her first marriage and her inability to accept her present happiness.

She reminisced about her closeness to her brother and her fierce and competitive dislike of her older sister. A masculine identification was indicated in this data, suggesting to the therapist that it was probably derived from identification with the aggressor. She had her first sexual relationship when she was 13 and married at 16 because she was pregnant. Current dreams indicated an ongoing desire for a more loving response from her first husband and a wish to see him, which her present husband refused to allow her to do. She related a nightmare in which she saw Frankenstein walking; this was what had led her to a private psychiatric consultation. The therapist associated her fear that she might hurt her crying child with her seeking of psychiatric assistance. In response, she complained that her husband was able to ignore the child's whining and crying because he was slightly deaf, although "He doesn't hear a lot of little things that I know he does." *The therapist missed the import of this point, and did not pursue its possible impact on her: the feeling of isolation caused by her husband's hearing difficulty, resulting in heightened irritation, dependency needs, and feelings of deprivation.*

Jealousy between her children was discussed, and the therapist made a mildly cathartic interpretation, indicating the universal phenomenon of jealousy that often leads to anger and the wish to hurt someone. She expanded upon her anger at her children, which was typically expressed in overconcern with their poor eating habits. She told of an episode in which one of the children would not eat dinner, but later wanted an apple. She refused him and he took an apple for himself: "At the time, I had a knife in my hand. He was bending down to the refrigerator getting the apple, and I had the impulse of doing away with him, and . . ."

The therapist empathized with the fear she experienced, and then described displacement of anger. He told her that it is often safer for us to show anger to people we are not afraid of, like our children, rather than our bosses. "It is remarkable that all through your first marriage you didn't really feel any anger about your husband having affairs." She then ventilated some anger combined with catharsis and insight. She told about her first husband's meticulousness, how she would joke while preparing a clean white shirt for him to wear each day, "Here I am ironing your shirt, and isn't it a big joke you will be going out in it with a girl."

She then recalled her own eating problems as a child, the quarrels with her mother, and her mother's efforts to "force food down my throat." She recalled the hospital psychiatrist's literal genital interpretation of her impulse to plunge a knife into her breast: The knife was a penis, her chest a vagina, and she was having intercourse with her chest. At the same time, he told her she needed at least ten electroshock treatments, and that she was on the borderline of being all right or seriously, mentally ill. At this point the therapist reassured her that she was in no danger of a breakdown. The patient returned to the depression she had experienced during her pregnancy and asked for an explanation of its cause. The therapist ascribed it to a fear that her husband would be angry and rejecting; therefore she became sad and guilty. In this way, he interpreted to some degree the deflection of hostility against herself. During this exchange, the patient made a parapraxis associating husband and father, but the therapist, while recognizing it, did not pursue it.

Aware that this session had to end soon, the therapist again reassured her about her ability to control her impulses. He reiterated her concern about "going off your rocker," and reminded her that she always had been able to control these frightening thoughts. He assured her that it is quite common for people to have these kinds of feelings about their children. He also reminded her of her excellent ability to "snap out of it," particularly when "you have had a chance to talk about it to someone outside of the family." She reflected, "I always thought I was weak, that I didn't have the ability to snap out of it."

The session ended with the therapist setting the limits for brief psychotherapy. "You and I will meet together at least four more times, and if there is need for further treatment, we will be able to arrange that. But I have a feeling that within the five visits together you will feel much better and much stronger."

SECOND SESSION

The patient started by commenting that she felt so relaxed that she questioned whether she needed to continue with therapy. The therapist inquired about her thoughts since they had last met. She expressed resentment for her first husband's now pregnant wife. Her expressions became slightly stronger in affect as she proceeded, moving from words like "aggravated" to "it burns me up." She felt that this woman cut her off from her own daughter and prevented the child from writing to her. The therapist helped her express her anger by suggesting the writing of an imaginary letter. "She should kiss the floor for me giving him the divorce for the life that she is leading now." At the same time, she acknowledged again her continued sexual attachment to him. She had told her present husband of this ongoing attachment. The therapist indicated how understanding her present husband must be. Her father had warned her that she might overtax her present husband's understanding, that "a man can just take so much." This brought to mind her initial disturbance and her father's efforts to get her to see a psychiatrist. The therapist interpreted the displacement to her child of rage which arose from the grievances associated with her first marriage. She asked, "Do you think it has anything to do with my childhood life?" referring to the difficulties between her parents, her fears that she was fated to repeat her parents' unhappy marriage, that her anger would lead to separation and loss, and that her husband would abandon her. As she reviewed the fate of the family members, it was evident that she was oppressed by the fear of separation and loss. "I think that way, and my kid sister says, she says that daddy and mommy broke up, your first marriage was bad; my older sister and her husband, they have money problems that they almost split up; my brother and his wife almost split up because my brother chased around, but now that has been solved and calmed down; my sister and her husband solved and calmed down, so my kid sister thinks, you know, she just got married in August, she thinks, well, here I come, you know?" Her own husband, however, had told her, "We are not going to split up, because you are not worrying about me chasing around." But she responded from the depth of her depression: "Well, maybe it is something else. And then, what comes in my mind? Death."

A 65 year-old relative had died during the past weekend. She identified strongly with his widow, saying that she would not be able to go on without her husband. The thoughts about the death of her present husband were intense, almost obsessive. The therapist elected not to touch upon him as a focus for her anger, judging that this would arouse too much anxiety. Instead, he interpreted the inward deflection of hostility and again directed it to the hostility against her first husband and his present wife. He mitigated the interpretation by generalizing that in her position he too would have been angry enough to have death wishes for the first husband.

The patient half denied, half admitted her rage. The therapist tried to work with the denial, pointing out that other women would have been enraged by her first husband's behavior; he questioned why she seemed not to care. They returned again to the quarrels between her parents, and her fear of expressing anger because it would disrupt the marriage. The therapist asked her, "Doesn't this strike you as funny? Your husband was two-timing you, he was spending a lot of money, obviously to support this other woman. You didn't get angry. But a little child cries and you get angry." She reflected her understanding of this paradox and commented on her lifelong tendency to restrain emotional expressions.

They went back to the separation of the parents, and at that point elicited anger at the mother for having left her father, and identification with the father who became so upset by the disruption in the marriage that he had consulted a psychiatrist. She acknowledged, "Any child would be angry if its mother left." The patient wondered if she had put herself in a situation that forced her to get married in order to get away from her mother, but then quickly indicated that she cared tremendously for her first husband. She recalled a dream from the previous night in which she had been making love with someone who was not her husband. The therapist interpreted, "By that you are really saying that instead of being angry at him, you would really like to like your first husband."

She recalls the day she left her first husband. She went to a beauty parlor, bought new clothes, and had supper with him. At supper he asked, "Why didn't you dress like that when we were together?" The therapist asked why she went to that trouble to make herself attractive, and she disclosed her feelings of competition with the other woman. She depicted herself as a ragamuffin who didn't have money to buy clothes because her husband was spending it on his mistress. The therapist contrasted the lack of anger at her first husband who treated her badly with the recurrent thoughts of hurting her present husband who treated her well and was understanding. She returned repeatedly to the narcissistic injury she had suffered from her first husband's indifference to her body and her clothes. Her present husband's perceptiveness, understanding, and concern had not mitigated this old injury.

She ruminated again about the injustice of being separated from her daughter by her first husband's present wife. She complained that her head felt heavy and confused. The therapist interpreted this feeling with the tendency to "feel something and be afraid to express it. You hold it in check until you feel like you are going to explode." He suggested that she felt she had been cheated. She responded that in her first marriage, "We only lived a common life, you know, we had our own apartment and that was that. But she has been to Canada, she has been to Spain, she has been all over the place." The therapist asked, "What would you like to do to her?" She replied, "I don't think I would like to kill her, but I would like to give her a good beating up, maybe." She laughed as she stated this in the freest expression of anger she had been capable of so far in the two sessions.

But she had frightened herself by expressing this anger and needed reassurance. Her thoughts turned to the oldest child. He was not her child, but her husband's. She feared she was unreasonable in chastising him. She also kept a distance between them, and didn't express as much affection for him as for her younger children. What did the therapist think of her as a person? The therapist reassured her within the context of interpreting the relationship between anger and depression. As she reflected further about her treatment of her stepson, her comments indicated improved self-esteem. She was able to see that the child liked her; therefore, she must have been expressing something to him other than anger.

THIRD SESSION

The close approach to her anger at the end of the last session had aroused anxiety. She opened this session with the seemingly mild complaint of having been nervous during the weekend. While trimming shelf paper, she had thought about a woman she met in the hospital who had cut her wrists. She thought of the woman having done it, but not of doing it to herself. She claimed she was able to think about this without being upset. The therapist assured her that it was possible to think of many things that seem frightening, though the thoughts themselves need not scare us. They discussed the sequence of events and thoughts several times as the therapist sought to improve further her ability to tolerate hostile feelings, and to assure her that feelings and thoughts need not lead to overt behavior.

They moved to a discussion of a manifestation of low self-esteem and inwardly deflected aggression. She described "an inferiority complex" in which she paid little attention to her appearance and clothes and devalued her own opinions. Yet, she was able to recall an encoutner with a friend who had differed with her about redecorating the kitchen, in which the patient had persisted in her own view. But when she wore a bathing suit, she thought she was overweight and unattractive and that everyone else looked more attractive, or that her breasts were not large enough to please her husband. But her husband always complimented her when she dressed up and told her how attractive she was to him. She was unable to tolerate too much positive self-evaluation: Her husband, she jokingly commented, should not do all that he did for her; "He should hit me on the head."

Her husband had observed that she was benefitting from this therapy. She had calmed down, and was redecorating the house. Also, she had been able to relate her present depression to her first marriage; when her present husband wanted to discuss what had transpired between her and the therapist, she was reluctant to tell him because she no longer wanted to dwell on her first marriage.

She and her husband had discussed their jealousies. She was jealous of her present husband's first wife, despite the fact that she was dead. Her husband had responded to this by saying, "You don't have to worry about me, but *he* [her first husband] is still walking around." The therapist encouraged her to explore her jealousy. She became franker, not only in admitting to experiencing it, but also in her ability to obtain some distance from it.

Denial set in, and she returned to a sense of mystification about depression, feeling that she was visited by it without cause or reason. The therapist reminded her that she had learned something about the role of anger in forming depression. She responded by becoming somewhat intra-punitive, feeling that she had abandoned her child to her first husband, and that people would feel she was repsonsible for the divorce. This account was followed by some working through of other experiences, feelings, and impulses that contributed to her depression.

She revealed an incestuous episode with her brother when she was about 13 years old that had troubled her for years. Her willingness to communicate this information during the third session suggested excellent rapport with the therapist and the effectiveness of the ongoing working-through process. It was one of the experiences in her life that had made her question her ability to control impulses. She commented that it was a terrible thing, because she had been very young. The therapist indirectly reassured her, "You were just a child." She commented that it had been "something new and exciting that I wanted to explore." It developed that she had had intercourse prior to this event; the therapist did not comment. She felt that her mother's emotional distance had contributed to her vulnerability to her brother's advances; if her mother had been more supportive, she would have been able to go to her for help.

She then described the family's characteristic withholding of affection. She acknowledged that she often was upset by many things she was unable to externalize.

The patient was implying that her early sexual behavior, including the episode with her brother, was a search for love. Her mother had been absent, her father inaccessible. Her own ability to express love was dammed up. The therapist encouraged her to communicate her love to her husband.

FOURTH SESSION

The therapy was arousing anxiety. Again, the patient complained at the beginning of the session, "I think I've got more problems now than I had when I first started with you." Over the weekend, at a New Year's party, she had begun urinating frequently. A physician had diagnosed it as cystitis and recommended a heating pad. She associated the urination with death, a friend having told her, "You pass your water before you die." Some hypersexuality appeared to be associated with the experience. She complained of climaxing but of not feeling satisfied, of having sexual desire all day long. She had been drinking alcohol the night before the frequent urination began.

With no evidence that her compelling need to urinate was organically based (her physician had not prescribed medication for infection), the therapist attempted to minimize her anxiety which associated urination with death. At the same time, he noted to himself the intra-punitive content of her fears. Compelling urination in this young woman suggested to him a number of determinants: intense anxiety; voyeuristic and/or exhibitionistic excitement, and phallic strivings or competitiveness. He attempted to return the discussion to the precipitating circumstances of the party.

For a moment, she appeared overcome with sexual intensity and complained, "I got that feeling again. I can't understand it; I can't cope with it." It developed that her husband didn't dance. During the party he had tended bar, and she, in her low-cut dress, had danced with many other men, including his brothers. She reluctantly admitted that dancing could be sexually exciting, but attempted to deny that this was her response, because she was dancing with "my nephews, my husband's brothers." The therapist suggested that this didn't make any difference, that dancing with these men could have generated sexual excitement which was frightening to her. He did not remind her of the incestuous episode with her brother.

A more specific precipitating event emerged. A nephew in the Army was going off to India, and this reminded her of her first marriage. He would be alone for about six months before his wife joined him.

Her sexual dissatisfaction troubled her; she had never felt this way before. The therapist, however, reminded her of her sexual dissatisfaction in her first marriage, her hurt pride, and self-devaluation. Also, there had been talk at the party about Christine Jorgenson, sexual perversion, and a woman who forced her son to submit to sodomy by her male friends. She reported a dream, the night after the party, of a photographer taking the clothes off a baby, sodomizing the infant, and then photographing it.

The therapist in succession suggested that anxiety, sexual excitement, and the need to repair the narcissistic injury she had suffered from her first husband's neglect could be the basis for her malaise. (The patient's dream offered rather strong support to both the voyeuristic and exhibitionistic elements of the phallic competitiveness hypothesis he was considering.)

The patient clearly was titillated by the discussion of perversions, and wondered if she would ever do something like that. The therapist reminded her that we are curious by nature. They worked for a while on her fear that a thought inevitably must lead to overt behavior. The therapist reminded her of her capacity for control, but she had begun to doubt this ability because of the sexual excitement she was experiencing. She was afraid she might cheat on her husband. The night before, she had visited friends who were entertaining a black man, and she had fantasized about going to bed with him. They discussed her fantasies about black men and their reputed larger penises. She compared herself to other women who deny that they have such thoughts and asked, "Who am I? A freak of nature?"

The therapist told her that curiosity is a driving force in the human personality, and that people are extremely curious about sex, sexual practices, and sex with people different than they might ordinarily know. He told her that people are curious about what it is like to be the opposite sex. He suggested that a woman is curious about what it is like to have an erection and an ejaculation, and that not being able to have these may make some women jealous. He reminded her that in talking about her childhood, she had described herself as a "tomboy," and that this is a way in which girls express their curiosity about what it is like to be a boy. Then he suggested that the urination urge might be a way of expressing that wish, "Here is something that is coming out of you." The patient acknowledged, "It really is." The therapist replied, "Similar to the way it comes out of a man, isn't it? It just gushed! Just the way a man comes."

She responded by saying that she was more frightened by the impulse to be unfaithful to her husband than she was by the wish to be phallic. This led to a recent experience of anger at her husband. Feeling ill, he had returned from the doctor somewhat angry and uncommunicative. He had been experiencing swollen glands and pains in his back and chest over a period of several weeks. She had been frightened that he might die, and she felt the threat of death all around her. She referred to his swollen glands as his "two balls," and reminded the therapist that her husband's first wife had died of a tumor. She then recalled some pornographic material her husband had brought home depicting women inserting candles and brushes into their vaginas. She wondered whether she would ever to something like that to herself. Her husband had explained to her that this is a form of masturbation for women, comparable to a man masturbating when he cannot have a woman.

Finally, she expressed her concern that they had only one more session before therapy had to end, and that she would be left with her sexual over-stimulation, anxiety, and depression. Another possible determinant had emerged for the exacerbation of anxiety: was it a plea to remain in contact with the therapist? He decided to offer reassurance then, but planned to do some work during the next session to help her understand that symptom formation may pursue secondary goals such as satisfying dependency needs or keeping one close to a loved one.

FIFTH SESSION

Urination pressure had ameliorated, as had the obsessional thoughts of using an instrument with which to masturbate. However, she remained preoccupied with the possibility of having an affair with a black man. The therapist offered a concept of hostility based on phallic envy. He had reviewed the preceding session for his own clarification and decided that hostility and anger at her husband were the principle dynamics of that session. His efforts at this meeting, possibly their last, would be toward working through this dynamic. He reasoned that there was little risk that this patient would not respond well to an intellectual approach since she had demonstrated a capacity to translate interpretations into personal, affective terms.

In the ensuing discussing, she was quick to agree that men are more fortunate than women because the sexual behavior of men is generally more accepted or more readily forgiven than that of women.

"It's a man's world," she commented. "If he does something bad, he won't get pushed in the gutter." At the same time that she continued to deny her resentment of this state of affairs, she acknowledged that she desired freedom comparable to that of men. She wanted to have a gay time without restrictions or recriminations, but felt that children hamper a woman's freedom to enjoy even a brief vacation. She communicated a mounting tone of complaint. She was plagued by thoughts of injuring her children. Was she displacing anger for her husband?

At this point a major dynamic of her depression emerged. Her husband, on their return from a brief vacation, during which she had worried about the children they had left at home, had said to her, "You had a good time, but your mind was at home because you were just left with me alone." She asked, "What makes you say that?" He replied, "Because, on account of me not hearing."

After years of urging, this past week he had acceded to her request and had been fitted with a hearing aid. His hearing difficulties had caused him to withdraw socially, which had tied her down and prevented her from having fun, from moving about as freely as she would have liked: "I'm afraid to have a good time because I know he is really not having a good time."

She added, "I have a resentment because, on account of you know, he can't hear well." Her husband was generally morose and withdrawn socially, but when he had a few drinks he forgot about his hearing difficulties, and "People can't believe he is the same person." The therapist made a connection between this description and her reaction to the New Year's party when he isolated himself from the fun by tending bar. She replied that her husband believed this connection was true and she was beginning to agree with him. She questioned her wish to explore new and unusual situations because of the possible effect on him. She had never seen an on-stage play. He was willing to take her. "He keeps saying, 'Come, I'll take you to a play,' but I don't want to go with him because I know he won't hear it." She described the quality of life in her home. "My whole house is at a high keel. The television is full blast for him to hear it. The three kids have to shout to him because he can't hear them, you know."

(It is important to recognize that their work during the preceding four sessions had centered on the related dynamics, although the most relevant content had not been recognized by the therapist. These dynamics dealt with her inward deflection of aggression, fear of poor impulse control, defensiveness, displacement of aggression, and the severity of her superego.)

She then described her husband's jealousy, his inclination to accuse her of flirting with other men. She described an increasing sense of frustration and anger over the past years because of his refusal to do anything about his hearing problem; her efforts to have some fun in spite of these limitations; and the way he watched her "like a hawk" while professing that he wanted her to enjoy herself. The therapist again guided her through the dynamics of anger withheld and suppressed, which generated depression as a result of its inward deflection toward the self.

Despite his infidelity, she and her first husband always enjoyed doing things together. She returned several times to her difficulties in getting her present husband to do anything about his hearing problem and her need to fight against his concern about the cost; to the effects on the children of her husband's isolation; and to the high-decibel level of conversation, radio, and television necessary for him to be able to hear. The therapist pointed out that the loudness of the radio and television must remind her of quarrelling and fighting, of voices raised in anger. She picked this up quickly and readily identified with it emotionally.

Several times they worked through her wish to be active and enjoy herself while at the same time confronted with a feeling of restriction, limitation of pleasure, and the need to control her behavior. The therapist pointed out how deprivation could generate a search for expression and gratification through fantasy, and how her fantasies had alarmed her and contributed to her sense of wrong-doing and guilt. Finally, he again helped her to work through the way in which anger is converted into depression.

He approached the task of terminating their therapeutic relationship. She felt she had been helped. The therapist asked her to telephone him at the end of the month to let him know how things were going. He led her to the matter of secondary gains, asking, "Haven't you ever made up some kind of excuse for seeing someone just because you wanted to see and talk to him?" She readily acknowledged this, and indicated that the best way to see the therapist would be to have a problem, because, "I look forward to coming to see you." Every night she had been saying to her husband, "Oh gosh, this is my last visit with the doctor." Her husband had assured her that she was much better now, to which she added, "Yeah, but I don't know. I says, at least I know that I was coming back, that there was a visit coming up." She ended saying, "I hope I don't get myself so that I get myself sick to come in."

FIRST FOLLOW-UP

Four months later, the patient was seen after she telephoned complaining of nervousness and a fear of insanity, precipitated by the experience of a neighbor who "snapped and lost her mind."

In the interval, she had become involved in a necking episode with a childhood friend; she had told her husband about this, who was upset about it. Her husband had been turning down requests for social activities, but was willing to go out with her alone. He refused to socialize in groups. She had had incestuous thoughts about her children, involving fantasies projected ahead to their adulthood. She also had masturbated with a brush handle.

She was reassured about her fantasies and reminded that she had been afraid to let herself have thoughts of this nature before. She recalled telling the therapist about her incestuous experience with her brother. The therapist suggested that she may even have had some fantasies about him. She acknowledged these and reported that they coincided with her compelling urge to urinate, and that she had had more fantasies since. She believed that these may have been involved in her need to return to the therapist. The therapist suggested to her that her need to tell her husband of her necking experience had been an expression of her anger at him for circumscribing her pleasure, and that a more constructive approach would have been to tell him that she had a real need for him to be more socially active together, and that his refusal to do so was related in some measure to her depression and anxiety. She should also insist that he get a proper hearing aid. As expected, she was noticeably reassured and calmed at the close of the session.

SECOND FOLLOW-UP

Three months after the first follow-up, the patient was contacted in order to secure her permission to use her case material for publication. Her appearance was strikingly different. She was smartly dressed and youthful appearing, and her hair was attractively groomed. She and several mothers in the neighborhood had entered a babysitting arrangement that provided each of them with one free day a week. She had been feeling "quite well." Occasionally, she had "bad thoughts," but was able to talk herself out of them by reviewing some of the topics discussed in her treatment, particularly her rivalry for men.

Following her strong and continued insistence, her husband had obtained a proper hearing aid and was now never without it. The television had been turned down to a reasonable volume. She didn't have to shout; he had a better time at parties; she was able to leave him and mix with other people. He was considering surgery that might obviate the need for a hearing aid, and despite the expense she was encouraging him to go ahead with it.

Sometimes she thought she might be "going crazy," but was helped by knowing that this fear was due to "bad thoughts." Again, she was able to control the feeling by reviewing the dynamics discussed in treatment. She was no longer bothered by disturbing sexual fantasies and was generally more comfortable.

AN IDENTIFICATION PROBLEM

The following case, dealing with manifest depression and a latent character neurosis, demonstrates the possibility of dealing with a relatively complex problem in brief psychotherapy.

Only a gifted writer can do justice to case histories. This account certainly seems pale compared to the actual life drama. Precipitated by the death of President Kennedy, this young woman was in a depression which at first seemed possibly suicidal. A private language developed very quickly between the therapist and this very bright and insightful patient that enabled a quick exchange of flashes of insight, at times even without full verbalization.

A great deal is left out of the account, otherwise a monograph rather than a precis would be necessary. For instance, nothing is detailed here regarding the fact that she interrupted her account of pleasing her mother with good grades with a dream of having sex with a man under the pretense of not being aware of it. In the therapist's mind the sequence was noted and led to an early hypothesis that men were identified with her mother, and that she always felt she had to pretend to submit to her mother with mixed wishes, fear, and guilt—probably resulting in character problems. But there was certainly not the time in brief therapy to choose this area of intervention; rather, the somewhat superficial observation was made that her reaction of disgust confirmed her guilt feelings. Similarly overdetermined features abound throughout, including the reasons given for form and methods of intervention, following the principles laid down earlier in this text. For instance, the therapist's statement, "The cure is not in becoming wild again," was made to strengthen the patient's superego at a point when the therapist was not yet sure how self-harming her reaction to guilt might be.

If this young woman should have problems in the future, it would be an indirect benefit of brief intervention that she would very promptly look for further and possibly more extensive help than was possible in the time limit imposed by the reality of her brief stay in the city where the therapy occurred.

FIRST SESSION

The patient, Fran, was an educated, intelligent young black woman who had just graduated from college with a degree in mathematics. She was going on to a job as dean of women for a college, and was in New york City to work temporarily as a mathematician.

She came to the clinic on the day that President Kennedy was assassinated. She explained that the loss of this most worthy life made her feel that she was wasting her own life. The therapist noted to himself her strong identification with both success and maleness, and also her apparently severe superego. The patient appeared tense, anxious, and depressed.

She talked about dating several men, even having an "understanding" with more than one of them. She had accepted marriage proposals, although she had not really wanted to.

In response to the therapist's request she catalogued her problems:

1. She was never satisfied that she had done her best.
2. She was overly concerned that people like and accept her.
3. She doubted that she was able to love, because she was so selfish.
4. She tended to become depressed.
5. She must be all things to people, so that she would go out of her way to write to men she didn't like in order to support them in their crises.
6. She was restless, searching, unsatisfied, and exceedingly active.
7. She could not control her sexual feelings.

(The therapist's earlier postulation of a severe superego was confirmed by some of these statements. Additionally, he perceived defensive efforts at placation and altruism, and some possible sources of her tension, anxiety, and depression.)

The patient's mother had always expected a great deal from her in all areas of performance. Her mother was the more dominant parent; as long as the patient could recall, her mother had worked. Though B grades were actually a more suitable level for her, she had strained to make A's to please her mother.

The patient interrupted this family account to tell of a recent "bad" dream: She had been in bed with a man who was having sex with her while she slept; she was not supposed to be aware of what was going on. Her expressed disgust with the dream confirmed the punitiveness of her conscience. By association she told of a recent affair with a man whom she had been distressed to discover was married. With the therapist's help she was able to see both the wish and the denial in the dream, though her disgust remained unmitigated.

The therapist began to formulate his conceptualization of the precipitating event from these preceding statements and from some additional references to the sense of freedom that being in New York suggested to her, "if I want to be wild, drinking, smoking, and having sexual relations." Free from the need to study and achieve, and away from both mother and professors, she was threatened by a loss of impulse control. Moreover, she was in conflict because the stay in the city would be a short one, and soon she would have to begin her employment and conduct herself in a manner befitting that role.

The therapist interpreted this concept to her and sought earlier related events. She recalled a party at age 14, at which she had become drunk. She had been disappointed because her father refused to escort her to the party. He came for her, carried her home like a "sack of potatoes," and stayed home from work the next day to nurse her. She had resolved then that people must not have this bad impression of her, and had begun to study in earnest.

Envy of her younger sister came to the fore, along with recollections of her father in a maternal role. Her father had been psychiatrically ill when her sister was born, and had stayed at home caring for the baby while her mother worked. Fran had been compelled to do the housekeeping while her father and the baby played together.

She had been wild as a child, using obscene language outside the home, seeing a young man in defiance of her parents' orders, and having intercourse at age 14 or 15. However, this behavior had stopped after the party episode.

Her mother was the stronger of the parents; she worked steadily and made all the decisions. By contrast, her father shopped, cooked, and did the family laundry. She witnessed little love between her parents. Indeed, she had believed for a time that her father was impotent as a result of an operation he had had, but only recently had learned that he had affairs. She related an episode in which she had taken the role of the controlling mother: Her father, absorbed in playing with her sister, had neglected to cook dinner, and her sister had not done her chores; Fran had yelled at them in reprimand.

She felt she was like her mother in that she was incapable of love. Fran modified this; her mother loved her, but didn't show it. She and her mother had been alone together for four years while her father was in the Army and before her sister was born. Her early memories were of her sister's birth and Fran's excitement in telling people about her arrival, and of her father at home with her sister.

With the session drawing to a close, the therapist summed up and offered an interpretation, along with a caution against acting out: "You feel unhappy and you are dissatisfied with yourself. You are in conflict between your moral sense and your sexual feelings. This is what makes you feel self-centered at times and then extremely self-sacrificing at other times. Until you were 14 you were wild, then you became moral, but with that you became unhappy. But the cure is not in becoming wild again."

Fran interjected that such behavior would make her feel too guilty, and that whatever pleasure or relief she might get from being wild would not be worth the guilt.

The therapist supported her in this observation and went on to bolster her self-esteem and foster the therapeutic alliance: "You are very bright and have the capacity for insight. We should be able to work this out very well and help you feel more comfortable."

SECOND SESSION

Fran complained of vague dreams during the past week that she could not recall in the therapy session. She associated them with the imminent visit of a man she liked, who wanted to marry her. But she had a powerful conflict about marrying. She made great efforts to convince a man what a good wife she would make, but then retreated when he began to show interest in marriage. If she had to sell herself, she felt she could not be as good as she tried to be, and so her efforts backfired. She had always felt that she had to prove her worthiness in the form of accomplishments: "Mother gave us gifts when we did well."

She saw the strong possibility of a connection between striving to obtain affection and praise through performance, and her complaints of restlessness and hyperactivity.

The therapist and Fran worked on her need for distance in relationships, as rooted in her fear of being hurt if she got too close, which in turn appeared to derive from the pain of the loss of her father to her sister. Her self-centeredness was a protection against disappointment. Fran recalled an episode when she was eight: swinging "wildly" from a chandelier, she had been knocked into unconsciousness. Insightfully, she observed that she feared death if she gave in to her impulses, that this fear was related to her fear of closeness.

The therapist hypothesized that early in life she had felt let down in her wish to be loved. She responded by postulating that she could recall little of her childhood because it was so unhappy.

An exchange followed about her tension, her drive for achievement, and her compulsive working habits. She used these drives and habits to discharge dammed up energy, and to avoid temptation. She dwelled upon her need to keep her hands busy, reviewed the forces that made her feel charged up (i.e., masturbation). By association she introduced an exhibitionistic element in her early wish to be a model, and some genital play when eight or nine during a visit to the country. On her return to the city she had been preoccupied with the experience for weeks. The therapist decided not to interrupt her with an interpretation of a possible link to her loss of consciousness in the chandelier episode which had occurred about the same time.

Fran recalled a repetitive dream of a man named Thelma—her aunt's name—chasing her while she was nude. She then recalled another dream about folds in drapery which was not really folded. Asked to associate the folds, she linked them directly to female genitalia.

The therapist told her that they would come back to the dream about Thelma, and that if they could understand what made her anxious when she was having this repetitive dream, they would understand her current fears.

THIRD SESSION

Fran opened the session by spontaneously introducing the Thelma dream; it was evident that she has been thinking about it a great deal. If she pursued sex directly, and therefore acknowledged her feelings and wishes, she felt overwhelmingly guilty; so she disguised her wish by being chased. The therapist asked her for the sources of the conflict and her guilt, which she related to her wish that the men she was with feel good about themselves. The therapist in turn related this to her compelling need to feel liked and accepted.

She then reflected that she had never really enjoyed intercourse, and that some need other than sex drove her to win and seduce men. She went back to the Thelma dream, and voluntarily picked up its homosexual theme. She recalled cuddling in bed with her sister, liking girls better than boys, and the tomboy phase of her childhood when she had fought with boys and tried to beat them at their own games such as ball and marbles. The therapist asked if this had anything to do with being dissatisfied with herself.

She responded with thoughts and feelings about the limited opportunities available in American society for a black person. The therapist inquired how she felt about him as a white. She stated that she felt comfortable with him; she felt that he understood and accepted her, and that this understanding reflected his acceptance. The therapist drew a link between her feelings of second-class status and being both black and female.

There followed a long sequence in which the conflict over release or containment of impulse was likened to the conflicts over professionalism or marriage, and seeking to please her mother while at the same time being sharply competitive with her. She acknowledged that she saw the common denominator between these conflicts and the second-class feeling that entered into them.

Fran said that the past week had been pleasant for her, that she had felt more comfortable, more stable, and especially more flexible about her work and social activities.

FOURTH SESSION

She was late because she had taken the wrong subway. She said that she was sleeping better. Her boyfriend was in town staying with her. She enjoyed the intimacy without guilt. There was no sexual intercourse. Her friends knew about the arrangement; again, she felt no guilt.

She related her wish to remain unmarried to the wish to be a bachelor, "to live like a man." However, she perceived men as essentially weak, like her father. Her mother was stronger, and, in fact, more masculine than her father. Her desire to remain unmarried and to be like a bachelor was a wish to be a strong and domineering man, which she associated with her mother. Her wish to be active like her mother compounded her ambivalence about being female. Also, because she felt she couldn't win her father and that she had lost him to her sister, her sense of worth was damaged by this loss.

She responded with more details about her father's feminine qualities, how he liked to set the girls' hair. She also recalled thoughts that he was not really her own father, which would explain her feeling that he didn't really love her, that her strenuous efforts to please men were based on her need and efforts to win her father's love and respect.

Fran's resistance was prominent in this session. She recited how practical she was, and how she didn't daydream. The therapist encouraged her to speculate about what she would do if she had a million dollars. She would feel absolutely free and able to do whatever she wanted whenever she wanted. Her boyfriend's professions of his love for her made her feel uncomfortable, especially his protestation that he couldn't live without her. She would prefer him to be more aloof and less solicitous.

The therapist took her back to the Thelma dream and told her that dreams may express wishes. He reminded her of her wish for a strong man. Perhaps she wished for a strong man who would boss and dominate her. Perhaps she would enjoy being overwhelmed. She recalled her excitement during intercourse with the married man; his behavior had been rather bossy and dominating. Perhaps this also explained why she had never had real pleasure during intercourse with other men. The therapist suggested that her mother's personality predisposed this condition in Fran: She looked for her mother's qualities in men and had contempt for "nice guys"; she got a thrill from "bastards." He reflected that it was a pity her reasoning worked that way because it alienated her from many worthy people, it limited her opportunities for meaningful relationships, and above all it put her in a rather demeaned position. Fran also related the mechanism to her father's gentleness.

FIFTH SESSION

Fran opened the session with the complaint that it had been a difficult week. Her boyfriend treated her too courteously, he was too kind, and he behaved as if she was fragile. The therapist interpreted: "You basically feel his actions suggest that you are weak, but you end up saying he's the weak one. You believe that being feminine is to be weak, while to get close to a man is to expose yourself to being hurt. So you exaggerate the other side; you equate nastiness with strength. You know, Franklin D. Roosevelt had difficulty firing people, and he was so tender he cried at movies, yet he was probably one of the strongest persons of our century so far. There was nothing weak about him.''

Fran commented on her conflictual admiration and resentment of her mother's strength. The therapist referred to her father's actual weaknesses, and his apparent dependency on and placation of her mother. The therapist pointed out that as role models Fran's father and mother contributed to her confusion of sexual ieentification. She responded with an expression of optimism: She was better in this respect, and many of the issues had been clarified for her. Although she did not feel completely different in all respects, she did feel less pressure to be all things to all people, and she felt less conflcit about her wishes and desires.

The therapist indicated that she would need to recall repeatedly what they had discussed, especially the origins of her need for approval. She would probably have to keep herself aware of and work at accepting more passivity in her relationships, especially with men she cared about, in the same way that she would have to work at counteracting her tendency to admire roughness.

Fran acknowledged that she had been excited by the primitive, tough aspects of camping, and of outdoor life in general. Participating in such activities made her feel competent and effective.

The therapist reflected upon the necessity to give up a measure of one thing to obtain something else one might want. Thus, to have a good relationship, she might have to give up a measure of freedom. To have a family, should that be what she wanted, at times she would probably have to agree to put out the lights if her husband wanted to sleep, or be home at specific times to feed the children. She would have to understand the trade-offs in these restrictions, or else find herself becoming depressed. Unless she kept herself aware of making these choices—that they weren't simply being imposed upon her—she would again feel the compulsion to prove that she couldn't be contained or dominated.

She indicated awareness of how detrimental such compensatory overreactions could be in marriage. As she and the therapist worked over this point, increasing evidence emerged that Fran sensed a physical danger in submitting to another person. The therapist interpreted this fear: She wished for, but was afraid to have a man (like her mother) on top of her in intercourse. Her anxiety became manifest, and again they worked through the many aspects of her activity–passivity conflict.

Sensing the session drawing to a close, she reviewed her feeling of progress. She had not been crying. Her sleeping had improved and she awoke more refreshed. The greatest improvement was that her depression had lifted noticeably. Moreover, she felt much less tension.

The therapist structured the future. She didn't have to get totally better all at once to feel that she had achieved a worthy goal in therapy. These things took time. She would have to keep working at it, but she now had tools that had not been available to her before. Nor did she have to feel that entering a marriage immediately was necessarily a major sign that she was better. She was young enough to enjoy her single freedom for several years, after which she would probably want to work toward settling down.

They discussed steps she might take if she encountered emotional trouble in the future. These included her use of the facilities around the college where she would be working, or a telephone call to this therapist. A mail follow-up report was agreed upon.

Six months later the therapist received a note from Fran stating that she was doing well and enjoying her job more than she had expected. She was continuing to date the man who had visited her in New York City, but was also seeing other men.

AN ACUTE ANXIETY ATTACK COMPLICATED BY CHARACTEROLOGICAL FEATURES

The following case history illustrates the treatment of a blue collar worker who first came to the hospital in an ambulance thinking he had had a heart attack; after further examination, he was sent to the psychiatric clinic where he was interviewed by a medical student. On the basis of the intake notes, and with his written permission, the man was accepted as a patient, and was interviewed behind a one-way mirror and simultaneously videotaped.

This method allows observers to be direct participants. At the same time the videotape can be used for playing over crucial portions of the sessions for renewed scrutiny of the patient's statements and behavior, and the therapist's interaction. Small segments can be discussed in exhaustive detail, including the formation of concise hypotheses to be tested for their predictive power against the videotaped records of future sessions.

This case also illustrates that we do not rigidly adhere to the five or six hour format. There was reason to add three more sessions as new material emerged and needed working through in conjunction with additional dynamic propositions.

Intake Notes by a Medical Student

Mr. F. was a 27-year-old, white male, divorced and now living with the woman he called his common-law wife. He had a five-year-old daughter by his first wife and a two-year-old daughter by his second.

CHIEF COMPLAINT

On April 8, 1973 the patient had a sudden onset of palpitations, tightening in his chest, sweating, severe diffuse anxiety, and the feeling of a heart attack which took him to the medical emergency clinic. There was, however, no medical problem. Several months later, he had numerous similar attacks and was generally worried about himself and these "bad thoughts."

PRESENT ILLNESS

The patient's first wife had suffered what the patient described as a severe depression following the birth of their daughter in 1968. The patient "couldn't buy this"; he didn't understand and couldn't tolerate her demanding sadness, and began having affairs and paying his first wife little attention. In 1971 his girlfriend became pregnant and a divorce, which had been in the air, became finalized. He immediately took up residence with his girlfriend, whom he now called his wife. He felt guilty about the way he treated his first wife. He had had second thoughts about the divorce before it went through but she wouldn't take him back.

In 1969 he got a job as a general manager of a large gas station. He started at $130 per week and was taught the job from scratch by the franchise owner of the station. He had to overcome anxiety about working with the tools of the job; when he was a boy his father, a mechanic, had constantly derided him for any ineptitude he had with tools. He succeeded in overcoming his anxiety and by 1972 was making $240 a week and was in firm control of his job. He reported a change that took place in his personality during the period he was succeeding in the job. Prior to this time he had been a little anxious and worried about his competence in various areas; as he became a successful manager he began to be tougher, more commanding, sarcastic, and argumentive, in his words "a smart ass." He reported that these qualities were similar to those manifested in his father's personality, qualities which the patient felt were important in his father's preventing him from developing any self-confidence.

The patient's attack on April 8, 1973 occurred just before his boss was due back from a three-week vacation. It consisted of severe anxiety with thoughts of having a heart attack which took him to the medical emergency clinic. His other attacks occurred mostly while driving; his fearful thoughts were of accidents and injury. These attacks came about when he was driving away after an argument with someone. Because of these attacks and because of the persisting severe anxiety, he had to leave his job, and after being essentially immobilized for a month, he took a job paying about $95 a week, pumping gas in another service station. In the past few months, he felt somewhat better but he continued to be very anxious and to have similar occasional attacks. He sought treatment because of these continuing symptoms and because his first wife had been telling him how much psychiatry had helped her.

RELATED HISTORY

The patient's father used to be a drug dealer and spent several periods in jail during the patient's childhood. He had been and still was a mechanic. According to the patient he had been "straight" for the past 20 years. The father's sarcasm and criticism of the patient as a boy had made him feel "like shit, lost, shunned," and "like a little boy." His mother had always been a "nervous, fearful person," more so since a mastectomy five years ago. The patient said with seeming contempt that she was a "wreck" and "a sin" to behold. Relations between the parents were characterized by the father's "shrewd" criticisms of the mother, after which he fell asleep, leaving her talking to herself. Other significant figures were an older cousin with whom the patient could talk about feelings that he could not express to his parents, and two older boys who lived upstairs in his building and took care of him in the Harlem streets where he grew up.

MENTAL STATUS

The patient presented himself as a very neat, clean-cut, cooperative young man in a sparkling clean gas station uniform. He related well to the interviewer. Affectively he was anxious and mildly agitated. He expressed a full range of affect although the predominant mood seemed to be anxiety. His speech was pressured and circumlocutious with an obsessional quality, especially when talking about his fears. There was no evidence of a thought disorder, hallucinations, or delusions. Sensorium was within normal limits.

In the course of the evaluation he became somewhat less anxious and seemed very motivated for treatment. He did have one attack as described above on the morning before coming to the therapy session; this attack occurred while driving, following an argument he had with an old man over a parking space. His last attack was two months prior to this one and also occurred while driving, following an argument he had with his father over his father's treatment of his mother.

PROGRESS NOTE

This 27-year-old man was originally seen for evaluation by a medical student, when the preceding case summary was prepared. Subsequent to the evaluation, the patient was seen by a therapist as a demonstration of brief and emergency psychotherapy. The sessions were usually videotaped. The patient was seen a total of five times for the basic therapy, and had follow-up sessions approximately one month apart. Therapy terminated with the therapist's invitation to call at any time the patient felt the need for it.

This case is especially instructive because it demonstrates the need for progressively better hypotheses, in order to understand the symptoms as the final common path of a variety of factors. It is important to understand why the patient had his anxiety attack exactly that Saturday at 10:30 A.M., and not before or after. Such understanding is an internal test of the validity of the therapist's hypotheses. It also demonstrates the working-through process in the course of treatment, and the fact that five sessions can apparently lead to increasing improvement and—to judge for the time being—some lasting improvement, if not total recovery.

From the data compiled at intake, we agreed as a first hypothesis that the patient had developed his anxiety attack precisely on the morning of April 8, because that was the day on which his boss returned from vacation. The patient had been left in charge of the gas station employing 28 people, and had apparently resented the return of this paternal figure. The intrapsychic awareness of this aggression manifested itself as signal anxiety. The patient somatized his anxiety in the form of a heart attack, which was what actually brought him to the emergency clinic of the hospital.

This hypothesis fits much of the history of an unusually threatening and dangerous father figure who had also belittled the patient—"He can't handle a screwdriver"—which he dealt with symbolically and which was also manifested in his difficulties with other men. After this anxiety attack the patient settled for a much inferior job as a gas station attendant, making $95 instead of $240 a week. This "demotion" was consistent with the effects of a success neurosis, "retiring from competition with father."

In the *first session* with the patient, it appeared, however, that the facts did not quite fit the case: The boss had not really returned from vacation to take over the main role again, he had only returned for a few hours and left again for another two-week vacation; the patient therefore had no real reason for feeling demoted. It also became clear that an important part of the symptomatology was concern for what would happen to his families—his wife and daughter from his first marriage, and his second, common-law wife and their daughter—if he should die.

In the *second session,* it appeared that the Wednesday prior to the "heart attack" the patient had given blood for the aunt of a friend and felt weak from that experience. This was apparently the predisposing factor in feeling sick, but the question remained as to why he didn't panic until Saturday. In the *third session* it emerged that Saturday morning a friend had kidded him because he had been told, upon his arrival at the hospital to donate blood, that he didn't need to give any more; enough had been collected. This news had made the patient feel somewhat a patsy, and had apparently aroused some anger, which may have contributed to having the anxiety attack just then—in response to another aggressive stimulus and the feeling of having to "give" instead of "getting." Even the episode with his friend did not seem sufficient to explain the specificity of the attack. In a *fourth session* it became clear that the patient had given blood on other occasions without any difficulties. What seemed to make this time different from other times was that prior to the blood donation he had had a quarrel with his first wife about supporting her. He apparently resented her demands and also felt guilty that he was not taking better care of the child of his first marriage. He identified with this child, especially because he was away from her in the same way his father had been away from him—when his father was in jail, he had missed him. Having given blood when his friend didn't have to, now took on further significance; specifically that the patient was generally fed up with having to support two families and two children when he felt he was not getting enough care for himself. At the same time he identified with the "deprived" child by wanting to be taken care of as a sick man. His concern that his family might be left unsupported if he died seemed like a projection: wishing he did not have to take care of them as well as giving in to his own passive oral desires to be taken care of by doctors and nurses.

On the crucial Saturday of the major attack the patient had occasion to acutely experience a conflict in his boss's absence. On the one hand he identified actively with his father by being cocky, aggressive, and assertive with his employees. On the other hand he had an increasing identification with the women in his life: his younger sister; his mother, who was always ill and complaining (in the last five years particularly); his daughters; and his first wife, whom he left soon after her second child was born (her hemorrhaging at that time had upset him especially).

There were several factors in his history that supported hypotheses of passive wishes. When his father was in jail he was really overprotected by his mother, two rather macho men who were living in the same house, and two brothers who would take him out with them. If a situation threatened to get tough in a bar they would put him in a cab and tell him to go home before trouble started.

His fears of harm related easily to a father who proudly told of his knife fights; these fears manifested themselves in his childhood neurotic fear of being bitten by sharks. At one point in his adolescence, however, he showed a tendency to counter-phobic moves; he actually decided to go shark fishing—an event which at the last minute was supposedly interfered with by other circumstances.

The ambivalent dependence on his mother also manifested itself in a mild agoraphobia; he mentioned only incidentally that he was frequently afraid to drive long distances and would become more anxious the farther he was from home base. At the same time this agoraphobia was combined with a fear of harm by aggression in that he would become particularly anxious when driving close to big trucks. Again, however, his counter-phobic tendencies became apparent as he told of sometimes forcing himself to drive between two trucks, despite great anxiety.

His attitude toward his mother was often dramatically illustrated; as soon as he mentioned her he would say, "Oh, forget about her." In the fourth session a particularly dramatic episode occurred in which he suddenly began to stutter heavily and was unable to say "mother." Though he related that he had had a speech impediment in his childhood, the therapist had heard no prior evidence of it in the patient's speech. The therapist then became interested in possible neurological aspects of his problems; it was later found that his younger sister was left-handed, and that the patient had experienced difficulty with skills involving fine coordiantion. The therapist became particularly concerned when the patient said that in the last few years it had become difficult for him to write the figure "5."

His father's statement that he couldn't handle a screwdriver now acquired more than symbolic significance and the therapist wondered if this patient didn't suffer from at least a minimal brain disorder. Because he claimed that a difficulty in writing the number five was of relatively recent onset, the therapist wanted a neurological examination including a soft-signs test, an EEG, etc., to assure that there was no newly developing pathology in addition to a possible minimal brain dysfunction. The patient was found to be essentially neurologically negative, but to the therapist's disappointment no EEG was performed, nor were soft signs investigated.

The therapist was left to specualte that such awkwardness as the patient may have felt was due to a minimal brain disorder and may have influenced his symptom choice in the form of somatization.

The *fifth interview* was spent on working through, as had been done on each of the previous interviews, but also involved was a systematic rereading of previous ground, with the patient stating much of it. Also discussed was how to behave like the intelligent adult male he was—that taking a managerial job might help him to resolve the conflict of wishing to be passive versus the wish to be an aggressive male like his father (which, in turn, produced fears of castration and identification with his daughter as part of his oral needs). The patient related that although he had recently lived with his in-laws, he had just moved into his own apartment, enjoyed it, and rarely worried. He was quite willing to terminate therapy with the idea that he should call the therapist if need be. He was given a definite appointment for a month later.

In this *follow-up interview,* the patient complained about some discomfort in his stomach, but otherwise stated that he had been feeling almost perfectly well, as his wife had told the therapist over the telephone when she made the appointment for him.

More information, however, was obtained. After the attack on the crucial Saturday morning, he returned to work for three weeks, not feeling quite all right, but nevertheless functioning as manager until one night when he saw Dragnet on TV: two cops were killed and their wives and children were left unprovided for. This specific show seemed to have set off his entire complex of notions about not being taken care of on one hand, and the wish not to have to take care of anyone on the other hand. It also reawakened fears of gangsters like his father. After he saw this Dragnet episode, he simply stayed home from May until November of that year, which revealed more pathology than previously was recognized. At first he insisted that his second wife do nothing but take care of him; then he insisted that she quit her job to stay home with him; and finally, he moved with her and their daughter to his own parents' home because he felt that his wife had to pay too much attention to his daughter, and he wanted her or his mother to be free to look after him in case he should be sick. Later he moved to his in-laws.

In this interview, in which the therapist wondered about his job situation, it became apparent that he had been on welfare for some time, and that he had acquired much secondary gain from the passivity involved in being on welfare. In fact, welfare was now supporting his first wife and daughter as well as contributing to his own support, so that he received as much as $200 a week, which was much better than living on the $95 that he had made as a gas station attendant. This situation of secondary gain was discussed with him and seemed important enough to warrant another therapy session.

A week later the patient reported feeling practically well all the time, only once feeling some gastric discomfort when his landlady and her husband would not come in for coffee. He understood clearly that this was a stomachache in response to feeling unloved. His passive oral desires were especially worked through. He had been coddled as a child, and he was angry over having to take care of the two families instead of being taken care of himself. Clearly his anger was in conflict with his superego. We found reason to believe that his success neurosis manifested itself frequently; as soon as everything seemed satisfactory, he would start to worry. His reluctance to take on an appropriate job again and increase his self-esteem by substituting a real income for welfare was also related in part to an Oedipal fear. It was agreed that he would call the therapist in a month.

In his *last session* with the therapist, the patient had had some relapse of feelings of discomfort, particularly with regard to driving too far from home. It was found that this fear had been precipitated after he saw a young boy run over by a car and killed. This provided the opportunity to discuss his identification with that boy and his fear of death as a form of passivity like sleep; his wish to be as close to home base and to his mother as possible; and his feeling of being endangered the further he travelled from her.

The patient reported at this session that he generally felt well, was enjoying life in his own apartment, had become manager of a baseball team, and was to be interviewed soon for a job as a gas station manager.

A capsule formulation of his problem was agreed on: namely, the necessity of not wishing to be a little girl, and not wishing to be taken care of; rather, to be an adult male who takes care of others and at the same time is not afraid of his male adult role as a form of competition with a father figure, of whom he was afraid.

The patient and therapist met by accident a little over a year after the last interview. The patient had taken a job in the neighborhood of the hospital and was generally feeling well and without anxiety symptoms. They parted on friendly terms. There is just the merest suspicion that finding a job so close to the hospital might have been part of a tranference dependence:

whether this actually was the case is not certain. One should not complain if, even with the help of some continued positive transference, he now lives without disturbance.

POSTSCRIPT

As a final diagnosis, we would have to record the following:

1. Anxiety attacks with somatization (heart attack, stomach pains).
2. Mild agoraphobia.
3. Success neurosis.
4. Possible minimal brain dysfunction in childhood, with poor control of small movements, and a stutter, with some adult residue.

This case report is useful for studying the acute presenting symptom—the anxiety attack that took Mr. F. to the emergency clinic with a supposed heart attack—as the final common path of complex, indicating factors. As new facts emerged the therapist did not hesitate to extend treatment to eight sessions.

At first the therapist was wrongly overimpressed with the role of a success neurosis in the precipitating attack. It appeared that the attack was related to the fact that a friend had induced him to be a blood donor but had not given blood himself. This aroused anger in the patient as well as the wish not to have to take care of his first wife and daughter, and to be taken care of himself (in the hospital). At the same time his fear of death was a projection of the wish to deprive the wife and daughter of his support by illness or death.

It seemed that he was feeling weak after having given the blood three days prior to his "heart attack." This feeling of weakness was related to his upset over the hemorrhages his first wife had in relation to pregnancy, his awareness of his mother's menstrual bleeding, and his father's history as a knife fighter.

To some extent at least, he recovered for about three weeks after his "heart attack," and returned to the job. The upsetting Dragnet show on television was the final blow and he regressed to staying at home and first demanding his wife's care and finally his mother's. His intermittent chances for a low-paying, undemanding job as a gas station attendant satisfied his success neurosis but was interfered with by the fact that he received twice as much in relief and unemployment compensation than he could demand on the job. Secondary gain from his passivity played a role and he then discussed a mild agoraphobia as an additional form of dependence on his mother. The farther he drove from his home base, the more anxious he felt. At the same time, his fears of being fallen on by big trucks reminds one of "Little Hans."

The awkwardness he experienced from minimal brain dysfunction as a child may well have provided a matrix for his feelings of helplessness, and added strength to his passive wishes.

Bibliography

1. Abraham, K. *Selected Papers on Psychoanalysis*. New York: Basic Books, 1953.
2. *Action for Mental Health*. Joint Commission on Mental Illness and Health. New York: Science Editions, 1961.
3. Alexander, F. and French, T. M. *Psychoanalytic Therapy*. New York: Ronald Press, 1946.
4. Allport, G. W. The functional autonomy of motives. *Amer. J. Psychol.* 50:141–156, 1937.
5. Altman, B. The process of brief therapy. In unpublished summary of lectures delivered by L. Bellak, Nassau Mental Health Center, New York, 1976.
6. Arieti, S. Studies of thought processes in contemporary psychiatry. *Am. J. Psychiat.* 120:58–64, 1963.
7. Bahn, A. K., Chandler, C. A., and Eisenberg, L. Diagnostic and demographic characteristics of patients seen in outpatient psychiatric clinics for an entire state (Maryland): Implication for the psychiatrist and the mental health planner. *Amer. J. Psychiat.* 117:769–778, 1961.
8. Balint, M., Ornstein, P. H., and Balint, E. *Focal Psychotherapy: An Example of Applied Psychoanalysis*. London: Tavistock Publications, 1972.
9. Barten, H. H. *Brief Therapies*. New York: Behavioral Publications, 1971.
10. Barten, H. H. and Barten, S. S. *Children and Their Parents in Brief Therapy*. New York: Behavioral Publications, 1973.
11. Bateson, G., Jackson, D., et al. Toward a theory of schizophrenia. *Behav. Sci.* 1:251–264, 1956.
12. Bellak, L. The use of oral barbiturates in psychotherapy. *Amer. J. Psychiat.* 11:849–850, 1949.
13. ———. Psychiatric aspects of tuberculosis. *Social Casework* 31:5, 1950.
14. ———. The emergency psychotherapy of depression. In *Specialized Techniques in Psychotherapy,* G. Bychowski and J. L. Despert, eds. New York: Basic Books, 1952.

15. ———. The Thematic Apperception Test and the Children's Apperception Test in Clinical Use. New York: Grune & Stratton, 1954, p. 282.

16. ———. Introduction to *Psychology of Physical Illness*. New York: Grune & Stratton, 1952.

17. ——— and Black, B. J. Rehabilitation of the mentally ill through controlled transitional employment. *Am. J. Orthopsychiat.* 26:285–296, 1956.

18. ——— and Haselkorn, F. Psychological aspects of cardiac illness and rehabilitation. *Social Casework.* 37:483–489, 1956.

19. ——— and Smith, B. B. An experimental exploration of the psychoanalytic process. *Psychoanal. Quart.* 25:385–414, 1956.

20. ———. The schizophrenic syndrome. In *Schizophrenia: A Review of the Syndrome.* New York: Logos Press, 1958.

21. ———. A community mental health center in a hospital. *Brit. J. Med Psychol.* 33:287, 1960.

22. ———. A general hospital as a focus of community psychiatry. *J. Amer. Med. Assoc.* 174:2214–2217, 1960.

23. ——— and Black, B. J. The rehabilitation of psychotics in the community. *Amer. J. Orthopsychiat.* 30:346–355, 1960.

24. ———. Research in psychoanalysis. *Psychoanal. Quart.* 30:519–549, 1961.

25. ———. Acting out: Some conceptual and therapeutic considerations. *Amer. J. Psychotherapy.* 17:375–389, 1963.

26. ——— ed. *Handbook of Community Psychiatry and Community Mental Health.* New York: Grune & Stratton, 1964.

27. ———. Depersonalization as a variant of self-awareness. In *Unfinished Tasks in the Behavioral Sciences,* A. Abrams, ed. Baltimore: Williams & Wilkins, 1964.

28. ———, Prola, M., Meyer, E. J., and Zuckerman, M. Psychiatry in the medical–surgical clinic. *Arch. Gen. Psychiat.* 10:267–269, 1964.

29. ——— and Chassan, J. C. An approach to the evaluation of drug effect during psychotherapy. A double-blind pilot study of a single case. *J. Nerv. Ment. Dis.* 139:20–30, 1964.

30. ———, Rosenberg, S., and Meyer, E. Factors related to improvement in brief psychotherapy, and An experimental study of brief psychotherapy. In *An Evaluation of the Results of the Psychotherapies,* S. Lesse, ed. Springfield, Illinois, Charles C. Thomas, 1968.

31. ———. Community mental health as a branch of mental health. In *Progress in Community Mental Health,* Vol. 1, L. Bellak and H. H. Barten, ed. and contr. New York: Grune & Stratton, 1969.

32. ———. *The Porcupine Dilemma.* New York: The Citadel Press, 1970.

33. ——— and Berneman, N. A systematic view of depression. *Am. J. Psychother.* 25:385, 1971.

34. ——— and Bellak, S. *The Senior Apperception Technique.* Larchmont, New York: C.P.S., Inc., 1973.

35. ———, Chassan, J., Gediman, H., and Hurvich, M. Ego-function assessment of analytic psychotherapy combined with drug therapy. *J. Nerv. Ment. Dis.* 157:465–469, 1973.

36. ———, Chassan, J., and Hurvich, M. An application of intense design to the study of drug effect on ego functions. Scientific Exhibit at the American Medi-

cal Association's 27th Clinical Convention. Anaheim, California, Dec. 1–4, 1973.

37. ———, Hurvich, M., and Gediman, H. *Ego Functions in Schizophrenics, Neurotics and Normals.* New York: John Wiley & Sons, 1973.

38. ———. Careers in Psychotherapy. *Dynam. Psychiat.* 7:232–247, 1974.

39. ——— and Meyers, B. Ego-function assessment and analyzability. *Intl. J. Psychoanal.* 2:413–427, 1975.

40. ———. What is psychotherapy? Invited address at the Annual Meeting of the American Psychiatric Association, May, 1976. Adapted for this text by L. Small.

41. ——— and Sheehey, M. The broad role of ego-function assessment. *Am. J. Psychiat.* 133:1259–1264, 1976.

42. ———. The broad role of Minimal Brain Dysfunction (MBD) in adult psychiatric disorders. *Psychiatic Ann.* 7:10, 1977.

43. Benjamin, J. E. Prediction and psychopathological theory. In *Dynamic Psychopathology in Childhood,* L. Jessner and E. Pavenstedt, eds. New York: Grune & Stratton, 1959.

44. Benson, H. *The Relaxation Response.* New York: William Morrow, 1975.

45. Beres, D. Ego deviation and the concept of schizophrenia. In *The Psychoanalytic Study of the Child,* Vol. XI. New York: International Universities Press, 1956.

46. Bergler, E. and Eidelberg, R. Further studies on depersonalization. *Psychiat. Quart.* 24:268, 1950.

47. Bertalanffy, L. von. General system theory. In *Main Currents in Modern Thought.* 2:75–83, 1955.

48. Bibring, C. Psychiatric principles in casework. *J. Social Casework* 30:230–235, 1949.

49. Bibring, E. The mechanism of depression. In *Affective Disorders,* P. Greenacre, ed. New York: International Universities Press, 1953.

50. Black, B. J. Psychiatric rehabilitation in the community. In *Handbook of Community Psychiatry,* L. Bellak, ed. New York: Grune & Stratton, 1964.

51. Blank, H. R. Depression, hypomania and depersonalization. *Psychoanal. Quart.* 23:20, 1954.

52. Blos, P. The concept of acting out in relation to the adolescent process. Presented at New York Psychoanalytic Society Meeting, September 25, 1962.

53. Bühler, K. *Die Geistige Entwicklung des Kindes,* 4th ed. Jena: Gustav Fischer, 1924.

54. Butler, J. M. Measuring the effectiveness of counseling and psychotherapy. *Personnel Guid. J.* 32:88–92, 1953.

55. Cameron, N. Experimental analysis of schizophrenic thinking. In *Language and Thought in Schizophrenia,* J. Kasanin, ed. New York: W. W. Norton, 1964.

56. Caplan, G. *An Approach to Community Mental Health.* New York: Grune & Stratton, 1961.

57. Ciompi, L., Ague, C., and Dauwalder, J. P. L'objectivation de changements psychodynamiques: experiences avec une version simplifee des 'Ego Strength Scales' de Bellak et al. Presented at the 10th International Congress of Psychotherapy. Paris, France, October, 1976.

58. Cole, J. The therapeutic efficacy of antidepressant drugs. *J.A.M.A.* 190:448–455, 1964.

59. Cole, I. E. *General Psychology.* New York: McGraw-Hill, 1939.

60. Deutsch, H. Acting out in the transference. In *Neuroses and Character Types.* New York: International Universities Press, 1965.

61. Diamond, S. A. neglected aspect of motivation. *Sociometry* 2:77–85, 1939.

61a. Durkheim, E. *Suicide.* New York: The Free Press, 1951.

62. Escalona, S. and Heider, G. M. *Prediction and Outcome.* New York: Basic Books, 1959.

63. Federn, P. The ego as subject and object in narcissism. In *Ego Psychology and the Psychoses,* E. Weiss, ed. New York: Basic Books, 1952.

64. ———. In *Ego Psychology and the Psychoses,* E. Weiss, ed. New York: Basic Books, 1952.

65. Fenichel, O. *The Psychoanalytic Theory of Neuroses.* New York: W. W. Norton, 1945.

66. ———. Brief psychotherapy. In *The Collected Papers of Otto Fenichel,* Vol. I. H. Fenichel and D. Rapaport, eds. New York: W. W. Norton, 1953.

67. ———. Organ libidinization accompanying the defense against drives. In *The Collected Papers of Otto Fenichel,* Vol. I. New York: W. W. Norton, 1953.

68. Frank, J. D. The role of hope in psychotherapy. *Intl. J. Psychiat.* Vol. 5, 1968.

69. Freeman, T., Cameron, J., and McGhie, A. *A Chronic Schizophrenia.* New York: International Universities Press, 1958.

70. Friedman, P. and Linn, L. Some psychiatric notes on the *Andrea Doria* disaster. *Amer. J. Psychiat.* 114:426–432, 1957.

71. Freud, A. *The Ego and the Mechanisms of Defense.* New York: International Universities Press, 1946.

72. Freud, S. *The Psychopathology of Everyday Life.* London: Ernest Benn, 1914.

73. ———. *Introductory Lectures to Psychoanalysis.* New York: Bori and Liveright, 1920.

74. ———. *The Ego and the Id.* London: Hogarth, 1947.

75. ———. Further recommendations in the techniques of psychoanalysis: Recollection, repetition, and working through. In *Collected Papers,* Vol. II. London: Hogarth, 1950.

76. ———. Fragment of an analysis of a case of hysteria ("Dora"). In *Standard Edition,* Vol. 7. London: Hogarth, 1953.

77. Gill, M. M., Newman, R. G., Redlich, F. C. and Sommers, M. *The Initial Interview in Psychiatric Practice.* New York: International Universities Press, 1954.

78. Greenacre, P. General problems of acting out. *Psychoanal. Quart.* 19:455, 1950.

79. Greenson, R. R. *The Technique and Practice of Psychoanalysis,* Vol. I. New York: International Universities Press, 1967.

80. Harris, R. E. and Christiansin, C. Predictions of response to brief psychotherapy. *J. Consult. Psychol.* 21:269–284, 1946.

81. Hartmann, H. Ein Fall von Depersonalization. *Z. Neurol. Psychiat.* 74:593, 1922.

82. ———. Comments on the psychoanalytic theory of the ego. In *The Psychoanalytic Study of the Child,* Vol. V. New York: International Universities Press, 1950.

83. ――――. Contributions to the metapsychology of schizophrenia. In *The Psychoanalytic Study of the Child,* Vol. VIII. New York: International Universities Press, 1953.

84. ――――. *Ego Psychology and the Problem of Adaptation.* New York: International Universities Press, 1958.

85. Herbart, C. P. As quoted in *Dictionary of Philosophy,* D. R. Runes, ed. New York: Philosophical Library, 1942.

85a. Hilberman, E. *The Rape Victim.* Washington, D.C.: American Psychiatric Association, 1976.

86. Hilgard, J. R. and Newman, M. F. Evidence for functional genesis in mental illness. *J. Nerv. Ment. Dis.* 132:1, 1961.

87. Hollingshead, A. B. and Redlich, F. C. *Social Class and Mental Illness: A Community Study.* New York: John Wiley & Sons, 1958.

88. Holt, R. R. Gauging primary and secondary processes in Rorschach responses. *J. Proj. Tech.* 20:14–25, 1956.

89. Jackson, D. Conjoint family therapy. Some considerations on theory, technique, and results. *Psychiatry* (Suppl.) 24:30–45, 1961.

90. Jacobson, E. On effect of disappointment on ego and superego formation in normal and depressive development. *Psychoanal. Rev.* 33:129–147, 1946.

91. ――――. Denial and repression. *J. Amer. Psychoanal. Ass.* 5:61, 1957.

92. ――――. Depersonalization. *J. Amer. Psychoanal. Ass.* 7:581, 1959.

93. ――――. *Psychotic Conflict and Reality.* New York: International Universities Press, 1967.

94. Jacobson, G. F., Strickler, M., and Morley, M. E. Generic and individual approaches to crisis intervention. *Am. J. Public Health.* 58:2, 1968.

95. ――――. Crisis theory and treatment strategy: Some socio-cultural and psychodynamic considerations. *J. Nerv. Ment. Dis.* 5:392–404, 1968.

96. Jonas, A. D. The emergence of epileptic equivalents in the era of tranquilizers. *Intl. J. Neuropsychiat.* 3:1, 1967.

97. Jones, E. *The Life and Work of Sigmund Freud,* Vol. III. New York: Basic Books, 1957.

98. Kaffman, M. Short-term family therapy. *Family Process* 2:216–234, 1963.

99. Kanner, L. A discussion on early infantile autism. *Dig. Neurol. Psychiat.* 19:158–159, 1951.

100. Kardiner, A. *The Traumatic Neuroses of War.* New York: Hoeber, 1941.

101. Katan, M. Schreber's prepsychotic phase. *Inter. J. Psycho-Anal.* 34:43–51, 1953.

102. Katz, M. M. and Lyerly, S. B. Methods for measuring adjustment and social behavior in the community I. Rationale, description, discriminative validity, and scale development. *Psychol. Reports* 13:503–535, 1963.

103. Kernberg, O. *Borderline conditions and Pathological Narcissism.* New York: Jason Aronson, 1975.

104. Kliman, G. *Psychological Emergencies in Childhood.* New York: Grune & Stratton, 1968.

105. Kovacs, M., Beck, A. T., and Weissman, A. The communication of suicidal intent. *Arch. Gen. Psychiat.* 33:2, 1976.

106. Kris, E. Danger and morale. *Amer. J. Orhtopsychiat.* 14:147–155, 1944.

107. ――――. *Psychoanalytic Explorations in Art.* New York: International Universities Press, 1952.

108. ———. The use of prediction in a longitudinal study. In *The Psychoanalytic Study of the Child,* Vol. XII. New York: International Universities Press, 1957.

109. Laing, R. *The Divided Self.* Chicago: Quadrangle, 1960.

110. Lemkau, P. V. and Crocetti, G. M. The Amsterdam municipal psychiatric service. *Amer. J. Psychiat.* 117:779–783, 1961.

111. Lewin, B. D. *The Psychoanalysis of Elation.* New York: W. W. Norton, 1950.

112. Lindemann, E. Symptomatology and management of acute grief. *Am. J. Psychiat.* 101:141–148, 1944.

113. Lord, E. Two sets of Rorschach records obtained before and after brief psychotherapy. *J. Consult. Psychol.* 14:134–139, 1950.

114. Lowenstein, R. Some remarks on defenses, autonomous ego, and psychoanalytic technique. *Intl. J. Psychoanal.* 35:189–193, 1954.

115. ———. Defensive organization and autonomous ego functions. *J. Am. Psychoanal. Assoc.* 15:795–809, 1967.

116. ———. Ego autonomy and psychoanalytic technique. *Psychoanal. Quar.* 41:1–22, 1972.

117. Mahler, M. On child psychosis and schizophrenia. In *The Psychoanalytic Study of the Child,* Vol. VII. New York: International Universities Press, 1952.

118. Malan, D. H. *A Study of Brief Psychotherapy.* London: Tavistock Publications, 1963.

119. Mann, R. D. *A Critique of P. E. Meehl's Clinical vs. Statistical Predictions.* Ann Arbor: University of Michigan Mental Health Research Institute, 1961.

120. Mann, J. *Time-Limited Psychotherapy.* Cambridge, Mass.: Harvard University Press, 1973.

121. May, P., Wexler, M., Salkan, J. and Schoop, T. Nonverbal techniques in the reestablishment of body image and self identity—a preliminary report. *Psychiat. Res. Rep.* 16:68–82, 1963.

122. Mednick, S. A learning theory approach to research in schizophrenia. 1958. In *Theories of Schizophrenia,* A. Buss and E. Buss, eds. New York: Atherton Press, 1969.

123. Meehl, P. E. *Clinical Versus Statistical Prediction: A Theoretical Analysis and a Review of the Evidence.* Minnesota: University of Minnesota Press, 1954.

124. Menninger, K. Regulatory services of the ego under major stress. *Int. J. Psycho-Anal.* 35:412–430, 1954.

125. ———. *Theory of Psychoanalytic Technique.* Menninger Clinic Monograph Series No. 12, The Menninger Foundation. New York: Basic Books, 1958.

126. Meyer, J. Konzentrative Entspannungsubungen nach Elsa Gindler und ihre Grundlage. *Zeitschrift fur Psychotherapie.* 11:4, 1961.

127. Mintz, E. On fostering development of some conflict-free ego functions. *Psychotherapy: Theory, Research, & Practice.* 2:84–88, 1965.

128. Monroe, R. R. *Episodic Behavioral Disorders.* Cambridge, Mass.: Harvard University Press, 1970.

129. Morton, R. B. An experiment in brief psychotherapy. *Psychol. Monogr.* 69:1, 1955.

130. Murray, H. A. *Explorations in Personality.* New York: Oxford University Press, 1938.

131. Nunberg, H. The synthetic function of the ego. *Int. J. Psycho-Anal.* 1931, 12.
132. ———. *Principles of Psychoanalysis.* New York: International Universities Press, 1955.
133. Oberndorf, D. P. The role of anxiety in depersonalization. *Int. J. Psychoanal.* 31:1, 1950.
134. Ostow, M. *Drugs in Psychoanalysis and Psychotherapy.* New York: Basic Books, 1962.
135. Parad, H. J., ed. *Crisis Intervention: Selected Readings.* New York: Family Service Association of America, 1965.
136. Parloff, M. B., Kelman, H. C., and Frank, J. D. Comfort effectiveness and self-awareness as criteria of improvement in psychotherapy. *Amer. J. Psychol.* 111:343–352, 1954.
137. Piaget, J. *Language and Thought.* London: Kegan Paul, 1932.
137a. Pinner, M. and Miller, B., eds. *When Doctors Are Patients.* New York: W. W. Norton, 1952.
138. Psychoanalysis and learning theory. Dr. C. Brenner's Section of the Kris Study Group. *Psychoanal. Quart.* 32:152–154, 1963.
139. Rapaport, D. *The Structure of Psychoanalytic Theory.* Psychological Issues Monograph No. 6. New York: International Universities Press, 1960.
140. Reich, A. Pathological forms of self-esteem regulations. In *Psychoanalytic Study of the Child,* Vol. XV. New York: International Universities Press, 1960.
141. Rosen, J. N. *Direct Analysis: Selected Papers.* New York: Grune & Stratton, 1953.
142. ———. *Direct Psychoanalytic Psychiatry.* New York: Grune & Stratton, 1962.
143. Rosenfeld, H. *Psychotic States: A Psychoanalytic Approach.* New York: International Universities Press, 1965.
144. Scheidlinger, S. The concept of identification in group psychotherapy. *Amer. J. Psychother.* 9:661–672, 1955.
145. Schilder, P. *The Image and Appearance of the Human Body.* New York: International Universities Press, 1950.
146. Schulsinger, F. and Achte, K. Decreased recidivism in Denmark and Finland. Special Report on Schizophrenia. Washington, D.C.: National Institute of Mental Health, 1971.
147. Searles, H. Integration and differentiation in schizophrenia. 1959. In *Collected Papers on Schizophrenia and Related Subjects.* New York: International Universities Press, 1965.
148. Sechehaye, M. *Symbolic Realization: A New Method of Psychotherapy Applied to a Case of Schizophrenia.* New York: International Universities Press, 1951.
149. Seward, J. P. The structure of functional autonomy. *Amer. Psychol.* 18:7–10, 1963.
150. Sharp, V. and Bellak, L. Ego-function assessment of the psychoanalytic process. *Psychoanal. Quar.,* 1978, in press.
151. Shneidman, E. S. and Farberow, N. L. *Clues to Suicide.* Public Health Reports 71:109–114, 1956.
152. Sifneos, P. E. *Short-Term Psychotherapy and Emotional Crisis.* Cambridge, Mass.: Harvard University Press, 1973.

153. Simon, J. The paradoxical effect of effort. *Br. J. Med. Psychol.* 40:375, 1967.
154. Singer, M. and Wynne, L. Principles for scoring communication defects and deviances in parents of schizophrenics: Rorschach and TAT scoring manuals. *Psychiatry.* 29:260, 1966.
155. Small, L. Personality determinants of vocational choice. *Psychol. Monogr.* 67:1, 1953.
156. ———. *The Briefer Psychotherapies.* New York, Brunner/Mazel, 1971.
157. ———. *Neuropsychodiagnosis in Psychotherapy.* New York: Brunner/Mazel, 1973.
158. Sollod, R. N. and Kaplan, H. S. The new sex therapy: an integration of behavioral, psychodynamic, and interpersonal approaches. In *Successful Psychotherapy,* J. L. Claghorn, ed. New York: Brunner/Mazel, 1976.
159. Spiegel, L. The self, the sense of self, and perception. In *Psychoanalytic Study of the Child,* Vol. XIV. New York: International Universities Press, 1959.
160. Spitz, R. Hospitalism, an inquiry into the genesis of psychiatric conditions in early childhood. In *The Psychoanalytic Study of the Child,* Vol. I. New York: International Universities Press, 1945.
161. ———. Anaclitic depression, an inquiry into the genesis of psychiatric conditions in early childhood. In *The Psychoanalytic Study of the Child,* Vol. II. New York: International Universities Press, 1946.
162. ———. Psychogenic diseases of infancy. In *The Psychoanalytic Study of the Child,* Vol. VI. New York: International Universities Press, 1950.
163. Stamm, J. Deprsonalization and the wish to sleep. *J. Amer. Psychoanal. Ass.* 10:762, 1962.
164. Sterman, M. B. Neurophysiologic and clinical studies of sensorimotor EEG biofeedback training: Some effects on epilepsy. *Seminars in Psychiatry.* 5:4, 1973.
165. Strupp, H. *Psychotherapists in Action.* New York: Grune & Stratton, 1960.
166. ———. *A Bibliography of Research in Psychotherapy.* Chapel Hill: University of North Carolina, 1964.
167. ———. *A Clinical Picture of Claustrophobia.* Film produced by the Veterans Administration.
168. Van Itallie, P. H. Over 19,000 suicides in the United States. *Pulse of Pharmacy* 17:3, 1963.
169. Waelder, R. *Basic Theory of Psychoanalysis.* New York: International Universities Press, 1960.
170. White, R. W. Motivation reconsidered: The concept of competence. *Psychol. Rev.* 66:297–333, 1959.
171. Whittington, H. C. Transference in brief psychotherapy: Experience in a college psychiatric clinic. *Psychiatric Quart.* 26:503–518, 1962.
172. Wolberg, L. R., ed. *Short-Term Psychotherapy.* New York: Grune & Stratton, 1965.
173. Woodworth, R. S. *Dynamic Psychology.* New York: Columbia University Press, 1918.
174. Zarensky, I. Psychological problems of kidney-transplanted adolescents. *Adolescence.* 10:37, 1975.

Index